T0163735

Who Do *You* Think You Are?

Praises for

Who Do *You* Think You Are?

Dr. Tina Thomas's work establishing the biological substrate of the nine Enneagram personality types could prove to be a major breakthrough in our field. While those of us who have worked with the spiritual and psychological implications of this system for many years have never doubted its objectivity and immense usefulness, it will be helpful to have an empirically based explanation of why the Enneagram is so able to capture, with precision and elegance, the personality categories that we see in human beings across cultures and in different ages. While other studies have validated the objectivity of the nine Enneagram personality types, no one before has attempted to ground the origin of personality in brain chemistry the way Dr. Thomas has. This is truly pioneering work that has many profound and practical applications.

—**Don Richard Riso**, bestselling author of
Personality Types and *The Wisdom of the Enneagram*

In this lively book, Dr. Thomas presents her audacious case for integrating the wide range of research on personality into "OBT" (One Big Theory) that has direct applications to everyday life and is illustrated with a multitude of vivid and compelling examples.

—**David C. Funder PhD**, Distinguished Professor,
Stanford University, 1979, author of *The Personality Puzzle*

Step aside Dr. Phil; move over Dr. Oz. I truly believe that Dr. Tina Thomas is to personality psychology what Einstein was to physics and what Watson and Crick were to biology.

—**Eric Schulze MD, PhD**, researcher, CEO
Lifetrack Medical Systems, certified Enneagram teacher

Dr. T has done it again! Her first book, *The Ultimate Edge: How to Be, Do or Get Anything You Want*, has innovative dynamic tools for goal achievement and success. And now, *Who Do You Think You Are?* is a revolutionary book that brings personal development to another level! Dr. T has an uncanny ability to combine the art of psychology and the science of biology to create elegant ways to increase self-compassion, improve relationships, and help people to become self-actualized.

—**Richard Tscherne PhD**, clinical psychologist,
Director of The Gestalt Institute and Relationship Center
of New York and author of *The Little Engine That Did It*

Dr. Tina Thomas' book, *Who Do You Think You Are?* is a fascinating exploration of the study of personality and the way self-knowledge can be used by readers to better their interactions with others. Readers will benefit from her intellectual, but conversational, style of writing and her thorough analysis of the subject. There seems to be little in the book that doesn't have a straightforward usefulness attached to it.

—**Denis Boyles**, author, former university lecturer, contributing and senior
editor of *Men's Health, National Lampoon*, and *The New York Times Magazine*

Who Do *You* Think You Are?

Understanding Personality From the Inside Out

DR. TINA THOMAS

New York

Who Do You Think *You* Are?

Understanding Personality From the Inside Out

© 2016 Tina Thomas.

All rights reserved. No portion of this book may be reproduced, stored in a retrieval system, or transmitted in any form or by any means—electronic, mechanical, photocopy, recording, scanning, or other—except for brief quotations in critical reviews or articles, without the prior written permission of the publisher.

Published in New York, New York, by Morgan James Publishing. Morgan James and The Entrepreneurial Publisher are trademarks of Morgan James, LLC.
www.MorganJamesPublishing.com

The Morgan James Speakers Group can bring authors to your live event. For more information or to book an event visit The Morgan James Speakers Group at
www.TheMorganJamesSpeakersGroup.com.

Notice: This book is not intended to replace recommendations or advice from physicians or other healthcare providers. Rather, it is intended to help you make informed decisions about your mental, physical, and emotional health and to cooperate with your healthcare provider in a joint quest for optimal wellness. If you suspect you have a medical or psychiatric problem, please seek advice from a competent healthcare provider.

Shelfie

A **free** eBook edition is available
with the purchase of this print book.

CLEARLY PRINT YOUR NAME ABOVE IN UPPER CASE

Instructions to claim your free eBook edition:
1. Download the Shelfie app for Android or iOS
2. Write your name in **UPPER CASE** above
3. Use the Shelfie app to submit a photo
4. Download your eBook to any device

ISBN 978-1-63047-656-4 paperback
ISBN 978-1-63047-657-1 eBook
Library of Congress Control Number:
2015907415

Cover Design by:
Rachel Lopez
www.r2cdesign.com

Interior Design by:
Bonnie Bushman
The Whole Caboodle Graphic Design

In an effort to support local communities and raise awareness and funds, Morgan James Publishing donates a percentage of all book sales for the life of each book to Habitat for Humanity Peninsula and Greater Williamsburg.

Get involved today, visit
www.MorganJamesBuilds.com

I dedicate this book to my grandchildren,

Caleb Thomas Bernard (a.k.a. "Bito") and Scout Amanda Bernard.

This book is my gift to the two of you,
to help create a dream I have for you and your friends.

It is my hope that one day you will experience a world
where people have learned how to get along.

I hope your generation will appreciate and enjoy
how and why we are all a little different,
and more importantly,
will come to understand
how in so many more ways, we are the same.

With love,
Mia

Contents

Foreword

When Tina Thomas and I became research partners, I had no idea just *how* amazing our journey would be both personally and professionally. I cannot tell you how many hours, days, and dollars were spent in the hope that we might crack the code of this elusive personality puzzle. It has been quite the journey.

During this journey, many of our friends and family members thought we were obsessed and fanatical. Considering that we were an Investigator and Enthusiast partnership, who felt, like the Blues Brothers, that we were "on a mission from God," perhaps our friends' and families' thoughts were not so farfetched.

So, imagine this scene. Years ago, before presenting at the International Enneagram Association conference, Tina and I went on an Alaskan cruise. We had dressed up for the night. I was in my tuxedo, and Tina was dressed in a voluptuous, black velvet, split-to-the-thigh dress. (She called it her Jessica Rabbit dress.) She looked absolutely stunning. We had a rich and amorous dinner, complete with wine and candles. After dinner, we proceeded to the dance floor and danced to some dreamy, romantic music.

Tina whispered in my ear, "Eric, are you thinking what I'm thinking?" I nodded. "Yes I am, Babelicious." We dashed off the dance floor, raced up the stairs of the ship (elevators were just too slow that night), flung open the door of our ocean-side balcony cabin, jumped into bed, grabbed our personal laptops, and said in unison, "Let's do this!" Then, we set about trying to figure out how dopamine fits into the personality equation. I kid you not. It was, in fact, the night we had a breakthrough in our theory on dopamine and its relationship to the amplification or attenuation of personality.

Crazy? Perhaps. Capricious? Somewhat. Brilliant? She most certainly is. Watching Tina tenaciously search for the answer to the underpinnings of this personality system, observing her uncanny and intuitive ability to help other people realize their dreams (including mine), and witnessing her teach compassion and love along the way has been a true honor and privilege. She is a faithful and dedicated "Scout Ant" and a tribute to her personality "tribe."

Also, for the record, I want everyone to be aware that the theory presented in this book is a heuristic model. That is to say, it comes from practical experience and observation. We realize it is just a first-pass construct of the main modulatory monoamine pathways. We realize that it needs more research, and we invite that. We also realize the primary mechanism influencing personality might not be these neurotransmitters themselves but rather their counterparts. (For instance, norepinephrine may not be what regulates the thinking process. It may actually be that GABA, its counterpart, does that.)

Having said all that, I see this contribution as a radically simple but extraordinarily profound theory that can change the course of human evolution. So . . . step aside Dr. Phil; move over Dr. Oz. I truly believe that Dr. Tina Thomas is to personality psychology what Einstein was to physics and what Watson and Crick were to biology.

One thing is for certain: I personally witnessed countless peoples' lives change dramatically for the better as they came to see themselves and others through the lens of this personality system. I invite you to be open to the possibility of a better life for yourself and for those you care about by reading this book and applying it to your life. The results will be nothing short of miraculous. That is a big thing for a scientist to say.

Live well and prosper.
Sincerely,
Eric Schulze, MD, PhD

Overview

In the personality psychology textbook *The Personality Puzzle*, author Dr. David Funder asks, "Why doesn't somebody just come up with the One Big Theory—you could call it the OBT—that explains everything now accounted for separately by trait, biological, psychoanalytic, humanistic, behavioral, and cognitive approaches?" According to Dr. Funder, a singular, elegant system would be able to see the truth in all approaches.

Now, Dr. "T" Tina Thomas boldly asserts that such a system does exist. The system, known as the Nine-Point Personality System (NPS), is a unifying paradigm of personality. In addition to serving as a framework that unites the six leading and often seemingly contradictory approaches to personality psychology, the NPS has a biological foundation, based on combinations of neurotransmitter activity. Dr. T also states that, just like the blind men and the elephant parable, everyone in the various fields of personality psychology has been telling the truth, but no one, to date, has presented a system accurate and broad enough to be inclusive. This book introduces the NPS as a unifying paradigm and, perhaps even more importantly, explores how ordinary people can utilize this information to create healthier and happier relationships and lives.

As Dr. T explains, "There is no such thing as a difficult person, just people with difficult personalities!" Those who come to understand personality and its biological basis never look at themselves or others in the same way again. Understanding personality this way will help *you* understand what motivates you and others. This will also improve your ability to communicate. You will learn how to adjust your internal and external environments to optimize your specific personality chemistry to become the person you always hoped you could be and create the life circumstances you only dreamed were possible. And, if that isn't extraordinary enough, this new knowledge will create more compassion within yourself *and* more peace within all the relationships you've ever had, have now, or will have in the future. Understanding personality from the inside out may be the single most important body of information you need to reach your full potential.

The Human Physics Series

Books written by Dr. "T" Tina Thomas in the Human Physics series include:

A Gentle Path: A Guide to Peace, Passion & Power, now revised and retitled *The Ultimate Edge: How to Be, Do and Get Anything You Want*
Who Do You Think You Are? Understanding Personality from the Inside Out

And five e-books:

How to Find the Perfect Partner
Radical Relationships
Burn Fat Forever. . . and Grow Younger Every Day!
The G-word
The Little Book (The Missing Pieces of AA's Big Book)

Why the name "Human Physics" series?

- **Physics** (from Wikipedia) is the science of matter and its motion, as well as space and time. It uses concepts such as energy, force, mass, and change. Physics is an experimental science, creating theories that are tested against observations. Broadly, it is the general scientific analysis of nature, with a goal of understanding how the universe behaves.

- **Human Physics** (a term coined by Dr. Tina Thomas), as presented in this series, is the study of human nature. It also uses concepts such as energy, force, mass, and change, along with terms such as imprints, thoughts, feelings, emotions, personality, and neurotransmitter pathways. It borrows and integrates concepts from physics, biology, chemistry, psychology, sociology, anthropology, philosophy, and life experience. Human physics is an experimental science, proposing theories that can be tested against observations and formal research. Broadly, it is both the art and general scientific analysis of human nature, with a goal of understanding what motivates us as human beings and what makes us behave the way we do. Its ultimate purpose is to create universal understanding so we may have a chance to create a healthier, more peaceful, and compassionate world.

Acknowledgments

Thanks to all my friends, family, and colleagues who helped me along the way—and gave me *lots* of great material!

The recipients of my unending gratitude include all my family members, who took written tests, endured interviews, listened to lectures, were subjected to pain threshold tests and electric shocks (okay, that was a little "over the top"), and even gave blood samples so that my co-researchers and I could explore the recesses of your personalities. I cannot thank you enough. You may now come back to my parties; they are safe(r) now!

Thanks to my most important personality "project" of all time, my son, Dr. Matt Bernard, my biggest skeptic and then supporter, who eventually helped me dissect this system and refine the theory.

Thanks also to Greg Gasperecz for always unconditionally supporting me and helping me to launch into this life-altering endeavor.

I am grateful to my academic mentor and friend, Dr. Sana Khan, who challenged me to become an ambassador for world peace. (This book is the next step, Sana!)

I shall always appreciate the help and vision of Jack Labanauskas, who saw where we were headed and helped us to get there. Thanks also to Dr. Catherine

Hebert, the amazing muse, who led us to divine inspiration, and to Dr. Gilda Reed, my most favorite professor of personality, who turned me on to Dr. David Funder and his incredibly rich and entertaining text, *The Personality Puzzle*. Dr. Funder coined the acronym OBT (One Big Theory) and inspired me to find it!

Thanks also to my special "sister from another mother," Dr. Haley Fox, for her countless hours of encouragement and awesome editing. Thank you, Dr. Timothy P. Rice, for your contributions and help with editing and especially with the narratives that became a critical part of this book. And *merci beaucoup* to Angie Kiesling for "getting" me (and my work), for your incredible professional editing, and for being my "book angel."

I would like to extend special thanks and recognition to my teachers, the late Don Riso and Russ Hudson, whose genius and extraordinary dedication to "the work" helped to point the way and upon whose shoulders this book stands.

Of course, if it hadn't been for you, Dr. Eric Schulze, this book never would have *begun*! Thank you for being my research partner so we could discover a key to deeper understanding and create a gift of hope for our fellow human beings. Perhaps we have contributed to world peace after all.

If it had not been for the support and tireless efforts of Aaron Anthony, this book may never have been *completed*!

And finally, thanks to Mom and Dad for providing the most fertile and loving soil in which this little "seven" could be planted and grown so that I could become all I was destined to be *and* have fun along the way!

Credits:

- **Russ Hudson** and the late **Don Riso** made seminal contributions to the development of the Enneagram personality typing system. These contributions include but are in no way limited to: the names and key words chosen to represent the types and subtypes, the addition of levels of functioning, the creation of the Harmonic and Hornevian triads, and the refinement of theories on integration and disintegration.
- **Dr. Eric Schulze** contributed to the development and refinement of the neurotransmitter theory of personality and pioneered his original theory of origin and etiology of social orientation.

- **Dr. Matthew Bernard** (my son, the doctor) also contributed to the development and refinement of the neurotransmitter theory of personality.
- **Dr. Daniel Amen** has done pioneering work on SPECT scans and identifying biomarkers of ADD (Attention Deficit Disorder) (and perhaps of personality, as well).
- **Elizabeth Wagele** created the visual animation for the neurotransmitters.
- **Gary Docken** contributed two drawings,
- **Jacqueline Cote-Sherman** of Flourish Design illustrated the three-dimensional NPS and the Periodic Table of Human Personality (the beautiful original color versions can be obtained through this link: http://tinathomas.com/nps-3d-model-periodic-table).
- **Charles Abadie** contributed the front cover photo.

Introduction

Wouldn't it be great if you understood yourself and others better? How would your life be less stressful if you could predict how and why other people react to certain situations? Can you imagine how much easier your life would be if you could communicate what you needed or wanted clearly?

This book is for anyone who has ever wondered, "Why am I the way I am?" or "Why is this person the way he is?" If you have ever been confused by someone you cared about or felt triggered by someone—a friend, child, co-worker, lover, or parent—and found yourself frustrated or hurt in your dealings with that challenging person, this book contains some surprising answers for you. This book is also for people who may be doing well in relationships but want to gain an even better understanding and sense of compassion for themselves and others.

I created this book *for you*, to save you time and make your life easier. Within these pages, I will share a chemical blueprint for personality and show you how to identify your specific personality formula so you can understand how these chemicals affect you—and how you can influence these chemicals to enhance your mental, physical, emotional, and spiritual health and happiness.

With this information, I guarantee:

1. You will be more accepting of yourself and everyone else you know.
2. You will learn how your personality influences *everything* you think, feel, and do.
3. Once you understand yourself, you are a hop, skip, and jump away from understanding and appreciating everyone else.
4. When I tell you, "You will find more peace with everyone you know," I mean you will have more peace in *any* relationship you are currently in, ever had, or ever will have in your life.
5. If you utilize this information, you can create a better life than you are currently living.

How can I make such bold statements? My confidence stems from my own personal experience and what I have witnessed countless times in the lives of people I have helped.

This book began percolating from a private practice I started years ago. Much of my work as a therapist involves teaching people about themselves and giving them tools to improve their relationships and realize their dreams. I became extremely successful in this area and informally known as a "professional fairy godmother." Clients shared with me that their results exceeded their wildest dreams. To achieve those results, they needed to understand and master a few basic principles.

While the principles themselves are easy enough to learn, the everyday application can be more challenging. Often clients hit an emotional brick wall that sounds something like this: "Dr. T, I hear what you are saying about my spouse and what I need to do to be at peace with him, but I don't like the idea that I'll have to do what you suggest to get what I want." To this I say, "Well, I don't like that it hurts my foot when I drop a bowling ball on it. But gravity follows the laws of physics, and if I don't understand that, don't accept it, and don't change my behavior because of what I know, I'll get hurt over and over again."

Certain laws govern human relationships, too. I call those laws the Laws of Human Physics. If you understand these laws, you can use them to your advantage to gain peace with yourself and everyone you know. If you refuse to acknowledge and honor these simple but powerful principles, you will find yourself repeatedly hurt and frustrated and will not get the results you want in an elegant way. People who accept this principle eventually sigh and say, "Okay, so what exactly do I need to do again?" After that, we are off and running. Accepting "what is" has allowed my clients to stop spending so much time and energy striving to achieve the impossible, and this acceptance frees them up to use their time and energy to create what they want within the parameters of what is indeed possible.

My first book in the Human Physics series, *A Gentle Path: A Guide to Peace, Passion & Power*, has now been revised and retitled *The Ultimate Edge: How to Be, Do and Get Anything You Want*. This book is an owner's manual for human beings on the basics of how your brain works and how to retrain your brain to create more peace, passion, and power in your life. It is a powerful book, full of helpful information, such as understanding the seven most misunderstood emotions, how unconscious self-sabotaging belief systems are created, and how you can discover and reprogram them for your benefit.

When I was writing *The Ultimate Edge*, I was serendipitously exposed to an elegant system of personality typing, known as the Enneagram. To be honest, at first, I was tempted to dismiss the system since it emerged out of an ancient tradition rather than a modern, scientific one, and I thought the name of the system, Enneagram (pronounced any-uh-gram) sounded too "New Age flakey-cakey." Being a woman in the South (and a blonde!) who wanted to be taken seriously, I gravitated toward ideas and systems that could be validated by science or at least had some reasonable credibility based on observation and experience.

Thankfully, I kept an open mind. I continued to be impressed with the Enneagram's precision and predictive power. I devoured the work of two world-renowned figures in the field—Don Riso and Russ Hudson, authors of *Personality Types*—who emphasized the fluidity and complexity of the system, and I wondered if those features pointed to a biological basis underlying personality.

As a Gestalt therapist, trained to help clients work through issues in a dynamic and elegant way, I was even more impressed by seeing how the knowledge of personality from the Enneagram perspective dramatically accelerated my clients' already fast-paced progress. It also added an element of self-mastery that was easy to grasp and fun to utilize. I was so intrigued by the system that I enrolled in Don Riso and Russ Hudson's Enneagram Teacher Training program—a three-week intensive training (over a period of a few months) that emphasized both theory and experiential learning.

After one week of training, based on the system's precision and predicative ability, I was convinced there had to be a biological basis to the Enneagram. During the second week of training, I met someone who suspected the same thing.

Enter Dr. Eric Schulze, a brilliant physician who was also convinced of the biological basis of the Enneagram. We became research partners—and ended up researching a bit more than personality. We found our work so engaging that we literally became engaged and eventually married! Ours would be a somewhat unconventional partnership from the beginning. To our guests' bemusement, alongside the traditional cake table and bar, we incorporated a blood-drawing table at our wedding reception (since we were looking for a correlation between genes and personality). Yes, it was quite a memorable wedding! Later, at our now infamous first Christmas party, we administered personality tests to our friends and family and then hooked them up to equipment to measure their brainwaves, heart rate, and skin responses while subjecting them to freezing, cold-water presser pain tests. The results were promising, but we needed a wider range of pain, so at our Fourth of July party, we repeated the "experiment." This time, we added nerve conduction testing equipment and administered electric shocks to induce more pain.

Now, I have a hard time convincing family and friends to attend my parties! Reflecting on one of those parties, my sister, Ann, suggested that Eric and I get our heads examined. And so we did. We visited Dr. Daniel Amen, the first psychiatrist to suggest that psychiatrists might do well to take SPECT[1] scans of

---

1   SPECT stands for Single-Photon Emission Computed Tomography. It is a nuclear medicine imaging technique that provides three-dimensional images; in this case, SPECT scans of the

their patients' brains to better diagnose and treat them. Dr. Amen eventually identified six types of ADD based on his extensive library of SPECT scans and notes on patient behavior and challenges. In reviewing his work, I began to suspect that Dr. Amen may have inadvertently identified biomarkers for personality. Based on his work and our knowledge of the Enneagram, I was able to predict which parts of Dr. Amen's, Eric's, and my brains would be hypo- and hyper-perfused—that is, I guessed in advance which parts of our brains would exhibit relatively low or high blood flow. At that point, we were satisfied enough to declare that yes, in fact, we believed we had "cracked the code" of personality. At the very least, we felt certain that we had a good enough and elegant theory worthy of more rigorous research.

Excited and encouraged by our SPECT scan results, Eric and I set up a research project at the International Enneagram Association conference. It was a larger and more controlled study on Enneagram types and biomarkers (brainwaves, heart rate, and galvanic skin response). Even before we applied statistical tools, we saw promising correlations. Unfortunately, our data was lost in Hurricane Katrina before we had time to formerly analyze it. Katrina brought more setbacks, and other life challenges followed. Eric developed a brain tumor, and although he recovered, years passed before he regained his balance; ultimately, he changed the direction of his life. Our wonderful marriage ended in divorce; it was a loving and compassionate separation—thanks to our knowledge of personality! Also around that time, I lost nearly everything I owned in a house fire. When it rains, it pours.

In the midst of those catastrophes, I managed to complete three years of postdoctoral education at Duke University. During that time, I adopted the practice of referring to the Enneagram with a more contemporary term, calling it the Nine-Point Personality System, or NPS. I also distinguished the NPS from the Enneagram in a few subtle but significant ways, which I explain in Chapter 3. Fellow researchers who viewed the Enneagram with the same skepticism I initially felt seemed a bit more open to conversation when I changed the name, but many remained skeptical. Some were intrigued but too entrenched in their

---

brain show relative blood flow, which reveals hypo- or hyper-perfused parts of the brain or levels of brain activity.

formal training to be open to the possibility of a new, unifying paradigm in personality psychology. One of my most respected mentors said to me one day, "Dr. Thomas, don't you think if your theory was true, we would know it by now?" I was incredulous, disillusioned, and disappointed by what I saw as inside-the-box thinking. I was reminded of physicist and Nobel Prize winner Max Planck's now famous quote: "Science advances slowly, one funeral at a time."

With the wind knocked out of my sails, I realized that researching this theory was a complex proposition that could take a lifetime or more. I faced a quandary. I had run out of time and resources to continue on this path, and even though the information was not yet supported by rigorous research, it remained compelling and extraordinarily useful in my professional practice.

One night, I had a conversation with a graduate student from Sweden interested in researching personality. She was hungry for a single book that could recap our conversation from earlier that day. I decided that immediate usefulness outweighed the long-term benefits of formal research. I reasoned that perhaps getting this information out to the public might actually spur the academic world to take a more serious look at this theory and system. I considered the condition of the world and the need for this information, regardless of whether we had the advanced technology to fully support the theory. So, ready or not, here I am, having now written all this down in my second book.

I hope *Who Do You Think You Are?* inspires more rigorous scientific research. I am well aware of the need for it. I am also aware that decades of practical experience and astute observation underlie the rich contents of each chapter. Ultimately, it will be up to *you* to accept the premises or not. Regardless, I do hope you will be open to how the information can help you transform, heal, and enrich your life on many levels, as have countless other people who now understand and embrace the NPS and the theory behind it. I hope you find the time spent reading this book as worthwhile as I have found the time spent writing it. Finally, I hope you learn a few new things about your own personality that will help you to live well, laugh often, and love always.

Warning!

What you are about to read could change your life forever. Once you have this information, you will never be able to see yourself or others in the same way (and that could be a very good thing!).

When you do you understand the material in this book, it will be difficult—some would go so far as to say immoral—not to at least *try* to use this new knowledge in your daily life. Understanding yourself and others through the lens of the NPS will challenge you to take a "higher road" in all your dealings with other human beings. No longer will you be able to sigh, rant and rave, or label others as crazy jerks or idiots. Instead, you may come to realize that whenever someone's actions upset you, it is because (1) you have unfinished emotional baggage (refer to my first book, *The Ultimate Edge*), or (2) you do not have enough information about the personality in front of you to make a fair judgment about his or her behavior.

Understanding personality will make your life much less stressful. Not only do your thoughts and attitudes have the power to affect the way *you* feel, but they can also influence the behaviors and attitudes of the people you deal with every day, personally and professionally. You know when someone is being real or faking it. People know when you are judging or accepting them. You don't even have to say a word. When you are genuinely comfortable with yourself and others, people around you begin to relax, and relationships, both personal and professional, can reach a higher and deeper level of communication and connection.

Think about this: if you take pride in feeling righteous and better than others, if you enjoy experiencing drama in your relationships, if you are determined to hold onto grudges and cannot forgive others for being human, then put this book down.

I am serious.

If you are undecided, take the following test. If you pass it, you may proceed with the hope that the information in this book will be extraordinarily enriching. Understanding this system of personality will, first and foremost, improve your relationship with yourself and then with those you care about. With some mindfulness, you will ultimately learn to see everyone with eyes of compassion. At that time, to borrow a phrase from the Moody Blues' song "A Question of Balance," "and then, you will be answered."

Here is a test to determine if this book can help you improve your past, present, and future relationships:

See this apple?

It is an average, good enough, basic red apple. But, at this particular moment, let's say you are in the mood for a juicier snack, like an orange. Yes, that's it; the more you think about it, the more you desire an orange. But alas, all you have is an apple, and you don't have the time to go to the grocery store to get your highly desired orange.

With the information above, answer the following two questions:

A. How much effort will you apply to try to turn this apple into an orange?
- a. All day.
- b. I know I can't do it, but I will spend time praying for a miracle that will transform the apple.
- c. No time at all. I simply can't turn an apple into an orange and won't waste my time trying.

B. How much time will you spend being upset that this apple cannot be an orange?

- ○ a. It will ruin my entire day.
- ○ b. I will take it personally but only for a few hours.
- ○ c. Less than a minute or two, or not at all.

If you answered "c" to both questions, you are capable of transcendent, self-actualizing peace. You have the ability to be at peace with *what is*; therefore, you are capable of being much more at peace with any relationship you have now, have had in the past, or will have in the future. If you are currently experiencing any upsets with people in your life, you may discover that the only thing you need to be less upset is a little more information. Believe it or not, I have learned that, with enough information, being upset with people and the baffling things they do is about as pointless as being upset with dogs for chasing cats or cats for chasing birds.

It's that simple. Please note that I didn't say *easy.* However, if you are capable of rational thought in one area of your life, it can be transferred to your emotional life, and more peace will be the result of that process. There are no exceptions to the rule. It is one of the laws of human physics. Period.

Intrigued? I hope so, because it happens quickly, and with a blink of your eye, your perceptions about yourself and your world can change, and you will be forever transformed. Once you have experienced that change, your life can never be the same. (Have you ever tried to "un-cook" an egg?)

If you answered "a" or "b" for either question above, this book is probably not for you—yet. I suggest you find a good therapist, come back in about a year, and try again at that time.

If you passed the test, fasten your seat belt and read on!

Chapter 1

Who Is the Ultimate You?

Who do you think you are?

Before you finish this book, it is my hope that you will be able to figure out which of the nine basic human personalities you have and what to do to become the ultimate version of yourself.

Do you have the ethical and principled personality known as the **Reformer**?

Or perhaps you have the positive high-energy personality designed to anticipate others' needs, known as the **Helper**?

Could you be the charming and chameleon-like **Achiever**, who is incredibly gifted at goal achievement?

Or the special, highly sensitive, and sometimes temperamental **Artist** personality who has special gifts and challenges?

Perhaps, you are more of a brainiac and have the **Observer** personality, someone who might be the next Albert Einstein or Bill Gates?

If you're having a hard time deciding, it's possible that you have the **Loyalist** personality—a true blue friend who can have challenges with anxiety and decisions from time to time.

Might you be the **Enthusiast**, clearly designed to be a free-range human, motivated to have fun and freedom?

Or possibly you may relate most to the **Challenger**, a dominant and straightforward personality that tends to intimidate others without even knowing it.

Or finally, could you be a **Peacemaker**—gentle and sweet, avoiding confrontation as much as possible and motivated to seek and create harmony?

I have no idea who you are right now, but if you were the *ultimate* you, I would recognize you in a heartbeat.

Whether famous or unknown, educated or not, rich or poor, if you are your ultimate self, you are by definition what Abraham Maslow[2] referred to as a self-actualized person; that is, someone living at the peak of human potential.

Would you like to read a description of the Ultimate You?[3] Regardless of your particular personality type, it goes something like this:

- You are alive, engaged, and spontaneous.
- You are comfortable with yourself, others, and nature. You accept your own human nature with all its flaws. You have a non-hostile sense of humor and a wonderful capacity to laugh at yourself. You accept the shortcomings of others and the contradictions of the human condition with humor and tolerance. You may even have shed what I call "Buddha tears," crying with compassion for the human condition.
- You are free from reliance on external authorities or other people. You are resourceful and independent and have a mission to fulfill in life, some task or problem outside of yourself you are uniquely equipped to pursue.
- You are sensitive to what is not authentic, to what is fake or dishonest. Your own interpersonal relationships are therefore profound and marked by deep, loving, unconditional bonds.

---

2   American psychologist Abraham Maslow (April 1, 1908–June 8, 1970) is best known for creating "Maslow's Hierarchy of Needs," a theory of psychological health predicated on fulfilling innate human needs within a hierarchy that begins with survival needs and culminates with self-actualization.

3   The "Ultimate You" description has been modified from Wikipedia's definition of self-actualization, http://en.wikipedia.org/wiki/Self-actualization.

- Despite your satisfying relationships with others, you also value solitude and are comfortable being alone.

- You constantly renew your appreciation of life's basic goodness and have frequent peak experiences marked by feelings of ecstasy, harmony, and deep meaning. During these times, you feel at one with the Universe, strong and calm, filled with light, beautiful and good—you get the picture. (For some of you, think Woodstock meets Jazz Festival in the middle of the desert at Burning Man. You know who you are!)

In short, you feel peaceful, passionate, accepted, loved, loving, and *alive*.

In this moment, if you do not feel like the Ultimate You living your ultimate life, then it is my hope that this book will bring you closer to that. On the other hand, if you do feel like you already *are* your ultimate self, I don't have to tell you that this peak condition in no way precludes you from seeking more information to help you grow even further, since, by definition, self-actualized people seek ongoing self-improvement. My experience tells me that you will be pleased with the time you spend with this book, and you will find it an extraordinary tool for attaining even higher levels of ability to create and manifest a greater capacity for awareness and compassion.

In the next few pages, you will find a test by Dr. Richard Boyum related to the characteristics of the self-actualized person. It might be interesting to take this test today and then retake it about six months after you have implemented some of the ideas from this book.

Once you understand the Nine-Point Personality System (NPS) and the theory of the biological basis of personality, you are well on your way to becoming more of who you are truly meant to be. Furthermore, once you understand the information in this book, I hope you will come to accept that we *all* do the best we can, given the resources we have. In other words, there is no such thing as a difficult person, just people with difficult (for you) personalities (sometimes in difficult situations).

Understanding personality from the "inside out"—that is, understanding how biology and environment create personality—will help you to understand what motivates you and others, allowing you to communicate more effectively (to get more of what *you* want) and listen better (to help other people get what *they* want, too). This process leads to more satisfying relationships because satisfying relationships depend upon your ability to understand others. The degree to which you understand your personality and the personalities of others is directly related to the degree to which your relationships (and life in general) feel easy or hard. The most elegant way of understanding yourself begins with understanding your personality, and your efforts to accomplish this will be rewarded with more compassion and peace for yourself and any relationships you have ever had, have now, or will have in the future.

If you think I'm overstating the importance of understanding personality, consider the possibility that personality affects *every* aspect of your life. Whether you realize it or not, personality affects how easy or difficult it is for you to fall asleep and stay asleep; it even affects the quality of your dreams. Personality affects how you see yourself, how you perceive others, and how others perceive you. It also affects how you experience your present, how you remember your past, and how you envision your future. It affects how you learn and how you communicate (or don't), which then affects your personal and business relationships. Personality affects how you motivate yourself. It influences your food choices and even what kinds of people you like or don't like.

So, what is this thing we call personality? Well, as long as humans have been human, there has been an ongoing debate about how we define personality. (Three factors? Sixteen? Who knows?) And, what creates personality? (Nature versus nurture? Both?) Put simply, the most elegant definition of personality, in my opinion, is the following: personality is an enduring pattern of how a person thinks, feels, and behaves. If we accept this definition, the next question that comes to mind is *what* creates the similarities and differences in how each of us feels, thinks, and behaves? And how do we account for our human inconsistency over time as well?

Dr. Funder, author of the textbook *The Personality Puzzle*, cites six differing perspectives or approaches in personality psychology that attempt to explain what creates personality.[4] Some of the approaches seem quite complementary

---

4   The six main approaches referred to are the Trait, Biological, Psychoanalytical, Behavioral, Cognitive, and Humanistic approaches (Funder, 2000).

while others seem wholly incompatible. What has been missing is a unifying framework large enough and elegant enough to make sense of all approaches. Such a framework, ideally, would not oppose or contradict the current traditions of personality psychology. Rather, it would help to explain how each approach is useful and how it relates to the other approaches.

Personality is an enduring pattern of how
a person thinks, feels, and behaves.

The well-known parable about six blind men who encounter an elephant for the first time ends with the six arguing vehemently over what an elephant "really is" based on each man's interpretation of his experience of the elephant. According to the tale, each man touches a different part of the elephant—the trunk, the tail, the leg, the tusks, the ear, and the side of the elephant—then walks away convinced that his "truth" is complete and that the other five men are wrong. Obviously, what they each lack is a larger perspective of the elephant in its entirety.

I think the various approaches to personality psychology are all telling the truth from their perspective, but the "elephant" is what Dr. Funder calls the

One Big Theory that unites and makes sense of all approaches. In his book, *The Personality Puzzle*, Dr. Funder questions, "Why doesn't somebody just come up with the One Big Theory—you could call it the OBT—that explains everything now accounted for separately by trait, biological, psychoanalytic, humanistic, behavioral, and cognitive approaches?"

I believe this book effectively outlines that OBT of personality psychology. I begin with a personality system that offers the most complete and accurate representation of human personality that currently exists, which leads to a biologically based theory, developed after more than thirty years of conducting literature searches and experiments, gathering data, and observing human behavior. The personality system and my supporting theory, when combined, are the NPS. The NPS is as simple and complex as the human beings it seeks to map, and I believe it is large enough, true enough, and elegant enough to serve as a unifying paradigm. Not only can it embrace all six of the approaches to personality that Dr. Funder describes, but it can actually *integrate* all of them and show how they work together and complement each other. In addition, this system is simultaneously a categorical and a trait-based system. (If you are interested, I explain in Chapter 7 what that means and what makes that so very cool and useful for therapists and researchers.) And, as if that weren't enough, the NPS is also a dynamic, three-dimensional, and fluid system that is extremely precise and even *predictive*.

The degree to which you understand your personality and the personalities of others is directly related to the degree to which your relationships (and life in general) feel easy or hard.

Here's a sneak peek at the nine core personalities identified through the NPS—we'll dig more deeply into what each personality looks like later in the book.

One—*The Reformer*—principled and orderly, and under stress becomes perfectionist and self-righteous

Two—*The Helper*—caring and generous, and under stress can become possessive and manipulative

Three—*The Achiever*—adaptable and ambitious, and under stress can become image-conscious and hostile

Four—*The Individualist*—intuitive and expressive, and under stress can become self-absorbed and depressive

Five—*The Investigator*—perceptive and original, and under stress can become detached and eccentric

Six—*The Loyalist*—engaging and committed, and under stress can become defensive and paranoid

Seven—*The Enthusiast*—enthusiastic and accomplished, and under stress can become scattered and manic

Eight—*The Challenger*—self-confident and decisive, and under stress can become dominating and combative

Nine—*The Peacemaker*—peaceful and reassuring, and under stress can become complacent and neglectful

Chicken? Egg? *Or Both?*

Although the media has yet to catch up with the "nature versus nurture" (a.k.a. "genes versus environment") debate regarding personality, science has shed important light on this issue and reached a consensus. It appears that personality is both (1) something we are born with and (2) something influenced by the environment. In fact, the question in personality psychology is not *whether* personality is biologically based and then affected by our environment, but *how much* of our personality is hard wired, and to what degree do our life experiences amplify or attenuate our personality traits.

This elegant system of personality may be the most true-to-life personality system to date. In this book, I will describe the NPS in a fair amount of detail and include the biological theory that I believe underlies it. Through the lens of this personality system, you can eventually find answers to the following questions you may have wondered about for most of your life, and along the way, you may use the answers to these questions to become the Ultimate You!

These questions include:

- Who am I?
- How did I become who I am?
- Am I a product of my genes or my surroundings?
- How much of my personality can I change?
- What are my true and most basic motivations?
- Can I change the parts of me that do not work well for me? How?
- How can I motivate myself?
- How can I help others make their dreams come true?
- Why can't my significant others, boss, or employees see situations the same way I do?
- Why do I crave carbohydrates under stress?
- Why do I behave one way in some situations and another way in other situations?
- What are my strengths and weaknesses as a person?
- How can I maximize my strengths and minimize my weaknesses?
- What type of personality should I seek as a suitable mate?
- What types of exercise, music, foods, employment, etc. best support and enhance my optimal self?
- What do I need to know about my children's personalities to help them become the healthiest people possible?
- Why do certain movie characters or even certain people seem "real" to me—or not?
- How can I get my significant other to understand what I need?
- Why do some people always seem happy while others struggle their entire lives with melancholy and depression?
- Why do I repeat the same patterns in my life, even though I feel I should know better?
- Why do people choose certain recreational activities, drugs, and experiences over others?
- Why are some people outgoing and others so shy and private?

- What do other people really expect of me?
- How do age and experience affect my personality?
- Why do people sometimes behave in ways that hurt me, anger me, disappoint me, and confuse me? Why do *I* sometimes behave in those ways?

Self-Actualization Assessment[5]

Listed below are a series of sixteen characteristics of a self-actualized person as described by Abraham Maslow. Self-actualization here is defined as being in the process of fulfilling one's potential.

After reading each characteristic, rate yourself on a scale from one to ten. Your results will give you both a linear and an intuitive representation of your strengths and weaknesses in moving toward self-actualization.

The highest total you can receive is 160 points. How close are you to this score? Remember to record your results today, and about six months from now, after completing this book and utilizing this information, take the test again and see if you notice any shifts toward becoming more of the Ultimate You.

1. I have a highly accurate perception of reality. I can accept the good with the bad, the highs and the lows.

   (not at all) 1 2 3 4 5 6 7 8 9 10 (strongly agree) _____

2. I am accepting of myself, others, and nature. I see reality as it is and accept responsibility for it. I am as objective as a subjective being can be.

   (not at all) 1 2 3 4 5 6 7 8 9 10 (strongly agree) _____

3. I am spontaneous and not hung up on being as others think I should be. I am capable of doing what feels good and natural for myself. I do not try to hurt others, but I respect myself and my needs.

   (not at all) 1 2 3 4 5 6 7 8 9 10 (strongly agree) _____

---

5   This assessment has been modified from a test created by Dr. Richard Boyum. Find the original here: http://www.selfcounseling.com/help/personalsuccess/selfactualization.html.

4. I am focused on problems outside of myself. I am concerned with others and the problems of society, and I am willing to work to try to alleviate some of those.

   (not at all) 1 2 3 4 5 6 7 8 9 10 (strongly agree) _____

5. For all my social-mindedness, I also enjoy times of quiet reflection and don't always need people around me.

   (not at all) 1 2 3 4 5 6 7 8 9 10 (strongly agree) _____

6. I am capable of doing things for myself and making decisions on my own. I believe in who and what I am.

   (not at all) 1 2 3 4 5 6 7 8 9 10 (strongly agree) _____

7. I experience joy in the simple and the natural. Natural sights like sunsets are beautiful to me, and I seek them out. I can still enjoy playing the games I played as a child, and I have fun in some of the same ways I did many years before.

   (not at all) 1 2 3 4 5 6 7 8 9 10 (strongly agree) _____

8. I have experiences in which I literally feel I am floating. I feel in tune or at one with the world around me. At times, I almost feel as if I am, for a moment, part of a different reality.

   (not at all) 1 2 3 4 5 6 7 8 9 10 (strongly agree) _____

9. I have a feeling of fellowship with all of humankind. I am aware of and sensitive to the people with whom I come into contact.

   (not at all) 1 2 3 4 5 6 7 8 9 10 (strongly agree) _____

10. I have deep and profound interpersonal relationships. I am capable of fusion, love, and more perfect identification than other people might consider possible. I have relatively few friends, but those relationships are deeply meaningful.

    (not at all) 1 2 3 4 5 6 7 8 9 10 (strongly agree) _____

11. I believe in equality among human beings, that every individual has a right to express himself, and each person has strengths and weaknesses.

    (not at all) 1 2 3 4 5 6 7 8 9 10 (strongly agree) _____

12. I know the difference between "means and ends" and "good and evil," and I do not twist these things in a way that hurts me or others.

    (not at all) 1 2 3 4 5 6 7 8 9 10 (strongly agree) _____

13. I like to laugh and joke, but not at the expense of others. I am generally seen as good-natured, even though I am capable of being serious.

    (not at all) 1 2 3 4 5 6 7 8 9 10 (strongly agree) _____

14. I am capable of being highly creative. (Creativity can be expressed in many dimensions, such as writing, speaking, playing, fantasies, or other creative outlets.)

    (not at all) 1 2 3 4 5 6 7 8 9 10 (strongly agree) _____

15. I am resistant to enculturation and have, in effect, transcended my culture. I have a strong individuality, and I can make decisions about what is best for me and those I care about.

    (not at all) 1 2 3 4 5 6 7 8 9 10 (strongly agree) _____

16. I am aware that I am not perfect, that I am as human as the next person, and that there are constantly new things to learn and new ways to grow. Although comfortable with myself, I never stop striving.

    (not at all) 1 2 3 4 5 6 7 8 9 10 (strongly agree) _____

TOTAL SCORE _____ Date: _____
TOTAL SCORE _____ Date: _____

Chapter 2

Neurotransmitters— the Key to YOU

L et's go back a moment to the definition of personality from Chapter 1: **Personality is an enduring pattern of how a person *thinks*, *feels*, and *behaves*.**

Put another way, we could say that personality is a way of thinking, feeling, and behaving that is relatively *consistent over time*. But we know that people are not entirely consistent. Human behavior fluctuates at times. What about us determines our personality *and* can account for the fluctuations we experience from time to time?

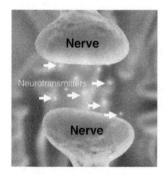

I believe the answer lies in our brain chemistry: neurotransmitters.

Neurotransmitters are simply chemicals stored in the nerves of the brain, and when released, their release stimulates the next nerve to release some of its neurotransmitters, which then stimulates the next nerve, until an entire chain of nerves is stimulated. This is how nerves communicate with one another. At the end of the completed chain of communication, one of three outcomes will be produced: a thought, a feeling, or an action. This is getting interesting, isn't it?

But it gets juicier . . .

If you were to cut a human brain in half and stain it with different dyes (don't try this at home!), you would discover three main pathways that run throughout the brain. (For those of you with technical backgrounds, these three pathways are the main monoaminergic modulating brain pathways.) Each pathway is regulated by a *single* neurotransmitter, and each neurotransmitter pathway originates in a separate location in the brain and then arborizes (branches out) throughout the entire brain.

I like the picture of three trees. It visually captures the essence of arborization. Just as the branches and leaves of the trees touch and affect each other, so do the neurotransmitter pathways in the brain. We don't understand the mechanisms completely, but even though they are distinct pathways, it appears that neurotransmitter pathways do communicate with and affect each other.

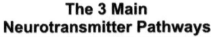

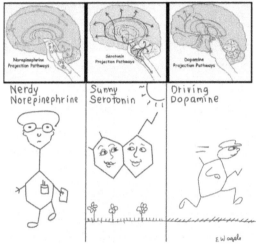

Norepinephrine regulates how we *think*.
Serotonin regulates how we *feel*.
Dopamine regulates how we *behave*.

By now, you may be able to appreciate that what we call personality may correspond with various combinations of high, medium, and low set points of the three main neurotransmitters. By set point, I mean the *usual* setting for the activity level of that neurotransmitter under normal circumstances.

Personality (how you think, feel, and behave) = various combinations of high, medium, and low set points of the three main neurotransmitters' activity in your brain.

To illustrate what I mean by a set point and how it works, let's look at blood pressure. We all have genetically determined set points for our blood pressure. If your blood pressure set point is 120/80, that means *most* of the time, under *normal* circumstances, your pressure will read at around 120 over 80 (give or take 10 to 15 points).

But what happens to your blood pressure when you are running late for an important event? It goes up, as it will with any number of stressors. But the elevation is only temporary. When that stressor goes away, your pressure should return to its usual range or set point.

On the other hand, think about what happens to your blood pressure when you are relaxing at the beach, without a care in the world. It probably goes down—but again, this is only a temporary dip. And, when that condition of luxurious relaxation goes away, your pressure will return right back to its set point.

To maintain good health, we should first know what our blood pressure set point is and then respond accordingly. The good news is that even if our blood pressure set point runs high, we can learn to manage it by monitoring it and making changes to our behavior (perhaps taking medication, lessening stressors, and/or adjusting our diet)—and we can even influence that set point by changing the way we *think* and *feel*.

In much the same way, neurotransmitters that help to shape personality have set points of high, medium, or low activity, and these set points have very specific effects on thinking, feeling, and behavior—and therefore on personality. Like blood pressure, neurotransmitter activity can fluctuate because of your choices and your changing circumstances. You may have temporary increases and decreases of the neurotransmitter activity in a single day or hour. Actually, neurotransmitters respond to your internal and external conditions every single moment. So, while your neurotransmitters affect the way you think, feel, and behave, just as with your blood pressure, the reverse is also true: how you think, feel, and behave can affect your neurotransmitter activity.

While your neurotransmitters affect the way you think, feel, and behave; the reverse is also true: you can influence your neurotransmitter activity by how you choose to think, feel, and behave.

Remember, just like blood pressure, these rises and drops in neurotransmitter levels are usually temporary, and when the optimal or stressful conditions go away, the neurotransmitters return to their set point, whatever that is for you. You will soon see that an understanding your set point will help to explain why and how your personality may temporarily "visit" another personality type, in a very specific pattern, depending on whether your conditions are optimal or suboptimal.

Let's explore the nature of these three main neurotransmitters, how they affect you, how to identify the set points in yourself and others, and what factors cause those neurotransmitter levels to rise and fall (which then amplify or weaken various personality traits).

Please note that the factors that increase or decrease the neurotransmitters are not compiled in an exhaustive list. Research is constantly adding new information to the relationship between our chemistry and the foods we eat, the music we listen to, the people we associate with, the way we exercise, and even how we express spirituality.

"Nerdy" Norepinephrine

Nerdy Norepinephrine

So let's start with "nerdy norepinephrine." **Norepinephrine** is considered the "thinking" neurotransmitter. It regulates how quickly and how often someone thinks and problem solves. Norepinephrine is literally a "brain adrenaline." If you think of the brain as an engine, the level of norepinephrine (let's call it "norep" for short) determines the brain's working idle speed. People who have a high set point of norep are people whose brain "engines" are set at a high idle. They are almost always revved up and ready to think!

As a stress hormone, norep affects parts of the brain where attention and responding actions are controlled. Very high levels of norep are associated with anxiety. (Interestingly, not all people with high norep are anxious. You'll learn why some are and some are not anxious a little later.)

People with high norep activity tend to speak fast and are sometimes perceived as high-strung. They may fidget and appear to have "nervous energy." High noreps are constant thinkers. They are the ones who report that they wake up in the morning and immediately start thinking about something. They think actively almost all day long and often have a hard time "turning their brain off," especially at night. Sleep can be a challenge—both falling asleep and staying asleep. Individuals with high norep also report active dreams that many times involve work or problem solving. If you ask someone who has a high norep set point what he is thinking about, you will most likely get a response that includes a chain of related thoughts. When it comes to problem solving, high norep types employ complex, option-oriented, and rapid thought for evaluating situations.

On the other hand, people who have a low norep set point are what we call "situation dependent" thinkers; that is, their general mental state is much more relaxed, and they don't actively problem solve unless a situation (or person) is in need of their attention. People who have a low norep set point tend to speak more slowly and may be perceived as "solid" or "steady." They usually don't have much difficulty falling and/or staying asleep. In fact, they often report that they "hit the pillow and fall asleep." Because they don't have an excess of brain adrenaline, they generally do not second-guess themselves and employ a well-developed instinct for evaluating situations and problem solving. These are the people who often say they make good "gut decisions." If you ask someone who has a low norep set point what she is thinking about, you will most likely get a response like "not much" or "nothing," and she means it! Very low levels of norepinephrine can be associated with loss of alertness, depression, and memory difficulties.

People who have a medium norep set point are called "intermittent" thinkers. Their ability to fall asleep easily varies, and they find themselves cycling in and out of daydreaming and active thinking throughout the day. People with a medium set point vary from relying on emotional, feeling-based methods to logical and strategic methods for evaluating situations and problem solving. If you ask someone who has a medium norep set point what he is thinking about, it's anybody's guess what the answer will be.

THINKING ABOUT THINKING

It can be a challenge to "type" oneself or another with respect to the norepinephrine set point. Almost everyone thinks most of the time, but active problem solving characterizes the kind of thinking norepinephrine elicits, and this is different than, say, daydreaming. Having a high norep set point myself, I assumed for most of my younger life that all people were like me and thought all the time in the intensely focused way that I thought. I now believe that, although the brain is constantly firing random thoughts, the difference between the norep types seems to lie in how much attention is paid to those thoughts. I liken it to a TV turned on in the living room that produces a constant source of noise in the background. The low norep types are like people who walk through the living room and barely notice any programs that happen to be on. The midrange norep types are like the people who catch a phrase or an image that interests them, sit for a while, and then move on to other areas of the house when they lose interest. The high noreps are the people who are glued to the screen most of the time and even have difficulty turning the TV off because something constantly captures their interest.

Under stress, a person with a high norepinephrine set point finds himself inclined to *think* of a solution to get out of the stressful situation. If no clear or obvious solution can be found, the stress level, and therefore the norep level, increases even more. In other words, constantly thinking about a problem that has no clear or obvious solution creates its own sensory overload, producing even more stress and igniting a vicious cycle. When this happens, falling asleep and staying asleep can become a challenge, adding even more stress to an already stressed mind and body.

Also, many people don't realize that hypoglycemia (low blood sugar), often the result of eating poorly, is a stressor to the body and causes an increase in norepinephrine. Many people who eat sweets and caffeine in response to feeling mental or physical low energy can unknowingly set off a roller coaster effect of high and low blood sugar levels with corresponding high and low norep levels; this wreaks havoc mentally, physically, and emotionally. Low serotonin levels complicate the process even more—sigh. (I'll address that in more depth in Chapter 6.)

Finally, caffeine has an effect on your adrenal glands, pushing them to release adrenaline and norepinephrine, which then causes your body to release its own stored sugars, and if your body overreacts with too much insulin, you are back to hypoglycemia and exhaustion and therefore more stress. So, a cup of Joe might kick-start that brain engine of yours and get it fired up, but do be careful: too much can leave you feeling anxious and jittery. Add a cigarette or two with that, and oh my, you are throwing kerosene on fire.

Some factors that **increase** *norepinephrine activity in all personality types include stress, sensory overload, caffeine, nicotine, and some antidepressants.*

It has also been noted that decreased levels of norep are associated with depression; some antidepressants are designed to increase norep levels to improve the sluggish thinking that often accompanies depression.

Some factors that **decrease** *norepinephrine activity in all personality types include repetitive muscle movement, gamma-aminobutyric acid (GABA), massage, some medications that help you sleep, and orgasms.*

One way to decrease the effect of norep is by doing repetitive muscle movement like walking, jogging, chanting, praying, or even chewing gum! Another way is to get a deep-tissue massage. You can also take GABA, an amino acid sold in health food stores as a supplement; it acts as a neurotransmitter, working like "brakes" on norep activity. Alcohol and some medications designed to help people sleep are believed to work by increasing GABA activity, which counters the effects of norep.

Another interesting activity shown to decrease norepinephrine is having an orgasm. That might explain why a person may describe himself as "brainless" after reaching a climax. (I tell people in my workshops that I'm not giving homework here—I'm just reporting what I have read in the research literature!)

The University of Washington states that the precursor of norepinephrine is tyrosine, which can be found in different foods. Ingesting foods with tyrosine can increase norep production in a person's brain. Nutrition Data lists that the seafood with the highest tyrosine content includes shrimp (1620 mg), tuna (1484 mg), cod (1476 mg), haddock (1467 mg), pollock (1426 mg), lobster (1392 mg), and snapper (1388 mg). Pork roast has 1606 mg of tyrosine, and chicken has 1500 mg; turkey has an even higher content with 1771 mg.

Dairy products also contain a significant amount of tyrosine. Cottage cheese has 1833 mg; cream cheese, 1528 mg; low-fat cheddar cheese, 1248 mg; Parmesan cheese, 1117 mg; provolone cheese, 1109 mg; and mozzarella cheese, 1105 mg. Plain yogurt has 1032 mg, and dry nonfat milk has 968 mg. Other sources of tyrosine include grains, fruits, vegetables, nuts, lima beans, avocados, almonds, sesame seeds, pumpkin seeds, and bananas. Soy protein has 2008 mg; tofu, 1321 mg; peanut flour, 1298 mg; seaweed, 2046 mg; spinach, 1483 mg; and beans have 1006 mg per serving.

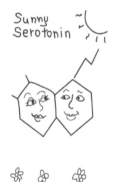

Sunny Serotonin

Now let's take a look at "sunny serotonin." **Serotonin** is known as the well-being neurotransmitter. The higher serotonin you have, the greater your sense of well-being.

People born with a high serotonin set point don't have to *try* to be positive; they are born with rose-colored glasses, wired to see the half-full glass. High serotonin activity is also associated with a high pain threshold and high pain tolerance.

By the way, the pain *threshold* is the point when a person first perceives pain; pain *tolerance* is how long a person can tolerate the pain—before saying "uncle" or passing out! People who have high pain thresholds are not necessarily aware of it, and, oddly enough, people who have low pain thresholds often report having high pain thresholds. The reason for this is somewhat muddled. Self-reporting might be unreliable because someone who has a high pain threshold may not experience pain often and therefore not think about pain very much. Someone with a low pain threshold, on the other hand, might wake up in the morning feeling pain but be able to push herself to go to work. In that process she may think, *Wow, I must have a high pain threshold because, despite my pain, I am able to push through it and do what I need to do.* But how could she possibly know that if she had a high pain threshold, she might not even have noticed the pain or felt it to that degree in the first place? She has nothing objective to compare it to. So, it makes self-reporting a little tricky. (Now you see why we decided to test pain tolerance and pain threshold with electric shocks that could be measured!)

Low serotonin activity levels are also associated with carbohydrate cravings, especially under stress. Personality types that appear to have low serotonin set points are usually the ones who describe themselves as "emotional eaters." Research now indicates a relationship between levels of serotonin and sunshine, so people who are already low in serotonin are believed to be more prone to depression known as seasonal affective disorder or SAD—now called recurrent major depressive disorder with seasonal pattern[6]—during the winter months when days are shorter and there is less serotonin-stimulating sunlight. So, keeping a sunny attitude may be easier to do by spending a little more time in a sunny environment. Even exposure to indirect sunlight (such as through a window) appears to improve one's mood according to researchers from the University of Pittsburgh and Carnegie Mellon University, who discovered that patients placed in bright rooms reported less perceived stress and took less medication per hour than patients in dim rooms.

People born with low serotonin set points are also what we call "reactive"; that is, they are more sensitive to their external and internal experiences and react more quickly and intensely (some would say more dramatically) than most people. So, a reactive person may be more keenly sensitive to sensory

---

6   American Psychiatric Association (2013). *Diagnostic and Statistical Manual of Mental Disorders* (Fifth ed.). Arlington, VA: American Psychiatric Publishing. pp. 123–154. ISBN 978-0-89042-555-8.

input—what he sees, hears, touches, tastes, etc. If, for example, he is exposed to music that most people experience as "loud," he could experience it as "blaring and obnoxious."

Reactive types are not only sensitive to their surrounding environment, but they are also more keenly sensitive to their internal environment (what they feel). So, something that most people experience as a little embarrassing might be experienced by a reactive person as "utterly humiliating."

Due to their heightened sensitivity, reactive types may tend to have a temper and/or experience anxiety. Once again, it is sometimes difficult for people to recognize their own reactivity. Not everyone who has a temper and/or anxiety identifies it as such. For instance, I once worked with a man named Bob, a very successful CEO and self-identified "carb craver." He used to say, "I never met a cookie I didn't like!" Bob asked me to help him figure out his personality type. He denied having any anger or anxiety, but after further questioning, I began to suspect that he had one of the reactive personality types.

I then asked him, given he would not acknowledge he had a temper, "Is it possible that people at work might perceive you as having a temper?"

He hesitated briefly then responded, "Well, yes. The people I work with might say that I have a temper."

"And why might that be?" I asked.

"Well, last month I threw my computer through my office window, and I think people thought I was having a temper tantrum."

"Well, what would *you* call that?" I inquired.

"Oh that?" he said. "That was just venting. That stupid computer was frustrating me, and I just had enough of it."

It turns out that Bob had a father who was also reactive and probably "self-medicating" with alcohol. Alcohol and anger do not mix well; as a result, Bob's father was often violently reactive. Bob grew up thinking that anger was a "bad" feeling. He was not taught that anger is a result of hurt or fear and can be a very useful emotion if expressed in a constructive way. When Bob was a child, he resolved never to "be angry" like his father. By not understanding the value of his reactivity and how to express it in a healthy way, Bob became the proverbial emotional pressure cooker. He constantly denied and tried to repress his upset feelings, but in time, with enough stress, pain, and/or fatigue, he would eventually succumb to uncontrolled, angry outbursts. Those outburst would be very uncomfortable for him, which then led him to attempt to "control it more," leading to more pressure and disastrous results.

Unfortunately, many cultures in our world perceive anger as a negative emotion, so there is a certain bias against people who are reactive. Reactivity, to those who are not reactive, can be experienced as overly dramatic. In fact, reactive types at low levels of functioning are often referred to as "drama queens," "obsessive-compulsive neurotics," or "bullies," depending on their precise personality types. Sometimes, as in the case of Bob, even the reactive people themselves judge their intense responsiveness in a less than positive light.

But there is incredible value in having this kind of sensitivity. Having a low serotonin set point makes it easier to see what is not right (seeing the half-empty glass), which makes for a very good troubleshooter. This kind of person can more easily anticipate what can go wrong and help to protect himself and others from harm in the process. Having low serotonin activity can also make a person more sensitive to beauty or lack of beauty in one's environment, lending an increased aesthetic sensibility and talent for tasteful decorating. Being sensitive to what is not "right" or fair can lead someone to take action to correct an injustice. Being sensitive to intense emotions can inspire poetry, music, or other expressive arts.

So, there we have it: high serotonin produces a sunny, positive outlook and a high pain threshold; low serotonin produces sensitive, reactive, and low threshold personalities. So, what about an average serotonin set point? As you might imagine, people born with average serotonin set points are what we call emotionally neutral. They are not particularly the positive outlook people, nor are they particularly reactive; they would probably describe themselves as emotionally "steady" realists.

A HUMBLING LESSON

Each set point, and especially the combinations of set points, has a specific effect that can be both a blessing and a curse, depending on a person's level of health and on the situation. I have to admit, I learned this lesson the hard way. Years ago, when Eric and I were still learning about this personality system, we were given an incredible opportunity to create a team of radiologists. We thought we were going to be smarter than God, so we created an entire team of neutral and nonreactive personality types. Our goal was to create a positive, happy, and harmonious group of radiologists; in other words, no reactives allowed.

What we created was an absolute disaster! Nine months after forming this group of radiologists, the entire practice imploded. By the time we realized that something was very wrong with our "harmonious" group, it was too late. In retrospect, we realized that all members, in the spirit of cooperation, and in an attempt to avoid conflict, never shared their concerns with each other. They were "yes people." Instead of saying "no" or expressing upsets, they routinely agreed to shifts and conditions they did not necessarily like.

With each attempt to be a "good team player," each doctor was inadvertently putting an emotional Band-Aid on top of a problem rather than addressing the concern. We pulled back the "bandages" of the group only to find a festering wound of unspoken disappointments, resentments, and disagreements that we had no idea existed. If only we had put just one reactive personality in our group, I am pretty sure that person would have served as the "canary in the coal mine," alerting us to his unhappiness with certain policies and procedures. That might have set a precedent and created permission for the other members to broach uncomfortable topics.

It was a costly lesson on many levels, but the take-home message was critically important: first of all, we were not smarter than God. (Imagine that!) There is a reason for biodiversity. Each one of our set points and combinations of set points has an advantage for survival. Understanding and respecting this ought to help all of us to appreciate, embrace, and celebrate our differences.

Factors that decrease serotonin activity include stress, pain, and fatigue in ALL personality types, but of course, types who have a naturally low set point are more prone to being affected by stress, pain, and fatigue. When anyone experiences one or more of those factors, it can drain the serotonin activity, making the person even more susceptible to—you guessed it—stress, pain, and fatigue.

The "big 3" factors that decrease serotonin activity in ALL personality types are stress, pain, and fatigue.

So, the next time someone is upset with you and maybe even yells at you, remember that he or she is not trying to be a jerk on purpose. I remind myself that the person before me must be experiencing some sort of stress, pain, and/or fatigue. Then I think, *Aww, his serotonin levels are depleted!* At that point, instead of feeling upset with this person, I feel compassion, and my behavior naturally reflects my attitude. I am much more kind and understanding and far less likely to take things personally. By being able to respond with compassion, I notice that instead of escalating into an argument or heated discussion, we move into a more civilized and pleasant form of communicating our differences.

Luckily, there are even more ways to increase serotonin activity than there are factors that decrease it. These include eating carbohydrates. But a word of caution here: in my quest to crack the code regarding fat in females after forty, I learned that eating carbohydrates, which may ease our mood in the short run, can really work against us in the long run. Carbohydrates are relatively new to our digestive tract (evolutionarily speaking). It follows that there is no such thing as an *essential* carbohydrate. Contrary to conventional thinking, we do not need to include carbohydrates for a balanced diet; we do not need carbohydrates to survive at all. In fact, as we age, carbohydrates can work against our survival by causing us to become insulin resistant, leading to obesity and other lethal conditions, such as diabetes, hypertension, stroke, Alzheimer's, and certain cancers. So, my recommendation here is to be aware that carbohydrate craving is a symptom of stress. Rather than reaching for a cookie or ice cream or pasta, substitute with another form of nurturing, and eat a piece of cheese or pepperoni so that your serotonin can return to a less depleted state.

Other factors that increase serotonin include positive thinking; "happy," uplifting music; antidepressants (such as selective serotonin reuptake inhibitors [SSRIs]); psychedelic drugs (such as Ecstasy); and kindness.

Some factors that increase serotonin activity are carbohydrates; positive thinking; "happy," uplifting music; most antidepressants; psychedelic drugs; and kindness.

One caveat regarding positive thinking: positive thoughts need to come from *within* the person in whom the serotonin is depleted. A well-intentioned (high serotonin) person chirping about the value of positive thinking does not often help a person in a depleted state. In fact, a serotonin-depleted person may experience the "help" as utterly annoying. It is a terribly difficult challenge to summon up positive thoughts from a depleted state since serotonin depletion creates emotional, mental, and physical dysphoria (the opposite of a feeling of well-being). The external world is experienced as heavier and darker, and a sense of hopelessness can overwhelm the brain. If that weren't bad enough, time itself seems to stretch out, creating the belief that this unpleasant state will last forever.

While it may be difficult to drum up a positive thought in the serotonin-depleted state, it may be slightly easier to perform a random act of kindness. Yes, believe it or not, simply being kind to someone, having someone be kind to us, or even observing someone being kind to another all increase serotonin levels and a sense of well-being.

GROWING UP IN A HIGH-SEROTONIN FAMILY

My mom, brother, and sister were all born with the Peacemaker personality; my dad and I are Enthusiasts. As you will come to learn, that's five out of five high-serotonin types. That's a lot of well-being under one roof!My parents were good parents. We were good kids. I was the oldest child, my brother came two years later, and my sister followed five years after that. To keep us in line, my brother and I got spanked a couple of times. By the time my sister came along, my parents had figured out that the easiest way to discipline us was to withhold compliments. That's right; you heard me—they would just stop complimenting us, and that's how we knew we were off track.

No alcoholism, no abuse, no drama. Some people might think it was almost boring. Like all families, we certainly had our disappointments and struggles, but what I remember most is lots of well-being and lots of love. In fact, growing up under my parents' roof, I only heard my mom raise her voice once and my dad twice.

My parents lovingly called each other "Tutti," and the only argument I witnessed as a child was at the dinner table. It occurred at least once a week and went something like this: "Here, Tutti, please, have the last bite," one parent would say to the other. "Oh no, Tutti, you have the last bite," the other would reply. "No, no, Tutti, you have the last bite!" And so it would go. We children would roll our eyes and say, "Would somebody just take the last bite, please?"

Years later, when both parents were nearing their eighties, married for over sixty years, they were still sweethearts. My dad had been through two heart attacks, and my mom had not completely recovered from three strokes. They now had a new "argument": "Here, Tutti, you die first," one parent would say to the other. "Oh no, Tutti, you die first; I don't want you to have to be the one left behind," the other would reply. "No, no, Tutti, .

continued on next page...

...continued from previous page

you go first; it's asking too much for you to go through all that grief . . ."
And so it would go. We adult children would roll our eyes again and say,
"Would both of you just go together, please? We don't know how we are
going to take care of the one who survives." So, that was life in the high-
serotonin lane for my childhood and adolescence

But what happens when someone with high serotonin raised in a high-
serotonin family "bubble" hits the real world? Well, it wasn't until I was in
nursing school that I learned not every child is raised in a healthy, happy,
loving family. And, it took years for me to realize that when someone
raises his voice in a disagreement, it doesn't mean he is "yelling" at me.
Notwithstanding those two adjustments, I would not trade my experience
for the world. I have never lived a day where I did not feel loved or grateful
to have been raised in such a rich and warm environment.

In my young adulthood, I used to wonder why people would "choose"
to be negative or "choose" to have poor self-esteem or "choose"
to be angry or anxious or abusive. It wasn't until much later that I
learned that depression, anxiety, poor self-esteem, angry outbursts,
alcoholism, and many other ailments were not choices but were
caused by chemical imbalances, sometimes created or exacerbated
by external circumstances. That made me even more keenly aware
of how fortunate I was to be born with high neurotransmitter set
points and then steeped in a rich stew of serotonin and love as
I matured.

Still later, I came to understand that to whom much is given, much
is required. What that means to me personally is that my "job" in this
world is to utilize my fortunate beginnings to help alleviate future suffering
in the world through education related to improving communication,
understanding personality, and teaching compassion—an effort that I
hope will contribute to increasing our world's supply of serotonin.

Driving Dopamine

Driving
Dopamine

Lastly, let's look at "driving dopamine." **Dopamine** is the neurotransmitter associated with behavioral activation or body energy that helps us to achieve our goals and get our rewards.

When it comes to personality, it appears that an average set point of dopamine contributes to energizing characteristics of the basic or core NPS type. A high dopamine set point seems to amplify the basic personality while a low dopamine set point dampens some of the core characteristics of the personality. Having either the high or low dopamine set points creates what we call "wings."

The "wing" is a personality type next to the main personality that complements and adds important, sometimes contradictory elements to the total personality. In real life, wings are harder to explain than they are to understand once you grasp the concept. This part of the personality (the wing) seems to fluctuate more than the other two aspects, the (norepinephrine-modulated) thinking and the (serotonin-modulated) feeling parts of the personality, which appear to be more enduring. Until you better understand the characteristics and internal motivations of the nine basic personality types, figuring out another person's type (or even your own) can be challenging. Trying to determine the wing can be even trickier. For now, it is only necessary for you to remember this: dopamine seems to be related to wings, which amplify or attenuate the personality. You will learn more about wings in "Basic Principles" in Chapter 3.

Factors that increase dopamine activity include physical movement, consumption of high-sugar and high-fat foods, and orgasms. Other factors include alcohol, caffeine, cocaine, nicotine, gambling, primal music, weightlifting, and anti-Parkinson's medications that increase L-dopa. To help your body produce more dopamine, you can also eat foods rich in tyrosine, a nonessential amino acid found in chicken, turkey, fish, peanuts, almonds, avocados, bananas, lima beans, sesame seeds, and pumpkin seeds. Monoamine oxidase **inhibitors** (MAOI) and SSRI drugs also increase concentrations of both dopamine and serotonin.

Factors that increase dopamine activity include primal music (like drumming), protein (especially red meat), high-sugar and high-fat foods, weightlifting, orgasms, alcohol, caffeine, cocaine, nicotine, and gambling. Other factors include medications that increase L-dopa and movement. Factors that decrease dopamine are decreased movement; chronic stress; B-vitamin, iron, and zinc deficiencies; estrogen deficiency (in women); excessive alcohol; narcotic consumption; and some antipsychotic medications.

A decrease in physical activity is associated with lowered levels of dopamine. Dopamine levels are also lowered by chronic stress; B-vitamin, iron, and zinc deficiencies; estrogen deficiency (in women); and excessive alcohol and narcotic consumption. Antipsychotic medication can also reduce dopamine activity.

WHEN ALL ELSE FAILS . . .
THERE'S ALWAYS CHOCOLATE

Chocolate has been highly valued in many cultures, and there is some evidence that chocolate, especially dark chocolate, may improve mood temporarily due to its high levels of sugar, fat, phenylethylamine, and caffeine. The sugar in chocolate is associated with a release of the neurotransmitter serotonin, and the fat and phenylethylamine are associated with an endorphin release. Chocolate also contains anadamine, which targets the same receptors as tetrahydrocannabinol (THC), the principal psychoactive constituent of the cannabis (marijuana) plant, and produces a cozy, euphoric feeling. The caffeine in chocolate adds a temporary stimulant effect, which makes chocolate the optimal "brain happiness food." It may also be why many choose chocolate when depressed, as it improves their overall state of mind.

Now, you have a basic understanding of the three main neurotransmitters and their effects on your body, mind, and behavior. You also have some information about how you can increase or decrease the effects of these neurotransmitters. In the next chapter, let's see what "magic" happens when we *combine* neurotransmitters.

Chapter 3

A New Theory Based
on an Ancient Symbol

Now that you have a basic understanding of the three main neurotransmitters, how they affect your body and mind, and how *you* can affect them, let's see what happens when we combine two of them.

For starters, if you were to take the high, medium, and low set points of norepinephrine and combine them with the high, medium, and low set points of serotonin, mathematically you would come out with nine possible combinations.

It would look something like this:

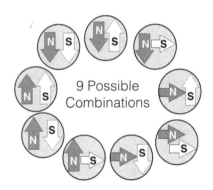

9 Possible
Combinations

Starting at the top right, the combinations are:

1. Low Norepinephrine / Average Serotonin
2. Average Norepinephrine / High Serotonin
3. Average Norepinephrine / Average Serotonin
4. Average Norepinephrine / Low Serotonin
5. High Norepinephrine / Average Serotonin
6. High Norepinephrine / Low Serotonin
7. High Norepinephrine / High Serotonin
8. Low Norepinephrine / Low Serotonin
9. Low Norepinephrine / High Serotonin

I believe these combinations are what yield the nine basic or core personality types of the NPS, each with its own specific motivation, basic fear, and communication style.

(You will find a more detailed description on each type in Chapter 4, "The Nine Types—Which One Are You?")

The 9-Point Personality System

You may be wondering how combining two different neurotransmitter set points can form the foundation of a personality. So, I am going to illustrate how three high norepinephrine set points each combine with a *different*

serotonin set point and create very different personalities as a result of those combinations. The three personalities are the Loyalist (6), Investigator (5), and Enthusiast (7). This triad of personalities is often referred to as the Thinking Triad in Enneagram circles.

High Norepinephrine / Low Serotonin

Recall from the previous chapter that norepinephrine is a brain adrenaline. Having a high norep set point is like having a "brain engine" set at a high resting idle. In other words, high norep creates a brain that is "revved up." Now, take that revved-up brain and run some low-octane fuel (low serotonin) or low well-being thoughts through it. What kind of thoughts do you think will be created with this combination of chemical set points?

Typically, the kinds of thoughts produced include questions like: "What can go wrong here?" "What's not right with this picture?" "Can I believe what this person is saying?" This kind of thinking is actually quite beneficial when it comes to troubleshooting because the low serotonin creates a sense of "well-being deficiency"—a feeling that something may be wrong, which then causes the brain to think and look for potential trouble and danger. Constant vigilance like this can lead to an overall state of anxiety and/or a reactive temper, a sense of always feeling "on edge."

This type of thinking and attitude characterizes the Loyalist, the sixth of the nine personalities. I think this personality may be the second hardest personality to have because it rests on top of a lot of mental energy, designed to be skeptical and somewhat suspicious. That is a perfect recipe for feelings of unrest and anxiety that seek relief by finding structure and security. If a Loyalist finds a person, family, religion, or organization that she can trust, it will create a sense of relief and security that will lead her to be extremely loyal and potentially self-sacrificing, sometimes even to her own detriment. We often say you can't find a better and more loyal friend than the Loyalist, hence their well-deserved name.

The Loyalist is designed to be a team player, and although she can be a good leader, she will generally feel more comfortable supporting others. We sometimes say tongue-in-cheek that the Loyalist has a "ricochet" brain; she can think on many different levels at the same time. But that can be exhausting. (It can also make reading a challenge. Many Loyalists report that the multi-level thinking action in their brain makes focusing attention in one place a struggle.) This ricochet-thinking may explain why Loyalists gravitate to structure and rules. If a higher authority sets up a system of structure and rules that the Loyalist believes in (or is loyal to), then following those rules helps keep the brain from bouncing around and having to question every single step of the way. Rules and order help calm the ricochet brain and create a sense of certainty and security, which also leads to a greater feeling of comfort and well-being.

High Norepinephrine / Average Serotonin

Now, let's try another combination. This time, we will start with the same revved-up (high norep) brain, but instead of running low octane fuel (low serotonin), let's see what happens if we run moderate octane (an average set point of serotonin) or emotionally neutral thoughts through it.

What kind of thoughts do you think this combination of chemical set points might create? Typically, people with this combination of set points ask emotionally neutral and curious questions like: "What makes this work?" "What happens when you add this to that?" "What would an alien think if they saw this object?"

This type of thinking and attitude characterizes the Investigator, the fifth of the nine personalities. This kind of personality reminds me a bit of the main character in the movie *E.T.* Remember how E.T., the alien, was tireless for knowledge ("Input! Input! Input!")? The Investigator has a similar motivation— an unending quest for knowledge.

With an emotionally neutral orientation, objects and ideas can sometimes be more interesting than emotional people. As a result, the Investigator can seem less than approachable and not so "warm and fuzzy." This type of personality is generally not very aware of cultural trends and fashions either, which is why the Investigator looks and behaves in a way that we refer to as "nerd-like." Investigators tend to be more practical and pragmatic than fashion-conscious.

High Norepinephrine / High Serotonin

Lastly, take the same revved-up brain, but this time, let's see what happens when we run high-octane (a high set point of serotonin) or positive outlook emotions through it. What kind of thoughts do you think will be created with this combination of chemical set points?

Typically, the kinds of thoughts produced include optimistic questions like: "What else can go *right*?" "What can I do to make the world a better place?" "Wouldn't it be great if we all got along?"

This type of thinking and attitude characterizes the Enthusiast, the seventh of the nine personalities. This personality, having a high mental speed and high well-being, is a very inquisitive type who seeks out novel information and experiences. The Enthusiast also tends to be a bit of a risk-taker, because he assumes (with all of that well-being-loaded serotonin circulating around) that everything will turn out just fine.

The Enthusiast does not have to "try" to be positive or seek out the half-full glass. He is born with (chemical) rose-colored glasses and naturally sees the bright side of things, even in some of the gloomiest situations.

So, there you have it: the Investigator, Loyalist, and Enthusiast All three personalities are constant active thinkers (high norepinephrine), but they are distinctly different due to the combining of high, medium, or low set points of serotonin.

In the next chapter, I will give a more detailed description of each of the nine personalities in the NPS, but for now, let's do a quick review of the six remaining norepinephrine/serotonin personality combinations.

First, let's look at the Challenger (8), Peacemaker (9), and Reformer (1) personalities (the low norep types). This triad is often referred to as the Gut Triad in Enneagram circles.

Low Norepinephrine with Low, High, and Medium Serotonin

The Challenger (8), Peacemaker (9), and Reformer (1) personalities all have low norepinephrine set points, and because of this, they all share similar thinking patterns. These three types typically sleep well; that is, they fall asleep easily and tend to sleep soundly. Because they have low set points of norepinephrine, they tend not to overthink ideas or second-guess themselves and therefore appear to make solid gut decisions that they usually feel pretty confident about. They are all "situation dependent" thinkers, meaning they are not actively thinking or problem solving unless a person or situation prompts them to focus their attention on whatever is needed in the moment.

So, taking the non-overthinking brain and running low serotonin through it creates the reactive, gut-response-driven Challenger.

Replace that with high serotonin, and you have a non-overthinking, very pleasant, and easygoing Peacemaker.

Replace that with average serotonin, and you get a non-overthinking, emotionally neutral realist, known as the Reformer, who sees the world simply and plainly and offers clear and uncomplicated visionary solutions.

Finally, we have the Helper (2), Achiever (3), and Individualist (4). This triad is often referred to as the Heart Triad in Enneagram circles.

Average Norepinephrine with High, Average, and Low Serotonin

The Helper (2), Achiever (3), and Individualist (4) all have average norepinephrine set points. We believe this creates a brain that cycles between active problem solving and daydreaming throughout the day, creating what you might call "intermittent thinkers."

Take this intermittent-thinking brain, couple it with high serotonin, and you get a positive-outlook "Helper" type who is motivated to take care of others and tends not to think much about her own personal needs.

Next, consider what happens when you have an average set point of norepinephrine with an average set point of serotonin. You get a creative, emotionally neutral (perhaps calculating?) Achiever. But (pay attention here) because *both* set points are in the average range, you also get a personality type that is only one step away from *every one* of the other eight personality types. Perhaps this formula accounts for the Achiever's ability to be chameleon-like and to morph into whatever she needs to be to achieve whatever goal she desires at any given point in time.

Lastly, combine the often-creative, intermittent-thinking brain with low serotonin, and you get an emotionally reactive, creative artist, the Individualist, who is keenly sensitive to both his internal and external worlds.

These nine personality types and the relationship between them is often represented by a symbol known as the Enneagram. The symbol itself is believed to be ancient, but no definitive reference to the origin of the symbol is known. (See Appendix A for a more detailed history.)

The Enneagram Symbol

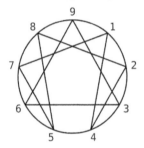

Incidentally, the symbol is not a satanic or cult symbol; rather, the lines in the figure mark the "integration" and "disintegration" paths that predict which personality type will temporarily "visit" another personality type (when the neurotransmitters temporarily rise and/or fall) due to optimal or stressful conditions—more on that later.

Now that you have an idea of where we're headed, but before learning about the specifics of each personality, let's step back a bit and review the language of the NPS and then review the basic principles of this elegant personality system. Later on, I will show you how to apply this information to yourself, your relationships, and your life.

I'm not just a number!

The Language of the Nine-Point Personality System

According to Professor Peter Austin, from the Linguistics Department School of Oriental and African Languages in London, it is estimated that there are over 6,900 languages in the world. I believe that when it comes to personality, there are only nine basic human "languages" you need to learn in order to become "fluent in human." This fluency will help you to more easily communicate what you want and also more easily understand what other people want and need.

If you have ever tried to learn how to speak a foreign language, you know it initially requires a lot of conscious effort, but ultimately, it becomes smooth and effortless. The same is true in learning this system. And, just as all languages have multiple words that may refer to the same object or situation, the NPS personality types go by many names and nicknames as well as numbers.

Have you ever been at a cocktail party where someone mentions that you remind her of a friend who is a Pisces or a Gemini? If you are not familiar with astrology, not only can it be confusing, it can actually be annoying. Or, how about someone who's into the DISC personality profile system? A DISC devotee might tell you that you're a strong "D" or an "I," or that you're totally a "blue," or you have a lot of "yellow" in your personality. If you're not familiar with the field of psychology or personality testing, you might be inclined to tell this person she has a lot of "B" and "S" and that she might as well be saying you have a Hamster or Pastrami personality.

Over the years, I have learned that initial conversations about the NPS with those who are not familiar with the system can be tedious, especially if I use the "super shortcut code" of numbers, as opposed to names of types. Say, for example, I were to say to you, "Hi, I'm Tina, and I am a three. I originally thought you were a two, but now that I've spent some time with you, I think you are a nine." If you have no experience at all with the system, this conversation might sound like, "Hi, I'm Tina, I'm a blah-blah-blah, and you're a blah-blah-blah." Pretty soon, your eyes might glaze over, and you may suddenly remember that you left an important load of laundry in your washing machine at home.

However, what if I were to say to you, "Hi, I'm Tina; I have the Achiever personality. I initially thought you had the Helper personality, but now that I've spent some time with you I think you may be a Peacemaker." You might intuitively get a general idea of where I was headed. It would not be too far of a stretch to guess that I might be a motivated and energetic person, and that I mistook you for someone with a rather strong, generous personality, but with more information, I now perceive you as a more mild-mannered, gentle sort.

The names, as opposed to the numbers, lend themselves to at least a hint of the nature of the personality types. Therefore, I have deliberately used the full names of the personality types in this book whenever I could, even though sometimes it's a little cumbersome. In real life, among friends and colleagues familiar with the system, we use the super shortcut language, or the number associated with each NPS type. For starters, it's just faster to say a one-syllable word like "four" than a six-syllable word like "Individualist." It's also simpler and more discreet in public. If, for instance, you are with a friend who is fluent in the system, you can more subtly raise four fingers to your cheek than mouth the word "in-di-vid-u-al-ist" when you are taking a guess at your waitress's personality. This is particularly useful when you don't want to be obvious about it—especially if your waitress is standing there taking your order!

Please note: there may be times in this book where you will see a reference to a personality type as a number and not with the formal name; on those occasions, it might be for the sake of alliteration, like a "serious social six" or a "flaming four," or for rhyming purposes, such as "I'm great, 'cuz I'm an eight" or finding the "fun for one," or simply because it's an exact quote or intimate reference.

Getting back to my question about being at a cocktail party and the conversation about astrology, throughout my entire life, I have been amused by how many professional astrologers were unable to determine my astrological sign. Many start with Sagittarius, then Leo, perhaps Taurus, then Aquarius. In fact, my actual astrological sign, Capricorn, is often one of the last ones they guess. The slow and plodding Capricorn is the antithesis of my personality. So, I am fond of telling people that I believe there are nine different types of Capricorns and nine different types of Aries and nine different types of Gemini and so forth. No amount of experience, in my opinion, can train someone to be precise in guessing a person's exact date of birth—which, by definition, is the only true confirmation of your astrological sign. However, when it comes to the

NPS, people can be trained to look for physical, mental, and emotional cues that are universally agreed upon, and with experience, some people can become phenomenally good at determining other peoples' NPS types.

Just as people who are exposed to a second language at a young age more easily learn it, I believe the same is true for learning the language of the NPS. If this system is taught to youngsters, it can be an easily assimilated and incredibly rich asset to life experience. I base this idea on what I have seen in the life of my grandson, Caleb. Caleb was born into a family that discussed personality and NPS types the way some families discuss the weather and current events. One day, when Caleb was five years old, he and I went to see the movie *Winnie the Pooh*. About thirty minutes into the movie, Caleb leaned over and whispered, "Mia, is Winnie the Pooh a nine?"

"Why, yes, he is, Caleb! Good job," I responded.

"What about Owl? Is he a one?"

"Yes." I nodded.

"So then is Eeyore a four?"

"Yes, actually, I believe he is!" I exclaimed.

"Hmmm, is Rabbit a six?"

"Yes, yes, he is!" I was excited and feeling proud.

Then, he asked, "What about Tigger? I'm thinking a seven with a six wing."

I almost dropped my box of popcorn and fell out of my chair. I was just amazed. It was like a personality Helen Keller moment. It was then that I realized just how intuitive and natural this system really is—so simple that a five-year-old could grasp it. That's when I thought, *This needs to eventually become a part of early childhood education.* And then, I thought, *No, this needs to become a part of everyday human language and understanding.* Someday, I hope this language will become as commonly used as concepts like "nuking" things in the microwave or "googling" a news story, concepts that did not even exist a few decades ago.

Basic Principles

The NPS is comprised of nine basic personality types, with each exhibiting a range of behaviors based upon nine discrete primary motivations. The constellation of behaviors is relatively distinct for each of the nine types and relatively specific to a type, depending upon the individual's level of functioning (how functional or dysfunctional a person is within their type).

Like most representational models that describe a dynamic system, the NPS is both simple and complex, depending on the level at which it is studied and applied. If you consider that all of art is based on three primary colors, then you quickly realize it is the mastery of the artist that can take those colors and create *The Mona Lisa* or the ceiling of the Sistine Chapel. Likewise, the NPS is based on simple constructs. With further study, and through observation of yourself and others, along with maturity and some understanding of psychology, you will begin to see this rich system as dynamic and as deep as the human beings it seeks to map.

The following basic principles underlie the modern NPS:

(1) There are nine basic personality types.

According to this system, a person has one and only one basic or core personality type (a result of the various combinations of norepinephrine and serotonin). It must be noted, however, as in any typology, that an individual will possess and have access to the traits of *all* types. Although this system suggests only nine *basic* types of personality, if "wing" influences (which we believe are related to the addition of various combinations of dopamine—to be discussed shortly) are taken into account, there are actually twenty-seven different possible combinations. In addition, if the social orientation system is overlaid, that yields fifty-four different combinations. From there, multiples of nine in exponential quantities (based on level of function) continue to multiply. Theoretically, this pattern will continue until one can ultimately find a unique pinpoint placement for each human being who has ever walked the planet!

Despite the infinite variety at the individual level, nine basic categories do seem to exist and are characterized by nine disparate internal motivations and nine distinct ways of processing information. Whether the NPS is the truest and most accurate typology system available remains to be seen. However, it is by far the most useful system I have personally experienced to date.

The following list summarizes the nine personality types using the titles assigned by Riso and Hudson. Each title is then followed by a brief descriptive word and three additional words that generally describe that specific type's basic personality characteristics at high, average, and low levels of functioning, respectively.

One—*The Reformer*—principled, orderly, perfectionist, and self-righteous
Two—*The Helper*—caring, generous, possessive, and manipulative
Three—*The Achiever*—adaptable, ambitious, image-conscious, and hostile
Four—*The Individualist*—intuitive, expressive, self-absorbed, and depressive
Five—*The Investigator*—perceptive, original, detached, and eccentric
Six—*The Loyalist*—engaging, committed, defensive, and paranoid
Seven—*The Enthusiast*—enthusiastic, accomplished, uninhibited, and manic
Eight—*The Challenger*—self-confident, decisive, dominating, and combative
Nine—*The Peacemaker*—peaceful, reassuring, complacent, and neglectful

(2) The types are universal.

All nine types occur in both males and females, cross-culturally. Although no formal research has yet been conducted related to the NPS system, Riso and Hudson conducted Enneagram certification programs around the world. To date, their books have been translated into twenty different languages. Riso and Hudson reported that members of all cultures who received their training embraced their typology system. They also reported that this acceptance and resonance occurred regardless of race, religion, age, or sex, gender, or sexual orientation.

In addition to observations of the universality of personality by clinicians who utilize the NPS, personality researchers Costa and McCrea researched patterns of co-variation among personality traits in English-speaking populations, and they compared the American factor structure with highly diverse cultures (German, Portuguese, Hebrew, Chinese, Korean, and Japanese samples). Their data strongly suggest that personality trait structure is universal.

While it appears that personality transcends cultures, different cultures may support or struggle with the various NPS types to a greater or lesser degree. Even the same culture can change over time and be more or less supportive of different personalities. During the 1940s and 1950s in the United States, for example, women who had the Helper, Peacemaker, or Loyalist personalities were highly regarded, since attributes of caretaking and peacemaking (important for homemaking) and loyalty were prized at that time. A female Enthusiast or Challenger, both of whom are considered strikingly independent, might have had some challenges in those days. However, in this day and age, she may find herself more highly regarded.

Even in "micro-cultures," such as the business world, small business organizations seem to take on as a group many of the personality traits, both strengths and weaknesses, of their founders. Riso and Hudson go so far as to say that countries may possess (or reflect?) an overall personality as well. They suggest that, currently, the United States is an Achiever country of average to low health (under stress), whose primary motivations are success and image rather than depth. Japan, they insist, is primarily a Loyalist country that reinforces the concept of "other" and values group goals and loyalty.

(3) No type is better than any other type.

Although some personality types, in certain situations and cultures, may be easier to have (and to be around), there is no inherently "better" or "best" type.

When it comes to personality traits, every blessing can be perceived as a curse and vice versa. Many times, it simply comes down to the situation at hand. For every personality type, there is a unique set of motivations, gifts, and talents, which, as a package, contain both assets and liabilities.

For example, the Investigator personality is well known for its ability to be analytical and rational. While working as a professor, for example, or in a culture that values intellectual creativity and a pragmatic approach, the Investigator can excel quickly and almost effortlessly. However, in romantic relationships, the very same qualities may become a barrier to emotional intimacy. Many a bewildered Investigator has reported confusion over emotional outbursts from his partner. Attempting to "problem solve" an emotional issue can result in his partner's escalating anger, and it often does not help when the Investigator gets flustered and asks her to "settle down" and "work things out logically." What she may have needed instead was to be held or heard on an emotional level with no need to "solve" a problem.

(4) All human beings have aspects of all personality types.

It is generally assumed that a radio has access to all local channels, but most people usually tune into a few favorite channels. In a similar way, if you have all three neurotransmitter pathways, then, theoretically, you have access to all aspects of personality, but like a favorite radio station, you will have a primary or "favored" personality (a biological set point) from which to operate and interact with the world. And, using the same radio analogy, you could still tune into other "stations" or personalities. Initially, this happens naturally based on optimal and suboptimal environmental conditions, but if you wish to, with practice and awareness, you can learn to access the various aspects of all those other personalities within yourself that you might only visit occasionally. Learning how to consciously access more of you creates greater "neuronal plasticity" (a fancy term for a more flexible brain). It helps you to understand others' points of view and to experience your world in a richer and more profound way. (See Chapter 6, "How to Utilize the NPS to Create an Awesome Life," for more instruction on how to do that.)

(5) The NPS is both diagnostic and prescriptive.

By knowing a person's NPS type, you can easily assess the level of functioning and the amount of stressors affecting them without the need to have a detailed history or current situational status. Not only is the NPS diagnostic in a manner that is neither judgmental nor emotionally charged, it is also prescriptive, meaning that it suggests areas of "homework," for example, mental and emotional exercises specific for each type that can help a person find balance and higher levels of functioning.

(6) The NPS has often been referred to as a spiritual entry-level tool.

Initially, a person may be so identified with her personality that she fails to recognize the automatic response she makes as a result of her genetic predisposition, combined with her unconscious conditioned response to the daily stressors of life. George Gurdjieff, an influential spiritual teacher of the early to mid-twentieth century, described this way of being as the "mechanical man." He taught that the individual was an undeveloped creation.

. . . man as we encounter him is an automaton. His thoughts, feelings, and deeds are little more than mechanical reactions to external and internal stimuli. He cannot do anything. In and around him, everything happens without the participation of his own authentic consciousness. But human beings are ignorant of this state of affairs, because of the pervasive influence of culture and education, which engrave in them the illusion of autonomous conscious selves. In short, man is asleep. There is no authentic "I am" in his presence, but only an egoism which masquerades as the authentic self, and whose machinations poorly imitate the normal human functions of thought, feeling, and will.[7]

At the very least, knowing one's place related to personality traits is useful for insight and improvement through therapy. Eventually, with awareness and some form of objective support, it is believed that a person can "dis-identify" with his personality and automatic responses to stressors and other people. In this way, the levels of functioning can be positively influenced to achieve states of actualization and happiness.

(7) It appears that personality is biologically based and influenced by environment.

The relative contribution of "nature versus nurture" in shaping a person's personality has fostered a longstanding debate between and among social scientists and biologists. Frequently, the two camps have argued for the primacy of one to the exclusion of the other. A more recent trend, however, is the recognition from scholars in all arenas of the social and biological sciences that complex behaviors and variation in personality can be attributed to an intricate interaction between heritable traits and environmental influences.

The NPS can be considered a diathesis stress model that suggests that an inherited tendency to express certain traits or behaviors (diathesis) may be activated under certain environmental conditions, such as external stressors.

---

7   Needleman Jacob (1996). G. I. Gurdjieff and His School, Professor of Philosophy, San Francisco State University, San Francisco, CA www.bmrc.berkeley.edu/people/misc/School. html

According to W. John Livesley, MD, PhD, and author of several books on personality and genetics,

> The genetic basis of normal and disordered personality is well established: All personality traits studied to date, assessed using self-report measures, have a substantial heritable component. Progress, albeit modest, is also being made toward identifying specific genes associated with personality traits.[8]

Mothers of multiple children report distinct differences in their children's personalities, even in utero. Most parents are bewildered at times by how different their children can be, in both temperament and style, with little variation in their environment to account for such extreme differences. However, the environment does appear to have an influence in enhancing positive attributes and exacerbating less desirable traits. As Zuckerman states,

> The fate of an early appearing personality trait will depend on its congruency or conflict with the family environment and future environments to which the individual is exposed. In other words, the environment may more directly impact the level of functioning, which has more plasticity than personality itself. The occurrence of gene-environment relationships of interaction and correlation suggest the need for clinicians to re-think ideas about the nature of the environment and the role of environmental influences in the development of personality and personality disorders.[9]

(8) There appears to be a continuum of functioning within each personality type.

This continuum accounts for the vast differences in how a personality will express itself. The continuum, which describes varying degrees of gradation of internal

---

8   Livesley, W. J. (1995). *The DSM-IV Personality Disorders*. The Guilford Press: New York, NY
9   Zuckerman, M. (1985). Psychobiology of Personality, Cambridge University Press: New York, NY

motivation, can be arbitrarily divided into nine "levels of function." In the popular literature, these are called "levels of health" or "levels of development."

The nine levels of functioning can be further grouped into three subdivisions of functioning: above average, average, and stressed. It may help to think of the continuum as a photographer's gray scale with many shades between all white and pure black (see diagram below).

Continuum of the Nine Levels of Function

Above Average	Level 1	😃
	Level 2	🙂
	Level 3	🙂
Average	Level 4	🙂
	Level 5	😐
	Level 6	😕
Stressed	Level 7	😟
	Level 8	🙁
	Level 9	🙁

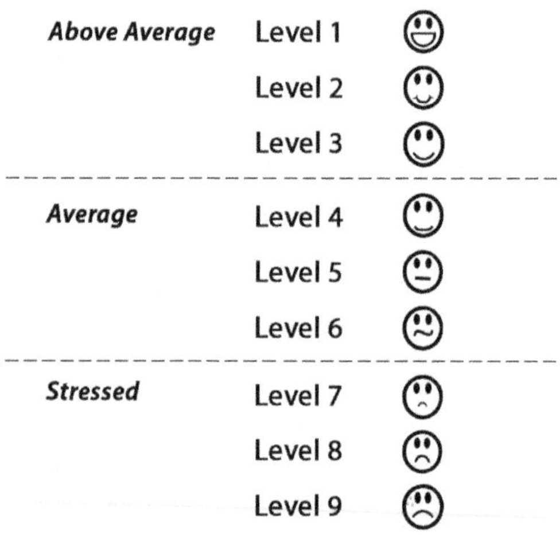

As stated previously, it appears that a person's personality type is genetically determined, and the environment influences the level of functioning for each personality type. The levels of functioning, originally influenced by environmental health of the immediate family, later extend to larger groups of people, such as school, work, and social organizations.

How a personality expresses itself is largely dependent on the level of functioning. For instance, the Challenger, at average levels of functioning, can be confrontational, domineering, and somewhat bossy in his manner of speaking and dealing with others. At stressed levels, and therefore low levels of functioning, the Challenger can become ruthless, bullying, and dictatorial. At above average levels, the same person is capable of being a magnanimous world Challenger, using his natural strengths to help and protect others. In fact, while some types dislike conflict (such as the Peacemaker and the Investigator) and try to avoid it, Challengers are energized by conflict and regard it as a challenge. This ability helps them overcome obstacles that would crush a less willful person.

Levels of functioning are generally stable over short periods of time, but they can change dramatically in either direction depending on the individual's internal perceptions and environmental stressors. It is possible, for instance, to be having a good day, performing at a high level of functioning, and then, when blindsided by an upsetting event, to quickly descend to a low level of functioning.

Examples of the range of functioning within the Challenger personality type include: Dr. Phil (above average), John Wayne (average), and Saddam Hussein (stressed).

A Three-Dimensional Representation of the Nine-Point Personality System
The beautiful original color version of the illustration can be obtained through this link: http://tinathomas.com/nps-3d-model-periodic-table

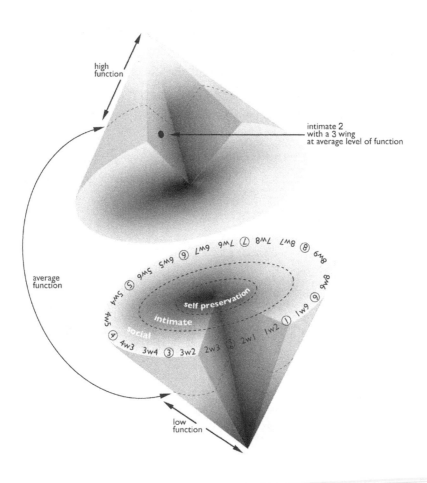

(9) There is a precise pattern of movement within this system under optimal and stressed conditions, referred to as integration and disintegration patterns.

The nine types of the NPS are not static categories. Each personality type can temporarily "visit" other personality types. Interestingly, Theodore Millon, an American psychologist known for his work on personality disorders, discovered, after creating his Millon Personality Inventory, that even traits of personality, while stable over time, tend to fluctuate during periods of personal growth and deterioration. Likewise, the expression of each NPS type is modified by optimal or stressed conditions in a predictable pattern. This results in the original personality temporarily accessing the traits and motivations of another personality. The personality pattern adopted depends on the "starting point"— that is, the original personality type and the direction of movement along a predetermined path, known as the path of integration or disintegration. (In some Enneagram schools, these paths are referred to as security points and stress points.)

The integration or security point of a given personality type is indicated by the number immediately after the personality type in the following sequence:

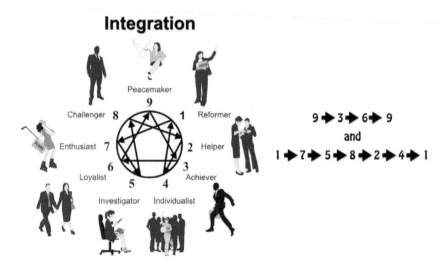

This pattern is observed when a person experiences optimal environmental conditions and/or when a person consciously chooses healthy patterns of thought and behavior.

The Nine-Point Personality System Type Direction of Integration
(Adapted from *Wisdom of the Enneagram,* Riso and Hudson)

Type	The Direction of Integration
1	Reformers become more spontaneous and joyful, like healthy Enthusiasts (7).
2	Helpers become more self-nurturing and emotionally aware, like healthy Individualists (4).
3	Achievers become more cooperative and committed to others, like healthy Loyalists (6).
4	Individualists become more objective and principled, like healthy Reformers (1).
5	Investigators become more self-confident and decisive, like healthy Challengers (8).
6	Loyalists become more relaxed and optimistic, like healthy Peacemakers (9).
7	Enthusiasts become more focused and profound, like healthy Investigators (5).
8	Challengers become more open-hearted and caring, like healthy Helpers (2).
9	Peacemakers become more self-developing and energetic, like healthy Achievers (3).

The disintegration or stress point of a given personality type is indicated by the number immediately after the personality type in the following sequence, which is exactly the reverse direction of integration:

Disintegration

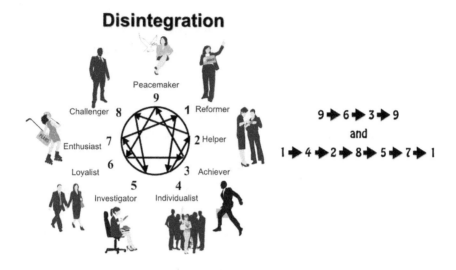

$$9 \rightarrow 6 \rightarrow 3 \rightarrow 9$$
and
$$1 \rightarrow 4 \rightarrow 2 \rightarrow 8 \rightarrow 5 \rightarrow 7 \rightarrow 1$$

This pattern is observed when a person is experiencing stressful environmental conditions and/or unconsciously chooses unhealthy patterns of thinking and behavior.

The Nine-Point Personality System Type Direction of Disintegration
(Adapted from *Wisdom of the Enneagram,* Riso and Hudson)

Type	The Direction of Disintegration
1	Methodical Reformers become moody and irrational, like low Individualists (4).
2	Caretaking Helpers become aggressive and dominating, like low Challengers (8).
3	Driven Achievers become disengaged and apathetic, like low Peacemakers (9).
4	Individualistic Individualists become over-involved and clingy, like low Helpers (2).
5	Detached Investigators become hyperactive and scattered, like low Enthusiasts (7).
6	Cooperative Loyalists become competitive and arrogant, like low Achievers (3).
7	Spontaneous, fun-loving Enthusiasts become perfectionist and critical, like low Reformers (1).

| 8 | Self-confident Challengers become secretive and fearful, like low Investigators (5). |
| 9 | Complacent Peacemakers become anxious and worried, like low Loyalists (6). |

To get a clearer picture of how this plays out, let's take a closer look at the lines of integration and disintegration for the Enthusiast (7). The integration line for the Enthusiast moves in the direction of the Investigator (5). The disintegration line for the Enthusiast moves in the direction of the Reformer (1). In practical terms, this means that the Enthusiast personality, which is motivated to experience fun and freedom, often through multiple and novel situations, has two potential directions of movement (in addition to vertical directions related to level of functioning).

Under optimal conditions, the Enthusiast may learn to better focus, an ability that comes easily for the high-functioning Investigator personality. In lay terms, NPS teachers say, "The Enthusiast learns to *visit* where the Investigator *lives*." By focusing on a limited number of options or development of skills, the Enthusiast may learn to channel her mental, physical, and emotional energies in an elegant and useful manner. Focusing enables the Enthusiast to more easily accomplish her goals and exercise her life skills. According to some Enthusiasts, learning to focus their time and attention is similar to taking bright but diffuse light and concentrating it into a powerful, single laser light beam.

The other direction the Enthusiast can take is in the path of *dis*integration, a direction observed during periods of high stress. At those times, the normally exuberant, playful, and easy-going Enthusiast personality begins to experience the lower functioning aspects of the Reformer personality. This includes a sense of rigidity and self-righteousness. In fact, Enthusiasts have reported that, in times of stress, they may feel judgmental and critical of other people who don't seem to understand the "right" way—that is, *their* particular way of living life and even having fun! (Chapter 4 includes a great story that illustrates that phenomenon perfectly.)

READY, AIM, FOCUS

With more than fifty-five years of experience as a card-carrying Enthusiast, I can say that I have a very full life. Let's just look at my career path. Not only am I a registered nurse and licensed social worker with a PhD in biopsychology and a post-doc with an all-but-dissertation master's degree at Duke University, but I have also been a bed-and-breakfast owner for almost twenty years, director of a cancer counseling center, owner of a solar business (which meant I had to get licensed as a general contractor), a business consultant (which involved getting licensed as a real estate agent), and an author and professional speaker. Along the way, I received certifications in Gestalt therapy; Enneagram teacher training; hypnotherapy; grief counseling; NLP; life, death, and transitioning counseling; psychoneuroimmunology; crisis counseling; Simonton-based therapy; conflict resolution; and the list goes on. I am currently director of the Gestalt Institute and Relationship Center in New Orleans and New York, and I continue to see private clients and do business consulting and public speaking.

Some might view this history as irregular and haphazard, but to me, it feels like a rich tapestry where one profession weaves into and enriches the other. I enjoy the "cross-pollination" effect of applying one paradigm of problem solving in one field to another. It's fun and exciting. Many people find it tiresome just to read about it.

Interestingly, I am often not aware that I myself am overwhelmed with the multitude of things I have to do (even if most of them are things I enjoy) until someone else mentions the number of balls I have in the air. (We haven't even talked about my personal life! Did I tell you that I taught myself Swahili, and now, I'm learning Italian? And that I love to dance and travel? That I have a reputation for making great costumes for Mardi Gras and Halloween? That I'm a gifted dog trainer? That I'm good with a chainsaw and tractor, too? And, I just became the Louisiana Senior

continued on next page...

...continued from previous page

Olympic Badminton champion in my age group this year, and—uh-oh, do you see what I mean?)

Sometimes, I get frustrated because there are so many *more* things I would like to do, and because I often have so many things going at one time, not everything gets finished or else it takes a long time to complete. For example, I have been trying to finish this very book for years. Granted, life has a way of stepping in and challenging even the best of intentions, but that excuse can only go so far.

This past Christmas, I took a three-week trip to Italy and France, in part to mourn the loss of my mom and also as an affirmation and celebration of her influence in my life. I had a significant moment in the Sistine Chapel during which I came to terms, once again, with the fleeting nature of the precious time we have here on earth. I vowed right then and there that when I returned home I would go on "lockdown"—no text chatting, personal emails, movies, stand-up comedy, going out to eat, etc. I would limit my non-book-writing time to only working out, seeing clients, and speaking engagements. My self-imposed lockdown would continue until my manuscript was complete. *Diffuse light focused to laser intensity.* I predicted it might take three to six months. I submitted the manuscript in three and a half weeks! Then, I vowed to repeat that lockdown process and finish four e-books that had been lying in varying states of "almost done-ness" for years. Now, they are off my to-do list as well. Thanks, Michael. (Michelangelo, that is—wink!)

(10) There is not always a "pure" personality type.

Notice that the NPS is arranged in a circle, and no matter what the basic type, it is positioned between two other types. The adjoining types are called "wings." All wings are "plus 1" (type + 1 = wing) or "minus 1" (type - 1 = wing) of the person's NPS type. In other words, if a person has an Individualist (4) personality, he may have either an Achiever (3) wing (that is, 4 minus 1) *or* an Investigator (5) wing (that is, 4 plus 1).

If You Had Wings

The wing modifies expression of the basic type. The identification of wings seems to have occurred simultaneously along with the observation of the NPS types. The wings may exert a mild, moderate, or heavy influence on the personality.

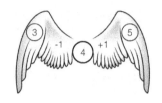

I believe that high, medium, and low set points of dopamine influence this aspect of personality. For example, it appears that a person who has a medium set point of dopamine will manifest a "core" expression of that personality.

Think of the types as colors in a color wheel; a "core" personality type would be equivalent to saying that person's personality is a "true blue." Having more or less dopamine within that personality type might manifest a more "blue-green" wing or "blue-red" wing.

So, for example, while the Helper and the Reformer both tend to be altruistic, the Helper is more emotionally expressive and the Reformer more emotionally neutral, so these traits are somewhat in conflict with each other. With a Helper who has a Reformer wing, the empathy and warmth of the Helper is counterbalanced by the restraint, objectivity, and idealism of the Reformer, making for a somewhat subdued version of the Helper, which we might call the Servant. The Servant is highly principled, with a strong conscience, and will often spend much time devoted to altruistic causes and do so with less self-regard than the core and host subtypes.

On the other hand, the Helper with an Achiever wing has been called the "Host/Hostess" and finds the traits of both personalities reinforcing each other rather than conflicting. Both personalities are motivated to use charm to win the affection of others, and both are considered high-energy personality types. In fact, this subtype is perhaps the most energetic of all and extremely friendly, serving others in extraordinary ways. They are usually perceived as exemplary and desirable people. They are usually more image-conscious and outgoing and tend to be more of a "gift giver" than a "servant."

As stated earlier, our best guess at this time is that dopamine set points range from very high to very low, and the particular space these set points occupy on

Position on Table	Name
Reformer (1) with a **Peacemaker** (9) wing	"The Idealist"
Reformer (1)	"The Reformer"
Reformer (1) with a **Helper** (2) wing	"The Advocate"
Helper (2) with a **Reformer** (1) wing	"The Servant"
Helper (2)	"The Helper"
Helper (2) with an **Achiever** (3) wing	"The Host/Hostess"
Achiever (3) with a **Helper** (2) wing	"The Charmer"
Achiever (3)	"The Achiever"
Achiever (3) with an **Individualist** (4) wing	"The Professional"
Individualist (4) with an **Achiever** (3) wing	"The Aristocrat"
Individualist (4)	"The Individualist"
Individualist (4) with an **Investigator** (5) wing	"The Bohemian"
Investigator (5) with an **Individualist** (4) wing	"The Iconoclast"
Investigator (5)	"The Investigator"
Investigator (5) with a **Loyalist** (6) wing	"The Problem Solver"
Loyalist (6) with an **Investigator** (5) wing	"The Defender"
Loyalist (6)	"The Loyalist"
Loyalist (6) with an **Enthusiast** (7) wing	"The Buddy"
Enthusiast (7) with a **Loyalist** (6) wing	"The Entertainer"
Enthusiast (7)	"The Enthusiast"
Enthusiast (7) with a **Challenger** (8) wing	"The Realist"
Challenger (8) with an **Enthusiast** (7) wing	"The Maverick"
Challenger (8)	"The Challenger"
Challenger (8) with a **Peacemaker** (9) wing	"The Bear"
Peacemaker (9) with a **Challenger** (8) wing	"The Referee"
Peacemaker (9)	"The Peacemaker"
Peacemaker (9) with a **Reformer** (1) wing	"The Dreamer"

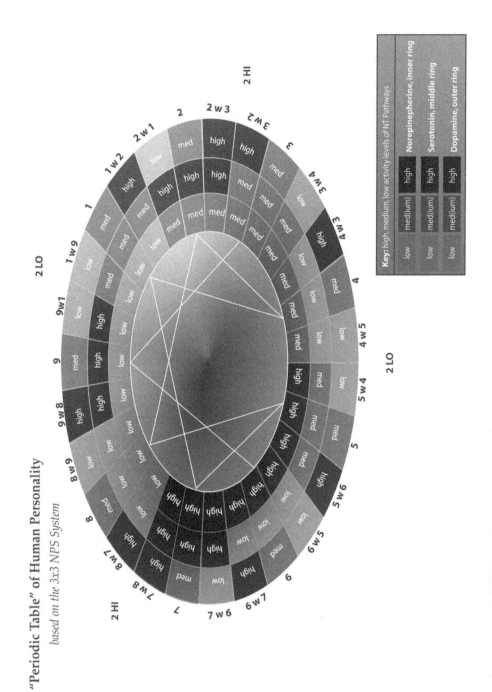

"Periodic Table" of Human Personality

based on the 3x3 NPS System

the continuum influence whether a wing exerts a high, medium, low, or no influence on the basic or core personality.

A more complete description of wings and all twenty-seven personality types (the nine basic and what Riso and Hudson refer to as the remaining eighteen subtypes) can be found in their comprehensive "bible"—I mean, book— *Personality Types: Using the Enneagram for Self-Discovery.*

To the right is a list of all twenty-seven types (the nine core NPS and eighteen subtypes or wing types) included in the Periodic Table of Human Personality:

Putting It All Together: The Periodic Table of Human Personality

On August 30, 2012, the world lost an amazing man. Don Richard Riso will always be considered a brilliant thinker and seminal contributor to the growing body of knowledge related to the Enneagram.

As I sat at the memorial service of Don in Stone Ridge, New York, I watched a video of his personal and professional path. I learned that, as a ten-year-old boy, Don was fascinated with Dmitri Mendeleev and the periodic table he created in 1869. Although incomplete at the time, Mendeleev's periodic table was orderly and helped to explain the natural and predictive laws of our world. The periodic table not only helped to explain the properties of elements, such as hydrogen and oxygen, but it also allowed us to predict what would happen if elements were combined. For example, combining two atoms of hydrogen with one atom of oxygen produces H_2O (water). Over time, Mendeleev's periodic table was refined and is now ubiquitous within the academic discipline of chemistry, with broad applications in physics, biology, engineering, and industry.

Don Riso and his partner, Russ Hudson, were pioneers and the world's leading authorities in observing and classifying the Enneagram personality types and identifying the levels of functioning. Another huge contribution they made was related to dividing the nine types into three different classifications (the Triads, which classify the types into mental groups; the Harmonic Triads, which classify the types into emotional groups; and their original creation, the Hornevian Triads, which classify the types into behaviors elicited by environmental stressors).

Riso and Hudson's brilliant work created the foundation that inspired us (Thomas and Schulze) to explore the biological basis of this system. Just as

Medeleev's periodic table describes the properties of the atoms, which, when combined, create specific elements with predictive qualities, we described the properties of the neurotransmitters, which we believe create the nine basic personalities. We think the addition of high, medium, and low combinations of dopamine account for the "wings," ultimately producing a total of twenty-seven more specific personality types, all of which have predictive patterns related to thought, emotion, and action.

From that, a chart could be crafted, which, in essence, could be considered (drum roll please) . . .

The Periodic Table of Human Personality
The beautiful original color version of the above illustration can be obtained through this link: http://tinathomas.com/nps-3d-model-periodic-table

What makes this theory and a Periodic Table of Human Personality revolutionary is that it has the potential not just to treat symptoms but also to predict the outcomes of treatment. In other words, understanding a person's symptoms through the lens of their individual biological baseline and then tailoring their treatment to that baseline offers the best chance for an optimal outcome. Using this system would move us away from cookie-cutter, "one-size-fits-all" treatments and toward individualized and specific therapies that could work in the most expedient way.

WHICH WAY TO UTOPIA?

If the perfect state of Utopia were located in central North America, let's say somewhere south of Kansas, how would you give directions to get there? If you lived in California, you would tell an inquiring traveler to head east. But if you told an inquiring traveler coming from New York to go east, she would end up in the Atlantic Ocean. The same principle holds true for the state of the Ultimate You (located very close to where you live). The journey to reach that state will be different for nine different types of people, and once having arrived, I bet even the destination may be experienced differently too.

The Periodic Table of Human Personality could be used to pinpoint the starting point of any given personality and help mental health professionals prescribe medications, diet, mental and physical exercises, and perhaps even music and lighting that would help modify the neurotransmitter set points for optimal functioning. This table could potentially predict what types of medications, for instance, might have specific side effects.

For example, let's take the case of Tom, a Loyalist who visited a psychiatrist with the complaint of depression. Traditionally, psychiatrists will offer prescriptions to relieve the symptoms and then adjust or change the medications accordingly based on observed side effects. But what if the psychiatrist were able to correctly assess Tom's basic personality chemistry? Is it possible that Tom could be spared a lot of frustration and potentially unpleasant side effects? I think the answer is yes.

Looking at the periodic table, Tom's set points are high norepinephrine, low serotonin, and average dopamine. For treatment of depression in this case, a medication that primarily increases serotonin and secondarily increases dopamine might be the drug of choice, since serotonin would increase Tom's feeling of well being, and a slight increase in dopamine would theoretically give him a little more pleasure and, potentially, a little more physical energy.

If, on the other hand, his psychiatrist was unaware of his baseline set points and selected a random medication used for treatment of depression that operated differently on the brain and its neurotransmitters, Tom would potentially have a very different result. If, for example, he gave Tom a medication that increased his norepinephrine more than serotonin, Tom might have a greater chance of experiencing side effects of nausea and anxiety.

Remember, there are also natural ways to influence neurotransmitters, with fewer potential side effects, and now that you have the information about how you can influence your chemistry, you can experiment with those alternative means of affecting your personality. And, if you are not getting the desired results and think you might require medication, you will find that you are much more informed and could work with your mental health provider to find the kind of chemical support you need temporarily or long-term. By sharing what you think your chemical set points are and giving feedback on how your treatment is affecting the way you think, feel, and behave, you can become a more informed and active partner with your mental health provider and, hopefully, achieve optimal mental, emotional, and spiritual health and physical fitness more expediently.

Enneagram versus Nine-Point Personality System

For scholars familiar with the Enneagram system, and for others curious about the differences between the current conventional Enneagram and the Thomas and Schulze theories that underlie the NPS, let me share a bit more detailed information.

In their book *Personality Types*, Riso and Hudson theorized that personalities are rooted in the relationship between the child and the parents. This differs from the theory of the NPS, which proposes that a person is *born with a genetically predetermined "set point" of high, medium, and low combinations of neurotransmitter activity levels that create what we refer to as personality*. In fact, Thomas and Schulze purport that the personality of the child influences the relationship with his or her parents (and the way the child perceives the relationship). We also believe that the way the child's personality initially expresses itself is more directly affected by the parents' or caretakers' level of health and functioning than by the parents' or caretakers' personality types. In contrast to Riso and Hudson's theory, Thomas's NPS theory states that it is the high, medium, and low combinations of neurotransmitters (namely norepinephrine and serotonin) that create the nine basic personality types.

Riso and Hudson divide the Enneagram into three sets of triads. One of those triads is based on each personality's primary way of dealing with stress. They refer to this division as the Hornevian types (based on the psychiatrist Karen Horney's work). According to their theory, three of the nine Enneagram personality types under stress are most likely predicted to move away from the stressor in order to handle the situation, three other types are predicted to move toward the stressor and take action, and the remaining three fall somewhere in the middle in trying to mediate the stressor. The NPS theorizes that the *dopamine set point amplifies or attenuates the basic personality* and accounts for the "wings" of each personality type. The relative high, medium, and low concentrations of dopamine, as they are distributed around the circle of the Enneagram, correlate fairly well (but not exactly) with the Hornevian types identified by Riso and Hudson.

Riso and Hudson use a term called "variant" that describes the way each personality interacts (or does not interact) with other people. Some other schools of the Enneagram use the term "subtype." The NPS uses the term "social orientation" as opposed to variant or subtype, because according to Thomas and Schulze that term seems less confusing. Social orientation appears to correlate with what traditional psychological models refer to as "attachment" styles. Within the social orientation framework, the terms (social, intimate, and self-preservation) seem to minimize confusion and are more value-neutral.

The teachers of the Enneagram generally believe that what Thomas and Schulze call "social orientation" is a learned or preferred way of relating to others. Dr. Eric Schulze's contribution to this theory is that social orientation is established as a result of the nature of the caretaking relationship with the child that most likely occurs in the first three years of the child's development.

Chapter 4

The Nine Types— Which One Are You?

S
o...who do you think you are? This chapter will hopefully give you an more in-depth understanding of the characteristics of the personality types. As you read about the various personality types, try to imagine how it most closely describes someone you know personally. For example, when you read about a personality known as the Reformer, if the description reminds you of your Uncle Lester, the next time you meet someone who reminds you of your Uncle Lester, there may be a good chance that that person might indeed have the Reformer personality. At least it's a good place to start.

Please note that it lies outside the scope of this book to fully detail the depth and breadth of each NPS type.[10] Nevertheless, the following descriptions will give you a general idea of the essential characteristics of each type.[11] The types and their various aliases are included, followed by each type's proposed neurotransmitter set points; a tagline (to make it easy to remember); "Basic

---

10 There are two books I recommend for in-depth descriptions, and they are *Personality Types* and *Wisdom of the Enneagram*; both books are by Riso and Hudson.

11 These descriptions are derived from Riso and Hudson (1999), Schreiber and Shannon (2000), Palmer (1989) and Havens (1995), and from personal and professional experience with many personalities.

Fear," "Basic Desire," "Key Motivation/s," "Favored Communication Style"; and a basic summary of that type. I will also provide a very brief description of the subtypes (as defined by Riso and Hudson) for each of the NPS personalities. As you may recall, these 18 personality subtypes (two per core or basic personality) are created from influences generated by the "wings," (the NPS types adjacent to the core personality type). As mentioned before, we think the core personality type is related to an average dopamine set point and that the wings are related to the high or low dopamine set point. I hope that highlighting a couple of the unique characteristics of the subtypes will help to give you a sense of the range of each personality and how it expresses itself when the wings are factored in for a deeper understanding of the richness of the NPS.

The examples of the various personalities are ranked from high functioning to low functioning. I have also included what I believe might be the biological "purpose" of each type. Looking for a biological purpose related to personality was inspired by E.O. Wilson,[12] a sociobiologist whose seminal work with ants and ant roles encouraged me to consider the correlation between human personality and ant roles, such as the leader ant, scout ant, fighter ant, worker ant, etc. Later, I expanded my search to explore other species for possible correlations of personality.

The core personalities and subtypes will have examples of well-known people, past and present, real and fictitious, who exemplify the range of the type described. Each section will then conclude with a narrative of a personal experience I have had with each type to help illustrate even more how the generalities and specifics of personality work together with a person's history and current circumstances to create a unique and memorable individual.

Following the section on type descriptions, I have included a "real world" application section that includes simple ways to remember the nine basic types, challenges of typing oneself and others, and tips for more accurate typing.

Recognizing that no one type is any better or worse than any other, it seemed appropriate to begin with the Challenger, since this type is also known as the Boss or the Leader.

---

12   Edward Osborne "E.O." Wilson (born June 10, 1929) is an American biologist, researcher (sociobiology, biodiversity), theorist (consilience, biophilia), naturalist (conservationist), and author of many books including *The Ants* (1990).

8. *The* CHALLENGER (a.k.a. the Boss or Leader)
LOW Norepinephrine—LOW Serotonin
The Powerful, Dominating Type: *"I'm eight, I'm great."*
Basic Fear: Being harmed or controlled by others
Basic Desire: To be self-reliant
Key Motivation: To be self-reliant, to dominate their environment, and to stay in control of their situation
Favored Communication Style: Imperatives

Challengers are self-confident and courageous. They are, to quote a phrase, our "natural-born leaders." They are resourceful and action-oriented. Challengers are dominant, powerful, assertive, and sometimes aggressive. They take charge and will not easily back down from a fight or difference of opinion. They want to be in control. Challengers tend to be out of touch with the tender, compassionate sides of themselves. They are natural leaders and are decisive, authoritative, and action-oriented. Unhealthy Challengers can be brutal, violent, and dictatorial. They tend to display open anger and a show of force. Integrated Challengers are courageous, self-confident, and willing to use their power for the support and protection of others.

Examples of the Challenger: Dr. Phil, Charlton Heston, Mike Wallace, Barbara Walters, Frank Sinatra, Bette Davis, Leona Helmsley, Ross Perot, Fidel Castro, and Saddam Hussein

• • • • •

When I think of the Challenger personality, I see an "armored teddy bear": a fierce and intimidating warrior with a marshmallow heart. I should know; I was married to an amazing, high-functioning Challenger for almost fifteen years. I was quite impressed with Greg Gasperecz when I first met him on the dance floor over thirty years ago, and even though we are no longer married, we have been dancing in one form or another ever since.

One of the features that characterize a Challenger is a straightforward, no-nonsense style. This type does not play mind games; basically, it's "what you see is what you get." People often ask me, "Why don't Challengers speak to other people like they want to be spoken to?" But the answer is that they do. They are not interested in social chatter or the weather. They don't want to hear about your feelings. They don't want to hear about how wonderful they are or how wonderful you are. They are designed to be alpha hunters. All you need to do is let them know what you want or need and when you want or need it; they will figure out how to get it. Please, for goodness's sake, don't try to tell a Challenger *how* to hunt. (You have been forewarned.)

Because they have low norepinephrine and low serotonin set points, Challengers are not designed to over-think. They react quickly and "from the gut" in a primal, responsive way. If you think about it, this can be extremely useful on a hunt. Let's say an alpha hunter sees that one of his fellow hunters is about to be charged from behind by an angry predator. The alpha hunter will immediately respond with a sharp, loud command, "Run!" or "Get down!" No second-guessing—seconds count; lives are on the line. It would be very costly if the alpha hunter paused and wondered, *Do I say something or not say something? You know, I don't want to hurt his self-esteem . . . I'm not sure how he's going to feel if I yell at him . . .*

A forceful and immediate "take charge" attitude and ability certainly serves a purpose in a hunting situation. It can also be quite useful in an operating room—"Paddles—stand back, everyone . . . charge!"—or in a military operation: "Don't shoot until I say so; do you understand?" However, this kind of direct, gruff, and sometimes overbearing presence does not always do so well in other contexts; for instance, when asking a secretary to do something, it may sound more like a command than a request. The same thing may happen with a spouse or children who feel like they are in a military camp rather than a home.

Greg was no exception to the rule here. Challengers speak in a way that I would describe as confident, from the gut. In other words, you won't hear Challengers presenting in a childlike, breathy, nasally, or whiny manner. Many times, their opinions are expressed as if they are facts. For example, a Challenger is more likely to say, "BMWs are the best made cars on the market," rather than, "I think BMWs are the best made cars on the market" or "I drive a BMW." The Challenger's tendency to express opinions as facts, coupled with their no-nonsense style can sometimes make them appear harsh, and their low serotonin set point can make them a little impatient and edgy.

Years ago, when my son, Matthew, and I decided to do a "family intervention" with Greg about his overbearing communication style, we approached him in a very gentle manner. "Greg," I began, "we want to talk to you about the way you sometimes seem a little rougher than we think you intend to be when you speak."

"What are you talking about?" he snapped back as he glared at both of us. All of a sudden, we felt like Dorothy and the Tin Man approaching the Wizard of Oz.

"Well," I stammered, "it's just that sometimes we think your style of speech seems a little harsher than you may intend it to be."

"I don't have any idea what you're talking about!" he retorted in a rather huffy tone.

I was incredulous and frustrated because our conversation was an example of the very situation we were trying to convey to him. But, being a good therapist, I invited him to be open to the possibility that there might be a disconnect between his communication style and his intention. Fortunately for us, he was a high-functioning Challenger who also had a very strong Enthusiast wing (so he was open to exploration and change).

It's easy to see how people who work or live with Challengers can feel intimidated, as Challengers often look stern and serious, especially when fulfilling their biological purpose. For example, once Greg and I were running late for a party. He was driving, and I could tell that he was intent on getting us to our destination as quickly and efficiently as possible. He was serious, quiet, and seemed extraordinarily focused. He almost looked angry. I thought of him as the alpha hunter and asked him, "Greg, do you feel like you are on a hunt right now?" He was concentrating so intently on getting us to our destination that he did not even hear my question—which, in fact, was the answer to my question!

If you ask a Challenger if they feel powerful or whether they think they intimidate people, they will usually look a little puzzled and respond, "Who, me? No, not at all." They might even find the question amusing. Most Challengers will tell you they just feel like they are being themselves. But if they were to look behind their path at work or in their relationships, they might see bodies strewn behind them from all the people they inadvertently bulldozed.

The reason for this is because people tend to project their way of relating onto others. Therefore, the straightforward Challenger assumes that everyone is being direct and forthcoming with him. If no one is overtly challenging his idea, he assumes everyone agrees, and he does not take into account that some people might be a little timid or uncomfortable about questioning his authority.

Challengers respect people who can stand toe-to-toe with them and share a different point of view—even though they will tell you they "know" they are right. I met a Challenger not that long ago in his mid-sixties who confided in me that he truly believed he was always right. It wasn't until he fell in love with a therapist and explored some of the more vulnerable aspects of himself that he realized there were many areas of his life still unexplored. He admitted he had sometimes relied on his gut decisions without enough information and was therefore not always right. It was quite a liberating relief to this particular Challenger, but also quite a surprise, to realize that, even though he was wired to believe he was always right, he was not.

Challengers present in a confident manner because they trust their gut and sense of knowing. Because of their low norepinephrine levels, they don't over-think issues, nor do they spend a lot of time analyzing themselves or others. I was at a party where two Challengers met for the first time. One of the Challengers said to me later about the other Challenger, "Wow, I really liked Lucy. She is a great gal."

I said to him, "Well, it's probably because you guys have the same Challenger personality. You probably resonated because you are both confident, powerful, no-nonsense people." To which he replied, "Yeah, whatever—I don't know about all that stuff; I just really liked her, that's all."

Speaking of confidence, I remember once being on the beach with Greg and observing his confident walk. "Greg," I asked him, "if your walk could talk, what do you think it would say?" As he was walking, he tilted his head and said, "Well, let's see . . . I guess it would say, 'You can walk in front of me, you can walk behind me, and certainly you can walk next to me, but you surely cannot walk where I am walking.'" I do believe that sums up not only the walk but also the attitude of the Challenger personality.

Although Challengers tend to avoid people who are weak, clingy, or whiny, they do respect and admire other Challengers and powerful people of all personality types. I believe that's one reason why Greg and I got along so well. (Greg, for the record, has the Challenger personality with the Enthusiast wing, and I have the mirror personality, the Enthusiast with the Challenger wing. Translated, that meant when it was time to make things happen, we met in Challenger Land, and when it was time to play, it was Enthusiast City all the way. We were quite the dynamic duo, and when we meet at Mardi Gras for our annual dance, you can still see that dynamic energy after all these years!)

When a Challenger is in a relationship where he does not feel like he has to take care of another person, it gives him a chance to relax and be vulnerable. Greg is an engineer, and during our marriage, he used to do environmental inspections. Grown men would become intimidated when he was on his inspection because he had the ability to shut down million-dollar operations and would not hesitate to do so, as his personality led him to be territorial and protective of the environment. He had a reputation as a really hard-nosed inspector. And yet, when he came home, he would close the door behind him, and I would get to experience the "marshmallow" under the armor as he would say to me in a sweet, childlike way, "Hewwo, Sweet One; could you kiss my wittle eye wids? I am vewy vewy tiwered."

Who would have known?

The Challenger with an Enthusiast wing (8 with a 7 wing)
HIGH dopamine —"The Maverick"

The Maverick is perhaps the most openly assertive subtype and is more blunt, realistic and extroverted than the Challenger with the Peacemaker wing. This personality presents as confident and self-assured. Mavericks tend to be bold in personal and business life, lack interest in working for others, and are not particularly comfortable with feeling dependent or vulnerable.

Examples: Lee Iacocca and Donald Trump

The Challenger with the Peacemaker wing (8 with a 9 wing)
LOW dopamine — "The Bear"
The Peacemaker influence manifests a generally softer, more accepting quality in the Bear. Bears still like to get things done their way, but more characteristically with a soft but firm voice and more casual demeanor. They present as a "reluctant dragon slayer"; that is, they are quite fine minding their own business and doing their own thing, but will pick up the sword if the villagers seek their help. (Think Bruce Willis and many of his movies where he is a basically a gentle man who reluctantly comes out of his peaceful, unassuming comfort zone to do whatever it takes to protect the underdog.)

Examples: Indira Ghandi and John Wayne

A CHALLENGER TO THE END:
THE LIFE AND DEATH OF MY UNCLE BOO

When I was five years old, my Aunt Patty and Uncle Pat, who were then sixteen years old, came to live with us because their parents (my grandparents) died within five months of each other, leaving them orphans. Even though they were more like sister and brother to us, my brother and I referred to Pat as "Uncle Boo" and to Patty as "Nanny." They were fraternal twins, and though they looked very similar, they couldn't have been more dissimilar in personality.

Nanny was talkative, anxious, and prone to self-doubt. In later years, we would learn that she had the Loyalist personality. Uncle Boo was a person of much fewer words and was more confident and domineering. When our family later learned what a Challenger was, there was no doubt in anyone's mind that Uncle Boo was the epitome of a Challenger. We also agreed that one Challenger was more than enough for any one family! He was neither loud nor boisterous, but he certainly was opinionated, and getting into a debate with him was usually a very unsatisfying experience because he was always "right" and resistance was futile. He didn't have to

continued on next page...

...continued from previous page

say it exactly, but everyone knew that when it came to Uncle Boo, it was "My way or the highway!"

Despite his crusty exterior, family members would describe Uncle Boo as a "lovable curmudgeon," especially many years later when he became a grandfather. He would wake up at five o'clock every morning to make pancakes for his three step-grandchildren, help them get dressed, and then take them to school on weekdays. On weekends, instead of going fishing or hunting, he would let them jump into bed and snuggle with him; he never tired of reading their favorite stories over and over again.

Uncle Boo had a heavy Peacemaker wing, (The Bear personality) meaning that even though he was reactive, it took a lot for him to get angry. He preferred to avoid getting upset, but when he did it was "game over."

At eighteen, Uncle Boo joined the Marines (the best branch of the military, of course). Then, he became a mounted police sergeant for the New Orleans Police Department—and of course, the mounted police were the best part of the NOPD. Uncle Boo received numerous medals of valor, but he shrugged them off as "just doing his job." I loved the story he told about a man threatening to jump off the Mississippi Bridge.

"There was a psychiatrist," said Uncle Boo. "You know, a shrink, who was trying to talk this jumper down, and he wasn't getting anywhere with the guy. I could tell the jumper was getting kind of antsy, and I was thinking, *This guy's gonna jump.* I looked at my watch. It was almost noon, and I was getting hungry. So I told my partner, 'Here, gimme a rope.' I tied the rope around my waist, and I just jumped out to the jumper. I grabbed him and brought him back to safety. They gave me a medal for it. But you know, really, I was just hungry. And, I was thinking, *If we wait for this shrink, and this guy jumps, we're going to end up having a lot more paperwork, and we're all going to end up missing lunch.*" That was Uncle Boo—a matter-of-fact, take-action, no-accolades, get-'er-done kind of guy.

continued on next page...

...continued from previous page

So, I was not surprised when I saw Uncle Boo embrace death in the same way he had embraced life. I learned that he was in hospice care, and I walked into his hospital room to find him lying quietly and watching TV, a bit bored and in a fair amount of discomfort. He was "doing dying" like he did everything else, just "taking it on the chin." He didn't believe in complaining, and like he said, those were the cards he was dealt. When I asked him how he was doing, his response was, "Well, kid, do you know what the difference is between a warrior and a killer?" I shook my head. He looked me straight in the eyes and said, "A warrior knows when it's time to put down his sword."

I took a deep breath. My Uncle Boo had just told me he was ready to die. He didn't really want to die because he loved taking care of his family, especially the grandkids, but he could see that after fighting cancer for eight years, his body had just become worn out and fighting for the sake of fighting was not in anyone's best interest. Uncle Boo was a true leader in every sense of the word.

For the next two months, I arranged to have family members sit with him practically around the clock so that he would have company and not be alone during his last few weeks. At first, he resisted the idea. "What? Why have people come and sit with me on deathwatch?" he protested. "What's the point? Everybody's got jobs and things to do." But once I was able to help him see that it was our way of honoring him for protecting us and being our Challenger for all his life, he was able to relax into the idea and receive our love.

Interestingly, he let me—an Enthusiast with a Challenger wing— spread my own Challenger wing and protect him during this process. I began to make decisions for him, like insisting that the hospital stop invasive, uncomfortable procedures and unnecessary medications. I told him when to increase his pain medications and made recommendations for how to handle communication with various family members. Because he had someone strong protecting him, he was able to give himself

continued on next page...

...continued from previous page

permission to let down his guard a bit and share some of the more vulnerable feelings he had not shared since he was thirteen years old. It was a precious time and a true period of grace for all of us. Ultimately, he confided in me, "You know, even though this was a little awkward at first, and even a little weird, it's been like a wide-awake funeral." And then, he got teary-eyed and choked up. "I can't thank you enough. I can go in peace now." Shortly after that conversation, he slipped into a coma. I continued my visits, with faith that he could still hear me, even though he might not be able to respond.

On three different occasions, to my amazement, Uncle Boo pulled himself out of his deep sleep to lend his Challenger hand—three times, in response to three different dilemmas I faced. On all three occasions, he began to stir gently and then more and more vigorously, as if straining to pull himself out of his deep stupor. He would then give me his best advice, and once he was certain I understood his instructions, he softly slipped back into a coma, sometimes snoring deeply as if satisfied that he had done his job of protecting his little sister/niece. Uncle Boo died like he lived because, as far as a Challenger goes, nothing is more important or satisfying than protecting those he loves.

Like I said, the Challenger is an armored teddy bear—a fierce and intimidating warrior with a marshmallow heart.

9. *The PEACEMAKER* (a.k.a. the Mediator)
LOW Norepinephrine—HIGH Serotonin
Pleasant, Easygoing Type: *"I'm nine, I'm fine."*
Basic Fear: Loss and separation
Basic Desire: To have inner stability, serenity, "peace of mind"
Key Motivation: To create harmony in their environment, to preserve things as they are, and to avoid conflicts and tension
Favored Communication Style: Epic stories

Peacemakers are receptive, peaceful, and capable of creating a harmonious atmosphere, which most find comforting. Peacemakers are easygoing and take life as it comes. They can see all points of view and readily replace their own wishes with those of others. Average Peacemakers have a tendency to get *too* accommodating, wanting to keep the peace rather than raise their own voice. Thus, they go along but don't develop their own identities. Unhealthy Peacemakers are seen by others as lazy and can be obstinate, ineffectual, and depersonalized. Their anger is sometimes expressed in passive-aggressive ways. Their desire to merge with and subjugate themselves to others can prevent them from becoming independent and fully functioning people. Integrated Peacemakers are excellent negotiators and counselors.

Examples: Mother Teresa, Joseph Campbell, Gerald Ford, Walter Cronkite, Garrison Keillor, Ron Howard, Jim Henson, Norman Rockwell, "Edith Bunker," and "Marge Simpson"

• • • • •

Here's a personality koan for you. Which personality is most representative of this statement: "Soft is stronger than hard, water than rock, love than violence"? If you guessed Peacemaker, you are correct! (Or else you were paying attention to the top of the page title?)

Indeed, water can, in time, wear down and through rock. You only have to look at the Grand Canyon to see the evidence. And, although violence may sometimes lead to a fleeting sense of triumph, in the end, love wins. Like the cypress that can bend with the strong forces of wind rather than be toppled over, the soft gentleness of the Peacemaker prevails.

Enter the sanctuary of the Peacemakers: Ohmmmm . . .

Peacemakers are, by far, the sweetest and easiest to be around of all the types. If you are having "issues" with a Peacemaker, you need to look in the mirror. Seriously. Having high serotonin and low norepinephrine creates generous measures of well being and mental calm. The extended periods of physical and mental tranquility this produces gives the Peacemaker what may be the easiest personality type to have—so long as the culture in which they reside embraces them.

Peacemakers are generally easy to recognize as well; a soft smile often graces their resting face, making them look like someone who has been smoking pot all their lives! Aside from their pleasant demeanor, the real tip-off is the way you will feel in the *presence* of a Peacemaker within only a few short minutes. Peacemakers are unpretentious and comfortable to be around. They exude a relaxed, accepting, unconditional sense of acceptance. Many people report that the experience of meeting a Peacemaker feels similar to "coming home," or the comfort of wearing an old pair of slippers, or the relaxed feeling one gets from seeing a dear friend.

Peacemakers are generally very agreeable and often do not have strong preferences. You may hear "whatever" sprinkled into their vocabulary quite often.

"Where would you like to go out to eat tonight?" "*Whatever* you want . . ."

"What movie would you like to go see?" "I don't know. *Whatever* . . ."

"What would you like to do this weekend?" "*Whatever*, it doesn't really matter . . ."

At first glance, it may seem odd to be that easygoing, but if you think about it, if someone is souped up on serotonin, high in well-being and low in norepinephrine—and therefore not over-thinking or having many ideas about things to do or explore—that person is going to be pretty relaxed, content, and "chilled out." So, it really doesn't matter what he does. To a Peacemaker, pizza is fine, but so is Chinese, and so is staying home to eat, especially if you cook.

That easygoing tendency and mantra of "whatever" often causes Peacemakers to merge with their partner or loved one. In fact, some Peacemakers will score highest in the same personality type (and even the wing) of their significant other. This makes them prone to codependency. (My favorite definition of codependency, by the way, is when you are in a near-death situation, and someone *else's* life flashes before your eyes!) So, Peacemakers need to be careful about identifying what their needs are and setting up their boundaries to make sure they remain true to themselves.

Because of the high sense of well-being, I believe the Peacemaker can tolerate mundane or unpleasant tasks more easily than other types. I often think of the Peacemaker as an affable worker ant. I can see the little worker ant in the ant pile, getting along with all the other ants and saying, "Sure, I'll carry the mud to here. Sure, I'll take the mud to there," over and over and over again—maybe even whistling a little ant tune as it goes about its merry way.

For humans, as with all traits, this can be a blessing or a curse. The blessing, of course, is that Peacemakers really are content with keeping the status quo, which is usually experienced by them as peaceful; the curse, therefore, is that change can be experienced as disruptive and the antithesis of peacemaking. Peacemakers are typically risk-aversive and "Protectors of the Holy Rut."

I have known many Peacemakers who have stayed in unpleasant, even abusive situations for longer than what was healthy for them,] simply because they were so resilient and buffered by their ability to tolerate those types of circumstances. Margie was a forty-two-year-old Peacemaker and mother of three children who came to see me because her oldest daughter was having persistent nightmares, and all three children were doing poorly in school despite extra tutoring. During our discussion of her children's issues, I learned that Margie had been in an emotionally abusive and negligent marriage for well over twenty years with a raging alcoholic. The degree of his alcoholism was so severe that he was unable to keep a regular job. She was therefore the source of financial support for the entire family. Not only was he a financial burden to her, he was also a poor role model for her children and extremely unpleasant (and sometimes dangerous) to be around when he was drinking.

Margie was quite a benevolent woman—so much so that her friends referred to her as "St. Margie." When I commented on how difficult it must be for her to be the sole provider for her family and to be under attack during her husband's bouts of drinking, she shrugged her shoulders and said, "Well, it's not pleasant. But you know, he had a very traumatic childhood, and he's been under a lot of stress for over a decade now." She minimized the negative impact her husband's behavior had on her and her children. At one point, I confronted her by saying, "Margie, I realize that you understand how your husband's history has influenced his current behavior. I realize that you are not judging him. And for that matter, neither am I. But do you think it's possible that you have been so *understanding* that perhaps you have become *over*-standing? And by that, I mean you have put so much effort into being understanding of your husband's situation that you may be neglecting your own personal needs and your children's needs."

This point of view had never occurred to her. It took her over a year to gather the courage to confront her husband, whom she feared would become even more violent. However, the day came when she was able to tap into her protective mother bear energy and, for the sake of her children, inform her husband that she was getting a divorce and that he needed to make arrangements to move out of the house. With her brother, a captain in the police force, standing next to her, she stood firm as she watched her husband pack his things and leave their home. The locks to her house were changed that afternoon. Much to her surprise and relief, she discovered that, within a week, he had flown to California to live with a woman he had been having an eight-year affair with.

Margie later said, "When I look back, I can't believe I was able to stay in that situation for so long, as bad as it was. But I'm telling you, when I was in the middle of it, it really didn't seem that bad. I would focus on the times when he didn't drink. I would tell myself it could be worse. I just kept putting one foot in front of the other and going to work and taking care of the children, trusting that everything would work out somehow, someway. My way of dealing with it was *not* dealing with it."

Speaking of not dealing with it, an old folk saying says, "You can't push a rope." And, never is that more true than with Peacemakers. Ropes are useful for tying things together, for uniting things, and even for pulling along, but everyone knows you can't push a rope. And you can't push a Peacemaker to do something he does not want to do. He just will not do it. Now remember, if a Peacemaker wants to avoid confrontation, he may tell you, "Yes, sure, I'll do that for you." But under his breath, he might mutter or silently think, *Sure, I'll do that when I feel like it, which may be never!* So sometimes, the power of Peacemakers comes not only from their ability to keep doing something over and over again but also in their power to dig in and *not* do something. Some people might call it stubbornness; others might call it passive-aggressiveness. But they are so darned pleasant when they dig in that it just feels like, well, like pushing a rope. I should know. My mother was a Peacemaker extraordinaire.

Mom (who was known to almost everyone as "Mamie") lived until she was eighty years old. She was truly the sweetest, most supportive person I have ever known. She was gentle and very Southern, a rare breed of refinement and authenticity.

Having the Enthusiast personality, I often tried to encourage my parents to try new experiences. I think she experienced it more like I was *pushing* them to try new experiences. But early on in that process, my mom taught me something about our differences and gave me a piece of advice that I was wise enough to follow, long before I understood the biological basis of personality.

It happened when I was twenty-five years old. I visited a rainforest in British Columbia for the very first time and found it to be such an amazing experience that when I came back home, I insisted that I be allowed to treat my parents to a trip to the rainforest. "That's a nice idea," replied my mom, "but we don't want to go, dear."

"I'll pay for everything—the flight, the hotels, your meals, your incidentals. All you and Dad have to do is show up."

"That's not the point, Tina. We simply don't want to go."

"You don't understand, Mom," I pleaded. "This is an amazing place. You and Dad work all the time. You need a vacation. You must go and experience it firsthand. It's a once-in-a-lifetime experience. It's like paradise over there."

"But we don't want to go, dear. It's like paradise right here," said my mom. She could see that I was getting exasperated, and finally, she said, "Listen, we appreciate that you want to help us, really we do. But we think we're happy. And even if we're not, we *think* we are." She paused, tilting her head with that little "So what are you going to do?" shrug, and then went on in her truly sincere and sweet manner, "So, do us all a favor, dear, and leave us alone. How about just helping the people who *ask* for your help, will you please?" And, she smiled that sweet smile that said "Really, that's all I can take, and it's time to change the subject now, okay?"

It wasn't until years later that I realized she really did know what she meant. She was perfectly fine and quite content and happy exactly where she was. Traveling, for her, meant exerting effort to gain nothing, as she was already happy at home. With no appreciable difference in happiness, why not just stay *home* and be happy? It was so much easier.

Perhaps the signature feature of Peacemakers is their desire for peace and harmony and for avoiding conflict and confrontation. Now, this is not to say that Peacemakers do not get frustrated, upset, or disappointed. It does take a lot for them to get to these places of discomfort, and when they express it, it's not always very comfortable for them to do so, and the message does not always transmit very well.

A few years ago, Mom confided in me her distress over an "argument" she had on the phone with her brother, Pat (my Uncle Boo, a Challenger). She said, "I was quite upset with your Uncle Boo yesterday, and today, I am feeling bad about it. I hope I didn't hurt his feelings because I really gave him a piece of my mind."

Later that day, I happened to be on the phone with Uncle Boo, and I mentioned, "Wow, I heard that Mom was really upset with you yesterday."

"Really?" he responded, "about what?" He was truly perplexed because, so far as he could recall, the conversation with her had been pleasant.

"Don't you remember discussing your decision to do such-and-such and having a bit of tension around the subject?" I asked, trying to help him remember.

He paused, as if searching his memory. "Oh yeah, vaguely. She didn't seem upset, though. I think she just said, 'I don't really like that idea.' But that's all

I remember about it. So, she's really anrgy, eh?" He almost seemed amused. "Nope," he chuckled, "I had no idea she was upset."

This example is probably made more extreme given that my Uncle Boo had the Challenger personality. The Challenger, if you recall, is very direct and would be less likely to hear a point of view that opposes his unless the other person was extremely blunt and straightforward. My mom, being soft-spoken and gentle, most likely couched her upset in her typical, sweet, Southern Peacemaker way, so the depth of her upset was obviously not conveyed. And, there was my Uncle Boo, totally clueless that my mom was upset with him, and on the other end of the spectrum, my mom, feeling guilty for being so "rough" on her brother. She was more like a kitty cat than a Tiger Woman. She was really the sweetest human being I've ever known.

The Peacemaker with the Reformer wing (9 with a 1 wing)
LOW dopamine — "The Dreamer"

Since Peacemakers repress their unpleasant emotions to maintain peace, and Reformers are emotionally self-controlled, The Dreamer tends to be a little more cerebral than the Comfort Seeker. They tend to be more interested in ideas and concepts. And, because they are more emotionally subdued, they present as a bit cooler and slightly detached. Due to their nature of being highly principled and having a high degree of integrity, under stress this subtype can have moments of righteous indignation.

Examples: Abraham Lincoln and Jimmy Stewart

The Peacemaker with the Challenger wing (9 with an 8 wing)
HIGH dopamine — "The Comfort Seeker"

The Comfort Seeker tends to be fundamentally oriented to others, is receptive, unselfconscious and agreeable. They possess a mellow, outgoing warmth and present as solid, grounded individuals. Comfort Seekers can be willful, some might say stubborn, in areas where they feel passion, and they will exert a gentle but strong force to accomplish their goals. They are sociable and rely on instincts like feelings and hunches for making decisions.

Examples: Ronald Ragan and Whoopi Goldberg

SWEET HOME ABITA SPRINGS AND MAMIE

Even though I have lived in several places over the years, I have kept my home in Abita Springs, Louisiana for well over twenty years. This is where our extended family comes for holidays throughout the year and what we all think of as our family's central gathering place. It is a modest country home situated in the middle of one hundred acres of partially wooded land.

When I first moved out to Abita, the land, house, and other structures were in pretty rough condition. I was told that my mother, a.k.a. Mamie, cried all the way back across Lake Pontchartrain Bridge, saying to my dad, a.k.a. Chief, "I know Tina Marie has done some crazy things, but this time, I'm really concerned about her. She may have gone too far."

Through a lot of blood, sweat, and tears, my husband, Greg, and I turned that rough, godforsaken piece of land and houses into an idyllic park-like place to live. Eventually, my mom and dad fell in love with Abita; then, they built a house on the land and lived the rest of their years together in their home, which they named "Summerplace."

Over the years, as my study of personality deepened, we would sit on their back porch and have discussions about personality, extending beyond people. Did animals have personality? Was it possible that even places reflected personality? As far as animal personality went, we felt pretty confident in its existence, and that was before the research began to surface showing that animals do seem to have personality. In fact, my parents had a chocolate Labrador retriever named Summer who was the sweetest, calmest, gentlest dog you would ever want to meet. So, we were certain that she was a Peacemaker. And if a piece of property or a place had, or reflected, human personality, then our land in Abita certainly had the Peacemaker personality, too. Because of the surrounding protected land, sometimes the quiet can be almost deafening. And, there is nothing like a clear, cold night when you look up in the sky to see countless bright, twinkling stars. Full moon nights create magical walks, complete with

continued on next page...

...continued from previous page

moon shadows wherever we go. Crisp fall mornings find deer strolling in the front "lawn," and springs bring robin redbreasts, woodpeckers, goldfinches, and a multitude of blue jays and rabbits.

For almost twenty years, my parents and I ran a small bed-and-breakfast called Abita Springs Be & Be. It consisted of two cabins with no televisions or electronic distractions. We also had a pool in the middle of the woods, with a hot tub spilling into it, a steam room, and private sauna. We wanted guests to feel like they were decades away from New Orleans. And indeed, they did.

Our slogan was "Abita Springs Be & Be . . . a quiet place to BE." It was a place designed so that guests could come and experience "being" rather than "doing," a place to relax and unwind and breathe. It was a place to get back in touch with oneself and/or one's partner. As innkeepers, we used to enjoy watching guests arrive, apologizing for being late. When they asked what they needed to do to check in, my dad would say, "Well, if you're here, you're checked in, and when you leave, you'll be checked out." In fewer than twenty-four hours, we would see those same harried, frazzled guests, often in their Be & Be robes, unwinding with a cup of coffee in hand, slowly tooling around the property in a golf cart, pausing to pick a few blueberries, or just sit and take it all in. We used to love to watch Abita do its magic on guests.

That magic, that serene, tranquil feeling, was the very same experience people would feel sitting next to my mom. So, you might be able to imagine what it was like for me to look outside my window upon a fresh spring morning, gaze across the field, and see my mom sitting quietly next to the "Mamie tree," named after her. I would do my journaling, get a cup of coffee, and if by chance she was still there, which she often was, I would take a stroll out to sit with her.

"Mind if I join you?" I might ask.

"Of course not," she would reply.

"So, what have you been thinking about?" I would inquire.

continued on next page...

...continued from previous page

"Oh, nothing." (Imagine that.) "Just sitting here." She might sigh and smile.

And then, I would sit next to her. I would put my head on her shoulder, or she would hold my hand. We might talk about something that was on my mind (because there was *always* something on my mind!), or we might laugh at the antics of the ducks in the pond before us. At other times, we just sat together in silence and absorbed the beauty and wonderment of it all.

Those were precious, priceless moments with my mom. Throughout the years, she reminded me on several occasions that when her time came to leave us on earth, and if I found myself missing her, I could always go to the Mamie tree and sit there, and she would be there.

I sit there often these days . . . even when I am not at home.

If you were not fortunate enough to have a Peacemaker as a parent, or to marry one, or have one for a brother or sister, I highly recommend you find one for a friend.

Peacemakers pull up a hammock . . . and . . . zzzzz . . .

1. *The REFORMER* (a.k.a. the Perfectionist, the Visionary)

LOW Norepinephrine—MEDIUM Serotonin

The Rational, Idealistic Type: *"One way."*

Basic Fear: Being defective

Basic Desire: To be good, to have integrity, to be balanced

Key Motivation: To be right, to strive higher and improve everything, to be consistent with their ideals

Favored Communication Style: Preach and teach

Reformers are reasonable, objective, and principled. They constantly strive to achieve high standards. Reformers strive for perfection in just about every aspect of their lives. At average levels, they can become judgmental of themselves and others, get angry when they or others don't meet their expectations, and see themselves as ethically superior. Unhealthy Reformers tend to be self-righteous, dogmatic, and punitive. Reformers might procrastinate for fear of making a mistake. Their thinking centers on what "should" or "must" be done. They tend to dichotomize, seeing things in black or white. Reformers often present with a quiet but solid sense of authority. Integrated Reformers can be critically astute and morally heroic.

Examples: John Paul II, Meryl Streep, Sandra Day O'Connor, John Bradshaw, Bill Moyers, Katherine Hepburn, Harrison Ford, George Harrison, Margaret Thatcher, Gene Siskel, William F. Buckley, the "Church Lady."

• • • • •

The Reformer is generally an easy personality to recognize because this person holds himself in a regal and erect manner. At lower levels of functioning, you may notice a certain physical and emotional rigidity along with tension in the jaw area. As an emotionally neutral personality, the Reformer presents as a rather serious person, and if an issue of injustice arises, an ethical and principled Reformer coming to the rescue will often be perceived as intense. Their favored speaking format is lecture, and when they speak, they tend to use a chopping motion while emphasizing key points.

The main motivation of a Reformer is to do the right thing for the right reason. These are the kind of people who would sacrifice themselves for the better of all (think Gandhi). A Reformer would vote for an increase in children's educational taxes if they believed it was worthwhile, even though they may not have children, and it wouldn't benefit them personally.

Most people would describe Reformers as perfectionistic and even rigid and judgmental at lower levels of functioning. They hold themselves to very high standards, even higher than they might expect of others.

Reformers use the imperative "should" more than any other type. We jokingly tease our Reformers and tell them they "should on" themselves as much as they "should on" everyone else! As low norepinephrine types, they do not over-think issues and rely on their gut to determine their moral compass. They are not generally adventurous and are quite comfortable in doing things one way as long as it's the right way.

Reformers present as solid and unflappable. Because of this, many other types report feeling calmed and soothed in their presence. I believe this is a rare personality type and that their biological purpose is to be a visionary, which is a more highly evolved role that does not show up in lower species. To be a visionary, one must have a sense of history and be able to project into the future. Being a visionary also involves developing one's own highly tuned morality apart from a cultural context.

Despite having a solid confidence in their gut decisions, one feature that is particularly refreshing in most average to above-average Reformers is their ability to be open to new ideas when those ideas are presented in a fair, sound, and logical manner. Reformers are not easily swayed by emotional or dogmatic rhetoric.

I worked with a Reformer named Charles (not his real name) who was the CEO of a fairly successful corporation. I met him at a mutual friend's cocktail party, and he asked me if I might meet with him and kick around a few ideas to help him improve his organization's efficiency. While his staff greatly admired and respected him—the organization was principled and already quite efficient, and profits were decent—employee retention was a challenge and a costly problem.

Organizations tend to reflect the personality of the founder, and the issues that the organization deals with frequently relate to the founder's personality. In this particular case, the organization as a whole was an ethical company, and it strove for high efficiency. Employees who were most highly valued were those who worked long hours, sometimes beyond what was physically healthy for them. The work environment was somewhat drab but clean, organized, and well managed. When I arrived at the headquarters, my overall impression was an immediate sense of uber seriousness and lack of joy. My suspicion was that the company did not need to be more efficient; it needed to be more relaxed and fun. My diagnosis: joy deficiency.

So I was not surprised at all when our first session began with Charles leading, "Okay, let's get to business, shall we?" and he launched into the statistics of his company's business. When he completed his report, I asked him how much fun he and his employees had at work. He looked at me with a somewhat puzzled look, as if that question did not compute. He sat across from me, erect in his wing chair. He looked visibly uncomfortable, tugged at his monogrammed shirt cuffs, brushed the unseen lint from his simple but tailored suit pants. "I'm not following you" was all he could muster. My confidence faltered, and I began to feel like Maria in the scene from *The Sound of Music* on her first visit with Captain von Trapp.

Our first session was interrupted several times with urgent phone calls and employees popping in with serious issues that needed to be handled immediately. So, my first suggestion was to move our sessions to my office. Interestingly, when the Reformer personality is at high levels of functioning, it temporarily "visits" my personality, the Enthusiast. I thought it was at the very least an interesting metaphor for what I hoped might happen in the long term for both Charles and his organization.

Initially, I dreaded our sessions. I can only describe them as dry. I often felt like we were two strangers speaking two foreign languages, and in a very real way, I think we were. I began to wonder if I was wasting his money and my time. He was more comfortable discussing ideas and philosophy. I wanted to get into personal dynamics and reach his inner child. He thought the whole inner child concept was "rubbish, no offense." I suggested he read my first book, *The Ultimate*

Edge: How to Be, Do and Get Anything You Want, which helped to explain the biology of the brain and the limbic system (in essence, the childlike part of the brain). If understood and manipulated skillfully, it can create powerful, dynamic change elegantly and quickly.

I did not expect to see him again. He read the book. He said he was hopeful. He showed up, always on time. In fact, Charles was extremely punctual, showing up five minutes before the session was to begin, waiting in his car approximately two minutes before the session, walking up to my office door one minute in advance, and then entering exactly on the hour. At one of our sessions, I noted his punctuality and commented that it might be an interesting "experiment" for him to experience the feeling of being less punctual. He seemed intrigued and even a little excited—looked at his watch, looked at me, and then said, "Okay then, exactly *how* late do you want me to be?" *Oh dear*, I thought, *this is going to be a long haul.* But actually, Charles was quite a dedicated adult learner and committed to his personal growth and that of his organization.

On a personal level, we eventually did reach his inner child, who was somewhat impish, had always wanted to play a musical instrument but was never allowed the opportunity, and secretly wanted to be a philanthropist. (How many five-year-old children even know what a philanthropist is, much less aspire to be one?) So, Charles took up playing the French horn, and we had some silly sessions, like showing up at the park and swinging on swings and sliding down the slides together. On an organizational level, we began slowly with simple things, like painting the walls of the offices with bright cheerful colors, implementing dress-down Fridays, and hosting a crawfish boil and employee birthday parties. We created educational programs for personality, communication, and customer service and an employees' reward system for *creative* (rather than efficient) ideas.

The day Charles showed up for a session in camping attire (all coordinated J. Crew, of course) because he was taking the rest of the day off and going on a weekend camping trip with his family was the day I began to think there was hope for him, his family, and his business. Sure enough, I started getting reports that his wife and children were delighted with their "new" husband and dad, although, at first, his wife wondered if he was having a midlife crisis or mistress. Employee retention increased dramatically. And much to Charles's delight and surprise, it seemed that the more fun his employees had, the more the company profits increased. It appeared that Charles and his organization were visiting his Enthusiast integration point more and more frequently and with more and more ease.

When we completed our work together, not only was Charles a much happier man, but he was also able to fulfill his secret dream of becoming wealthy enough to be a generous philanthropist. Mission accomplished.

The Reformer with the Peacemaker wing (1 with a 9 wing)
LOW dopamine — "The Idealist"
The Reformer's natural idealism is heightened in subtype known as the Idealist. The Peacemaker's tendency to avoid conflict is naturally at odds with the Reformers need to promote change. This combination creates a resistance to being affected by others and creates a somewhat detached sense of being an outsider evaluator of the culture. The Reformer can be a perceived as a little more formal, some might say distant, than the other Reformer subtype, the Advocate.

Examples: Al Gore and Mr. Spock in Star Trek

The Reformer with the Helper wing (1 with a 2 wing)
HIGH dopamine — "The Advocate"
The Advocate is committed to follow a righteous path, and the Helper wing adds warmth and a degree of interpersonal focus on people, compensating for the Reformer's emotional control. Advocates present as a little more passionate and action oriented than the Idealists.

Examples: Mahatma Gandhi, Joan of Arc and Ralph Nader

JUDGE NOT, LEST YE BE JUDGED

One of my most humbling lessons in life involved a Reformer named Nancy. She was a friend of a friend of mine, and I used to refer to her as Nancy the No-Fun Nun because she was so serious and conservative. My friend invited Nancy to fly into New Orleans for the Jazz Festival and

continued on next page...

...continued from previous page

then got a stomach virus the day after Nancy arrived. As a huge favor to my friend (and I do mean huge), I agreed to take Nancy to the Jazz Festival, which just so happens to be one of my most favorite things to do in the whole world. I often arrive first thing in the morning, and other than lunch and a nap under an oak tree, I dance the entire day.

So once we arrived at the Fest, being my happy little Enthusiast self, I began to my heart out. After about two hours, I began to feel a little awkward and sorry for Nancy because she had been sitting stiffly and looking uncomfortable on the hard metal bleachers the entire time I was out on the dance floor. It had been raining at the Fest that day, and conditions were somewhat sloppy. I sensed that she didn't feel comfortable mucking about in the mud, but I was determined I was not going to cut my own day short for her sake, and I was not going to allow her attitude to rain on my parade; after all, there was more than enough rain for the both of us!

Nancy looked at me disapprovingly as I danced in my uninhibited, freestyle manner. I noticed a sense of superiority rising within me, and I began to judge her lack of personal freedom. Then, I felt a wave of righteousness welling up.

I thought smugly that it was a shame she did not know how to have fun, but luckily *I* knew the "right way" to enjoy Jazz Fest. Poor Nancy. Amazing me. Why couldn't everyone in the world learn my way? It would be such a better world if we didn't have such stick-in-the-mud people like Nancy.

From the corner of my eye, I smirked at her thin, erect figure appearing stick-like against the background of mud at the fairgrounds. "Wow," I scoffed to myself, "Literally a stick in the mud!" My righteousness turned to wickedness. I was so clever. I was so "right." Poor little Nancy would always be stuck, and I would always be free. The more I danced, the more she frowned. At some point, I felt like I was dancing just to watch her frown.

continued on next page...

...continued from previous page

When the band finished their set, I reluctantly returned to my guest. She frowned as she looked at my white dress, now spotted with flecks of dirt and grass, and commented, "You are an amazing dancer. Your movements are so fluid and expressive, and you are just a beautiful woman. It's a shame it was raining today. I hope your dress isn't ruined. That dress would have been the perfect Jazz Fest dress on a sunny day."

I felt ashamed and embarrassed when I realized that her look of disapproval was actually related to how muddy and messy the dance stage had become and how it had affected my dress. My heart melted. I smiled. I appreciated her concern and sense of aesthetics for the "perfect" Jazz Fest outfit. In a moment of clarity, I saw my shadow—I had become as disapproving and judgmental of her as I thought she was of me; I was stuck in my own sense of "rightness" about the "right way" of living. I had become my own version of a stick in the mud!

My heart melted for both of us. I was reminded of how challenging it can be to be a Reformer of average to low functioning, regardless of whether someone is born with that personality or, in my case, was temporarily visiting it. From that day forward, I began to appreciate the struggles, authenticity, and high ideals of the Reformers I meet, and also the Reformer inside of me!

Good job, number one . . . now, it's time to have some fun!

2. *The HELPER* (a.k.a. the Caretaker, the Giver)
MEDIUM Norepinephrine—HIGH Serotonin
The Caring, Nurturing Type: *"Tea for two—I'll serve you."*
Basic Fear: Being unwanted
Basic Desire: To be loved unconditionally
Key Motivation: To be loved, to express their feelings for others, to be needed and appreciated, to get others to respond to them, to vindicate their claims about themselves
Favored Communication Style: Help and advice

Helpers are compassionate, caring, generous, and thoughtful, often going out of their way to help other people. Helpers are wired to be self-sacrificing and enjoy giving and nurturing others. They like to offer compliments and advice. They seek to be loved and appreciated by becoming indispensable to others and, in the process, tend to be unaware of their own needs. Average Helpers need to be needed and sometimes remind others of their service to elicit gratitude from them. Unhealthy Helpers are manipulative, coercive, and possessive with significant others. They can become angry and resentful when not appreciated for their sacrifices. Integrated Helpers are empathetic, warm, loving, genuinely caring, and supportive.

Examples: Eleanor Roosevelt, Lionel Ritchie, Luciano Pavarotti, Lillian Carter, Sammy Davis Jr., Martin Sheen, Robert Fulghum, Jack Paar, Sally Jessy Raphael, Bishop Desmond Tutu, John Candy and "Del Griffith" (played by John Candy) in Planes, Trains and Autombiles.

• • • • •

Faster than a speeding bullet when you need a friend. More powerful than a locomotive to lend you a hand. Able to leap over grocery store lines to get you chicken soup in a single bound. Look over there: It's a bird! It's a plane! No, it's the Helper!

NOTE: When one of my friends edited the personality type narratives, he commented that the Helper narrative was relatively short compared to the other types, but he also said that it was sweet.

"Hmmm," I replied, "short and sweet, eh? Well, that's describes my former mother-in-law, who just happens to have the Helper personality. So, that's just perfect. I think I'll keep the narrative just the way it is!"

And so, I did.

The Helper personality is another one of those rare personality types that is truly extraordinary in the amount of high energy and exuberance this person possesses. I would dare say the Helper (especially with the Hero wing) is the highest-energy personality type of all.

Because of their high energy and intense motivation to help others, Helpers remain ready to offer help and advice to anyone who seems in need. This can sometimes be perceived by others as overbearing and intrusive.

High in serotonin and wired to anticipate other peoples' needs, the Helper aspires to be the Super Friend, Super Mother, Super Dad, Super Teacher, etc. Biologically speaking, the Helper is like a worker bee; taking care of others seems to be its main function. Therefore, Helpers do not tend to be very introspective or aware of their own needs. But if you listen carefully to how they anticipate your needs, you might get a clue as to what they actually need too. For instance, when a Helper asks, "Are you hungry?" it is very likely that he may need to eat. If a Helper asks, "Are you cold?" chances are he might need a sweater.

Many friends and family have been frustrated to learn that if a Helper has to ask for what he wants and gets it, somehow it doesn't count nearly as much as if it were given to him without his asking for it. Take the case of a middle-aged couple I saw a few years ago. Harry was a Loyalist, and Lisa was a Helper. Harry complained that Lisa complained all the time, and Lisa complained that she was not feeling loved.

I asked her, "How would you know if you were loved? What would help you to feel loved?"

To which she responded, "I need affection, like hugs. Then, I would feel loved."

Lisa had to go to the bathroom in the middle of our session, which worked out really well. I asked Harry, "Is there a reason you don't hug Lisa?"

He looked exasperated and said, "I *do* hug her. I hug her and kiss her about thirty times a day! I literally counted for a week just to be sure I was not being a negligent husband."

So then, I asked him, "Does she have to ask for a hug?"

He thought for a moment. "Well, yes, I guess so. I'm usually busy. So yes, she'll ask me for a hug, but I *always* give her a hug when she asks for one."

"Okay, I think I know what you need to do," I said. "This week, I want you to give Lisa three hugs a day without her having to ask for them. Do you think you can do that?"

"Sure. That's nothing," he said, and off they went.

The next week we had our final session because the couple informed me that their marital issues had cleared up "magically." Lisa was giddy and feeling quite loved. On the way out, Harry paused, shrugged his shoulders, and said, "You're a genius! I can't believe it was that easy!" I winked at him, shrugged my shoulders, and smiled. Well, I'd like to think I was a genius, but really, it's just a matter of being fluent in Human, and in this case, it was being fluent in "Helper-ese"—the language of Helper love.

Lisa had been anticipating Harry's needs, but he did not realize he needed to anticipate her needs as well. Apparently, part of the Helper's interpersonal dynamics is not having self-permission to ask to have their personal needs met. Over time, anticipating others' needs and not having their own needs met can be exhausting, and eventually, it can deplete the Helper's internal resources, at which point they can degenerate into self-sacrificing martyrs. And, nobody wants that to happen, as martyrs can be quite unpleasant to be around. On the other hand, if you offer a Helper half the generosity she offers you, she will be a pleasant companion indeed.

The Helper with the Reformer wing (2 with a 1 wing)
LOW dopamine — "The Servant"

The Servant has a heightened sense of altruism. With the Helper traits of warm emotional and personal connection and the Reformer's traits of rational self-control, the Servant strives for love through goodness and selfless service.

At times, Servants may experience conflict between their principles and their hearts.

Examples: Alan Alda and Ann Landers

The Helper with the Achiever wing (2 with a 3 wing)
HIGH dopamine — "The Host/Hostess"
The traits of the Helper and the Achiever in the Host/Hostess create a subtype that easily relates to people and seeks intimacy and personal connection. The Host/Hostess has social grace and desires to win the affection of others. Charming, friendly and outgoing, they enjoy the attention of others, are self-assured, and exude a sense of well-being and self-enjoyment. Their free-spirited attitude can lead to mistyping them as an Enthusiast. The Host/Hostess' genuine warmth and ability to communicate makes them more a gift giver (either actual gifts or gifts of time, attention or energy) than a Servant.

Examples: Barbara Bush and Richard Simmons

MY ARMENIAN HELPER MOTHER-IN-LAW

My Armenian Helper mother-in-law was one of the most colorful and larger-than-life characters ever to have graced this planet. She was not particularly large in stature, but her booming voice, hearty laugh, and bold presence filled the room as soon as she entered. She was a gregarious and social person. For her sixtieth birthday, she hosted her own party for "five hundred of my closest and dearest friends" (which was pretty impressive to me, since I could count my closest and dearest friends on one hand).

Even though she was thirty years older than my husband, we were always sure to get a good week's rest to prepare for her visits because of her boundless energy and schedule of activities that began almost immediately upon entering our home. Her entrance went something like this: "Ooh, hello darlings! It's *so good* to see you; it's been so long. Why, you look fabulous! It's so great to be here. Oh, listen, how about if I clean your microwave?"

continued on next page...

...continued from previous page

"Well, we don't really need to clean our microwave," I would venture. "We are just glad to see you."

"No, no, no, I insist! I didn't come across the country just to sit here like a bump on a log. Please, let me be of service! Let me help. I haven't cleaned your microwave since the last time I was here. Look, it'll only take twenty minutes."

"Okay, if you insist."

She would literally beam and say, "And then, right after that, I'm going to trim those houseplants of yours. My, it looks like they haven't been trimmed since the last time I was here!"

"Really, really," my husband and I would insist, "you don't have to do that; we just want to enjoy your company, Mom."

But Mom was undaunted. She would continue, "Don't be silly, you kids. I know you work so hard. It's the least I can do to help out around here."

And so, we would go Saturday, Sunday, Monday, and Tuesday, but we could set our calendar by her visit, knowing that by Wednesday morning she would start showing signs of wear. "Do you want to stay home today?" she would ask us.

"What's the matter, Mom? You're looking a little tired. Would you like us to take you out to eat tonight?"

"No, no, *I'm* fine, fine. Don't worry about *me.*"

"But you haven't come out of your room all morning," we'd say.

"Well, my back's just hurting from cleaning the microwave and trimming those houseplants and cooking Eric's favorite Armenian dishes all week . . ." And so, her dip into martyrdom would begin. We would then discuss how dangerous it was for her to give and give and give and not let us take care of her. After a couple of hours of intensive "family therapy," a few tears, lots of hugs, and an evening out to eat, all would be well. And, she would promise that on her next visit she would remember to let us take care of her.

continued on next page...

...continued from previous page

But you know, sometimes personality just trumps the best of intentions, and the very next year, and the year after that, every visit began with:

"Ooh, hello darlings! It's *so good* to see you; it's been so long. Why, you look fabulous! It's so great to be here. Oh, listen, how about if I clean your microwave?"

The Helper . . . you just gotta hug her!

3. *The ACHIEVER* (a.k.a. Achiever, Hero)
MEDIUM Norepinephrine—MEDIUM Serotonin
Success-Oriented, Pragmatic Type: "Three's a crowd (-pleaser)."
Basic Fear: Being worthless.
Basic Desire: To feel valuable and worthwhile.
Key Motivation: To be affirmed, to distinguish themselves from others, to have attention, to be admired, and to impress others
Favored Communication Style: Promotion

Achievers are adaptable, energetic, and ambitious, and they desire to improve themselves. They are the chameleons who know how to fit in and can learn from modeling others. Achievers are goal oriented. They seek to be loved for their performance and achievement. At average levels, they often identify themselves by the role they play in life, such as parent, teacher, or winner, and are masters of appearance. They can become overly competitive, image conscious, and obsessed with comparative status. Unhealthy Achievers can be devious, exploitative, or sociopathic and have difficulty dealing with failure. Integrated Achievers can be effective, competent leaders, inspirational heroes, and captains of winning teams.

Examples: John F Kennedy, Jimmy Carter, Jane Pauley, Michael Landon, Tom Cruise, Sharon Stone, Dick Clark, Sylvester Stallone, Arnold Schwarzenegger, Kathy Lee Gifford, O.J. Simpson, and Jeffrey Dahmer.

• • • • •

The Achiever personality is a fascinating personality type. Charming and often quite accomplished, at high levels of functioning, the Achiever can perform superhuman feats. Achievers make things happen!

This personality is designed to achieve and be a Hero. At low levels of functioning, it can be, well, pretty scary (this is actually true for all types). In theory, the Achiever has average set points in all three neurotransmitters, making it only one step away from every other personality type. Because of this, I have often wondered if the Achiever might have been the original human personality, or the "stem cell" human, from which all other personality types evolved, as our species developed and our personality roles became more complex.

Regardless of this personality's origin, being biologically only "one step away" from any other personality type may account for why the Achiever is also known as the Chameleon. The Achiever is well known for her keen ability to morph into, or mirror, any of the other personalities. In fact, Tony Robbins, a famous celebrity Achiever, mentors his many followers (most likely without even realizing it) in Achiever personality strategies. For example, one of the success strategies he teaches is to find a role model and then adopt that role model's behavior and attitude. In other words, he teaches people how to be a chameleon, how to "fake it till you make it." He also teaches how to adopt a success-oriented mindset, which works well for Achievers in general. Many of Tony's suggestions involve disregarding how one feels and concentrating solely on results, which is easier to accomplish if a person is somewhat disconnected from his feelings in the first place.

Achievers are very driven and goal oriented; in fact, we often say tongue-in-cheek that if you are in a jungle and it's between you and an Achiever, you can kiss your fanny goodbye. Achievers are designed to survive. So, getting mad at an Achiever for pushing ahead in a competition (even if it's just five o'clock traffic), or for driving himself or others harder than the average person, might be a little shortsighted. It would be like getting upset with a cat for chasing a bird and forgetting that that same drive and ambition put a man on the moon (John F. Kennedy).

Achievers can be charming at all levels of functioning. Charming is a prerequisite, but here's another somewhat amusing way to identify an Achiever (get ready for this one): good hair! (Think Bill Clinton and the $75 haircut.) One possible observation might be that Achievers are tuned into culture, fashion, and trends. They make cool "cool."

I remember years ago when an Achiever colleague used the acronym TMI ("too much information") for the first time. I knew that within a short period of time I would be hearing "TMI" everywhere. And guess what? OMG—I was right! (I also saw "OMG" for the first time in a text from that same colleague and knew it would be an acronym of the future!)

This same friend struggled with his chameleon identity for many years when it came time to give a party. He wasn't sure which personality he should bring to the party, given his varied range of friends. Then one day, he realized he could take on the persona of "host," and he became able to unabashedly host parties with as many different personality types as he had friends.

One of the distinctive features of the Achiever personality, especially a young Achiever, is that he is not well connected to his heart. The heart is very much like the rudder of a ship and helps to guide a person on his journey in life. A person who is disconnected in this way may be at a disadvantage when it comes to making adjustments and corrections to stay true to himself and his life's purpose. For instance, if something feels good, then he knows that he wants to do more of it, but if it feels bad, then he wants to do less of it. And if he is not well connected, he may not know when he is acting "on purpose" or "off purpose." Instead of being able to use his internal rudder as a guide, he might have to rely on external cues. Especially as a youngster, the Achiever tends to use external cues, such as those evident in the culture surrounding him, to help him determine the right or appropriate way to be.

For example, an Achiever growing up in India might aspire to be a holy guru; an Achiever growing up in the Bronx might want to be the biggest, baddest gang leader; and an Achiever growing up in the Heartland might want to be president of the United States, a CEO, or an NFL football player.

The biological advantage to not being well connected to one's heart could be that, at high levels of stress (life-and-death, kill-or-be-killed situations), low levels of functioning (including high psychopathy) allow for ruthless, primal, "heartless" action. At low levels of functioning, a murderous Achiever could be so disconnected from her emotions that a person could hook her up to biofeedback equipment and interrogate her, and she could give socially appropriate verbal responses while not showing any telling responses on the biofeedback equipment. This paints the picture of a true heartless sociopath.

Even though an Achiever's wiring might seem best for primal "survival of the fittest," in a more evolved society—one that requires compassion and teamwork and a spirit of helping our multi-challenged members—Achievers may have to adapt, and so they do.

As noted, the ability to access and express emotions can be an enormous challenge for Achievers. As adaptive as this may be in a life-or-death situation, it is quite a disadvantage in other contexts, such as when a person wants to create and maintain intimacy. After all, intimacy involves sharing one's innermost feelings with another human being.

The Achiever with the Helper wing (3 with a 2 wing)
HIGH dopamine — "The Star"
The somewhat driven and high energy Star possesses extraordinary social skills and enjoys being the center of attention. They are often extremely charming and sociable. They tend to be highly popular and pride themselves on interpersonal skills and attractiveness. With the Helper wing, there is an emphasis on reaching out to others and making a difference in others' lives. They aspire to be leaders and heroes of their organization and/or community.

Examples: Bill Clinton, Tony Robbins and Whitney Houston

The Achiever with the Individualist wing (3 with a 4 wing)
LOW dopamine — "The Professional"
The Professional is a complex subtype, since the Achiever is essentially an interpersonal type, whereas the Individualist is more socially withdrawn. Professionals are more emotionally vulnerable than the Stars and tend to be intuitive and self-aware, which gives them more potential for developing their emotional lives. They often spend a great deal of time honing their craft in order to excel in their chosen field of endeavor and therefore usually become self-assured and outstanding in some way.

Examples: Richard Gere, Bono and Sting

MY SON, THE DOCTOR

Matthew Thomas Bernard is an Achiever with a Helper wing; he is also my one and only son. When Matthew was young, I was in nursing school, and his father was a teacher, so he was surrounded by educational influences. He also had a vision problem that required he wear corrective lenses. The visual effect of his glasses, combined with his articulate manner, earned him the nickname "the little professor" at his daycare.

By the time he was twelve years old, he had developed quite an intellectual image. That year, he attended a Halloween party and decided to dress up as a "nerd." He put a piece of masking tape around his glasses and buttoned his top shirt button. He was really pleased with his costume and thought everyone was going to think it was funny. No one laughed. The other kids did not know he was in costume, and poor Matt was very embarrassed. This is how he learned that children actually thought of him as a nerd. He was mortified. He immediately went on a campaign to reinvent himself.

In my humble opinion, he went too far. Whatever his idea of a "not nerd" was, Matt certainly became that. As a teenager, his favorite ad in a body-building magazine read, "It is rumored that there are those who walk among us who can change themselves at will." And, change himself he did. By the time he was sixteen years old, he had taken on the visual persona of a hoodlum, even though he was still a "good kid." But he had achieved his purpose; no one would dare to think of him and the word "nerd" in the same sentence anymore.

I didn't like him as a hoodlum. I didn't like his friends. He started smoking. (There was no telling *what* he was smoking.) He seemed to always have a bit of an "edgy" attitude. But he kept his grades up and a part-time job, and for all practical purposes, he was still a good kid. At the peak of his rebellion, Matt stormed out of the house one afternoon,

continued on next page...

...continued from previous page

slamming the door behind him and exclaiming, "I hope to God I never have a family like this. I can't wait till I get out in the real world, where I can have real freedom."

When he returned that evening, I remember telling him, "You know, son, I think you have more freedom in this family than you do in the real world."

"Yeah, right," he said in his most disgusted tone.

Not long after that, he made it clear that he no longer wanted to go to an all-male Catholic high school. He transferred to a co-ed public school, where he excelled and skipped an entire grade of high school. That put him in college one year younger than all the other freshmen. The pressure was on. Now, he had to live up to the image he had created.

One night, his stepfather and I came home to find this message on our answering machine: "Mom, Dad, this is Matt—I'm, uh, basically in jail." Matt had two such overnight stays in jail, and one incident resulted in a visit to the emergency room for injuries from a fall caused by drunkenness. To us, Matt seemed a bit lost. My friends assured me it was all part of growing up, but I wondered if he would live through it. Sometimes I wondered if *I* would live through it. One of my saddest moments as a parent was picking him up at jail and looking through the bars of his cell. "Yes, officer," I said as I gazed at Matt, his eyes staring at the floor. "Yes, that is my son."

Actually though, as heartbreaking as it was for us as parents, I think Matt had a lot of fun that semester, and he certainly had opportunities for growing and maturing because he was living on his own. He failed his first semester of college, not because he didn't do well academically but because he didn't show up to take his finals, thinking he could charm his professors into letting him take his final exams at a time that was more convenient for him. It didn't take him long to realize that the "real world" clearly did not offer more freedom, as he had imagined it would.

continued on next page...

...*continued from previous page*

And then, another life-altering event happened—this one eclipsing the Halloween party by a lifetime. Matthew learned that he was going to be a father. Realizing he was about to be responsible for another life, it was like some internal biological switch flipped on. Watching Matt then was like watching a real-life *Rocky* movie. A tribute to his tribe (the Achiever tribe that is), he systematically set about reinventing himself again. When he told me he was planning to go to medical school, I said, "Look, Matt, if you make it into medical school, I'll help you out financially and any other way I can, okay?" He looked a little incredulous and said, "Mom, I didn't say *if* I go to medical school, I said *when*." He said it with such certainty that I gulped; I knew from the bottom of my being that there was no question my son was going to be a doctor.

This time, he went even more dramatically from God-knows-what to Dr. Matthew Bernard. Taking the best from his mom (including information related to psychology, mental health, personality, dealing with death and dying) and the best from his dad (including gentleness, steadiness, and determination) and combining it with his own skill sets and personality created an amazing physician.

One of my proudest moments as a parent was the day Matthew shared with me his decision about his career choice in medicine. For several months, he was torn between the high-paying, high-pressured field of orthopedic medicine and the not-as-lucrative but equally satisfying field of emergency medicine, which would allow for more flexibility and a better quality of life for him and his family. "You know, Mom," he said. "It ultimately was an easy decision. My personality wanted me to go into orthopedics, but my heart wants me to go into emergency medicine." So, he followed his heart. And then, his emergency room team followed him. He became the youngest medical director of an emergency room ever hired. His youth brought energy, passion, and vision, and his leadership skills included charisma, courage, and confidence to lead his team from

continued on next page...

...continued from previous page

the lowest-ranked department in the LSU system to the highest-ranked department in one year! When he learned that he was nominated as Physician of the Year, he humbly said, "Why, that's quite an honor, but it was truly a team effort. I just got to be the quarterback, doing what I love."

Yes, I am proud of my son, Matthew, the doctor—but not just because I am his mother. He is an amazing physician, an incredible leader, a compassionate healer, a wonderful husband, a great grandson, a loving son, a terrific dad, and an awesome example of what a high-functioning Achiever can be. I am most proud because he took some tough times and challenges and, with sheer will and a lot of sweat and tears and sleepless nights, created a dream come true for himself and his family. Now he and his team save lives on a daily basis. Yes, officer, that's my son, the doctor, my Hero.

The Achiever can be anything he wants to be (just don't get in his way)!

4. *The INDIVIDUALIST* (a.k.a. Artist, Romantic)

MEDIUM Norepinephrine—LOW Serotonin

The Sensitive Type: *"Four-lorn and four-gotten."*

Basic Fear: To have no identity or personal significance

Basic Desire: To find themselves and their significance (to create an identity)

Key Motivation: To express themselves and their individuality, to create and surround themselves with beauty, and to attract a "rescuer"

Favored Communication Style: Personal stories, parables, analogies, and metaphors

Individualists are individualistic, emotionally sensitive, and self-expressive. They share their feelings in such a way that others can relate. Individualists feel everything deeply. They tend to be sensitive and artistic in either a traditional or non-traditional sense (artist to home decorator). Individualists have a sense of being special and often feel misunderstood by others. At average levels they may become too aware of their negative emotions and imagination and lack in self-esteem. At lower levels of functioning, they can be sad and tragic. Unhealthy Individualists can be withdrawn and depressed. They may appear self-absorbed and aloof. Integrated Individualists are creative and intuitive and able to help other people deal with emotionally painful situations.

Examples: Jackie Onassis, Ingmar Bergman, Alan Watts, Paul Simon, Tennessee Williams, Edgar Allan Poe, Annie Lennox, Virginia Woolf, Judy Garland, and "Blanche DuBois."

• • • • •

The Individualist, in my opinion, poses the most difficult challenges a personality can have. This one, let's just say, didn't win the chemical lottery. This personality feels things more deeply than all the other personalities combined. Being an Individualist is like having a Ferrari for a personality. It requires high maintenance, excellent fuel, and an optimal driver, but when all conditions are met, nothing on the road performs quite like it!

Unfortunately, the Individualist has a reputation for being a drama queen or king. At low levels of functioning—that is, when the Individualist's mental health has been compromised—you may hear family members saying, "We feel like we are walking on eggshells." Even from a young age, this child's emotional reactivity can upset the family to such a degree that she can control the family dynamics.

All people with this personality report having a little world inside their heads—a little romantic, imagined world, very different from the actual reality the rest of us experience day by day. And when someone is operating at a very low level of functioning, that imagined world can translate to poor reality testing. For example, a low-functioning Individualist with an eating disorder might imagine her body as fat rather than emaciated. Another might think he's the most giving and wonderful father in the world, while everyone else is thinking, *Are you kidding? He drops the kids off all the time; he's at the hair salon every day!* (Now remember, we are talking here about an Individualist at the lowest, most unhealthy level of functioning.)

At this unhealthy place, the Individualist also becomes prone to almost everything that can go wrong emotionally—depression, suicide, alcoholism, substance abuse, and (in females) eating disorders and cutting. Even when the Individualist does not suffer from a specific diagnosis, many do complain of a sense of longing, a sense of being poorly understood (or not understood at all), and a sense that something is missing (neurotransmitters perhaps?). Many report self-loathing, a feeling of being fatally flawed.

Judy Garland, an Individualist who unfortunately committed suicide, once reflected upon the lyrics to "Somewhere over the Rainbow," sharing her sense that "somewhere, out there" eluded her and existed far from her own grasp. A huge challenge for many people with this personality is the sense that "what I have now in my current situation is okay, but maybe something out there is better." They often have a sense that even though their circumstances seem fine, "something is missing."

If you ask me, all this is a high price of admission. What is the gift?

Individualists are sensitive to everything—and I mean everything—sensitive to food, sensitive to medication, sensitive to light and sound, to "energies" and the ethereal. They are highly intuitive and sensitive to the experiences of others. They are sensitive to their internal environments too. They are highly introspective. And from that sensitivity, they create music and poetry, beauty and art.

So the gift then, or the biological purpose of an Individualist, seems to lie in their ability to take that sensitivity and create art that illustrates human experience. No animals in the "lower species" create art that we know of. No other species seems to be smitten with ritual, as the Individualist seems to be.

When I read Matthew Alper's book, *The "God" Part of the Brain*, I learned that a specific part of the brain located in the left temporal lobe, when simulated with a trans-cranial magnet, can induce spiritual and/or religious experiences. For that to happen, some believe there must be something akin to a "God gene," and given that nature is very conservative (it doesn't just create a part of the body arbitrarily), there must be some important role here pertinent to our survival as a species. If there is a God gene, it likely exists to enable human beings to experience a spiritual connection, and the Individualist above all the other personalities surely has it.

Now, I don't want to get into a philosophical debate on the existence of God. But what I do now believe is that it is the biological job of the Individualist to help the rest of us connect with God, whoever or whatever that may be; to connect with a sense of something greater than ourselves, something transcendent, often through the arts—music, dance, poetry, sculpture, prose, and performance art.

In the more romantically and spiritually oriented cultures, the Individualist personality is more respected and revered than it is, say, in the United States, where Individualists are expected to "get a real job."

Given that the Individualist, like the Loyalist (6) and the Challenger (8)—only perhaps even more so—falls into one of those "sucks-to-be-you" categories of more reactive personalities, she possesses a low level of serotonin, the well-being neurotransmitter. But those who see the Individualist in this way only see part of the picture. True Individualists feel deeply, and they can sink pretty darned low and suffer from their tendency to tune in to both inner and outer influences. Individualists are super-sensitive and, as noted above, prone to clinical depression. On the other hand, when things are going well, when the creative juices are flowing and the Individualist can live into his purpose, take that human experience, and shape it into an art form, he soars.

High highs and low lows can seem like a roller coaster, but for a high-functioning Individualist, these two things tend to balance out. Put in the words of an Individualist I know: "Ah, 'tis the fate of the Artist to swing low into the depths, feel the pain of it, scoop up the treasures that lie hidden there, and finally give them over to the world." The art really does belong to the world, after all, not to the Individualist. And for the mature Individualist, great satisfaction comes from connecting with humanity by giving their art over for the enrichment of others.

I once asked an Individualist friend of mine, "Be honest. If you could experience joy and happiness *all the time*, wouldn't you choose to do so?" After considering this for a moment, she responded, "No, I could not live that way." I pressed her. "But if you *had* to choose between joy and pain, wouldn't you choose joy?" She answered, "What would be the point? I relish joy, of course. But I could never fully appreciate joy without having had an experience of sorrow. How can a person see light without knowing shadow? Joy without pain would be—boring. Besides, I would lose my artistic motivation. Human suffering offers rich material to transform on the way back to joy."

When we consider the importance of the balance between joy and suffering in the life of the Individualist, it raises some questions regarding the ethics of medicating people to adjust neurotransmitter levels. In Western culture in particular, the appetite for suffering is quite low, as is the tolerance for edgy, "out-there" personalities. Artists often "starve" in our culture—unless they are particularly accomplished and able to find a rare niche of acceptance. Consequently, Individualists may feel inclined to medicate that awful sensitivity and depressed mood rather than find their redemption in art. One cannot help but wonder at what cost to the world these choices come.

I am not suggesting we avoid medicating depression, an effort that can save lives. I only suggest we consider the whole person when making decisions such as this, and also that we consider how well (or how poorly) our culture has supported the Individualist to date, and whether there may be room for improvement in the way we value a personality so critical to humankind and so enriching for the human experience.

The Individualist with the Achiever wing (4 with a 3 wing)
HIGH dopamine — "The Aristocrat"

Individualists are often introverted and withdrawn, and Achievers are competitive and driven to succeed. The Aristocrat blends those two personalities in a manner that creates a subtype that is both emotionally volatile and contradictory. The Aristocrat presents as edgier; and has a somewhat sultry, more seductive and worldly presence than the Bohemian. Their reactivity is usually expressed with anger rather than anxiety. Aristocrats are generally ambitious and accomplished people, particularly in the arts, and tend to be more emotionally and financially extravagant.

Examples: The Artist formerly known as Prince, Michael Jackson, Tchaikovsky, Madonna and Bono

The Individualist with the Investigator wing (4 with a 5 wing)
LOW dopamine — "The Bohemian"

The Bohemian tends to be more reclusive and less ambitious than the Aristocrat, with more of an intellectual depth and intensity. The Bohemian presents as a softer and gentler version of the Individualist. When Bohemians are reactive they experience anxiety rather than a temper. They are intuitive, insightful and emotionally sensitive and tend to create more for themselves than for their audiences.

Examples: Johnny Depp, Bob Dylan and Anne Rice

MY "SPECIAL" CLIENT

One of the common characteristics of the Individualist is that they find their own *special* way of being unique in the world. I have a client named Paul, a forty-two-year-old Individualist, who smiles as he shares, "I relish my uniqueness. When I was five years old, my mother took me to a toy store once, and there were four purple water pistols on the shelf along

continued on next page...

...continued from previous page

with one red pistol. Purple was my absolute favorite color, but I chose the red pistol because I didn't want to be like the other children. It was important to me even then that I was perceived as 'special.' My friend, Larry, teases me and says I am indeed special. He calls me a flaming 'four' with a four wing!"

Paul is an editor at a university press and first came to see me for anger management. He almost lost his job due to his angry outbursts with the interns at the publishing company. Fortunately, he was able to maintain his position due to his years of faithful service, outstanding performance, *and* a letter from me stating that I would agree to help him learn how to manage his emotional states. At the time, he suffered from moderate to severe depression, especially in the wintertime, when he is vulnerable to SAD (seasonal affective disorder). He self-medicated with pizza and beer and taking naps in his darkened living room with his cat, Daisy, on his chest.

Paul is a man of modest means. His house is in an unassuming suburb of New Orleans, but enter his living room and he has rich, dark maroon ceiling-to-floor drapes that puddle on the floor and describe a man with more elegant tastes than the world around him. He has one bedroom in his house dedicated entirely to war games he plays on Sunday afternoons with his intellectual buddies, who enjoy sparring and debating world history and current events and flaunting their superior intellectual genius before each other.

Paul is quite resistant to assimilating into this century. For example, he insists on keeping his archaic cell phone, now held together with a rubber band and a piece of tape. Whenever I text him I have to keep my messages to under 180 characters or he receives them as "blanks." He takes great pride that he is not one of the "sheeple" (people who follow trends like sheep just for the sake of it). He lives as though trapped in a period of time and place that does not appreciate his eccentric mannerisms and attitude. For example, Paul doesn't say "goodbye" when leaving my

continued on next page...

...continued from previous page

office but rather "Fare thee well, good lady" as his parting salutation. Renaissance festivals would surely be too low-brow for his taste, and yet, the way he carries himself and his manner of speaking would fit into the Renaissance era so perfectly.

I have observed that Individualists are incredibly good with words. They are simply fascinated with language, communication, and all things related to words. Many write poetry, scribble lyrics, or journal. Their peers often describe them as "wordsmiths." And, God bless you if you happen to be on the other side of a hurt (and therefore angry) low-functioning Individualist who verbally lashes out at you. You will stand before her with your heart in your hand bleeding, wondering how she sliced and diced you in seconds. (Contrast this to the way a low-functioning Challenger might express his anger, which might be to bluntly say something like "I don't like you. You're stupid.")

Low-functioning Individualists can be extremely injured by the words of others, sometimes perceiving insult where none was intended. But ironically, they may seem oblivious to the surgical precision with which they can attack and hurt *others'* feelings. I often tease my Individualists and say they need to get their words licensed like boxers need to license their hands as weapons.

As a wordsmith, Paul is in a class of his own (and I know he'd be tickled to hear that). He is a word wizard. Sometimes, in our sessions, when he is describing a setting or a person with whom he has taken offense, his ranting and raving is near hypnotic. More than once, I have found myself losing track of his story as I become entranced by his melodic flow or the way he strings his carefully chosen words together. His vocabulary is so rich that I have to Google at *least* one word per session. Because of his quick wit and broad knowledge of current events, historical facts, and strong politically conservative opinions, some people might be taken aback by what appears to be (and likely is) a bit of an intellectual arrogance.

continued on next page...

...continued from previous page

At the same time, when it comes to intimate relationships, particularly with women, Paul is shy and socially awkward. For that reason, I suggested that he meet me at a Toastmaster's meeting to become more comfortable with *intimate* public speaking, which is quite different from lecturing on one's familiar topic. I was somewhat hesitant to bring him because of his intellectual and verbal prowess, concerned that he might be intimidating to members of the club who are simply trying to build their confidence in public speaking. I was pleasantly surprised to observe that he was absolutely kindhearted with the other members. He laughed with them at their not particularly sophisticated attempts at humor, and he refrained from peppering his comments with polysyllabic words. Later, I mentioned how much gentler he appeared than I had anticipated. He responded, "Well, I felt secure—I didn't have to prove anything to anyone. They were all good people trying to better themselves."

Paul initiated his divorce with his former wife years ago, but he still mourns the marriage as he looks back, thinking he may have made a mistake. It seems the longer he is away from his ex-wife, the more he longs for the stability and comfort of their relationship. Since his divorce, he has had several relationships, and after each one is over, he continues to mourn and long for them as well. He almost "courts" them by sending birthday presents and flowers on special occasions. However, they do not seem to respond in kind.

Many Individualists struggle with feelings of jealousy in romantic relationships and also in non-romantic personal and professional situations. Paul was eventually able to identify that he was actually jealous of his interns, many of whom came from privileged backgrounds. He judged that they were "spoiled brats," often missing deadlines and behaving indifferently to how their actions impacted others at the press. He believed they were squandering their many gifts of wealth and family support. (Paul's father died when he was four years old, and his mother struggled to raise him and his sisters. After his father's death, the family

continued on next page...

...continued from previous page

was forced to move to an apartment in a less desirable neighborhood, and Paul often felt helpless watching the toll that financial stress took on his mother.)

Paul began to realize that his angry outbursts were actually jealousy and judgments that were leaking out when he was tired and/or hungry. Once he learned to manage his anger at work, he was able to gather enough emotional energy to seek a new long-term lover. He seems mostly attracted to Individualist women who dress in "special ways." Paul describes his preferences this way: "I like kooky, creative, moody women with a sense of style and fashion. I don't care for slatterns [unkept women] who sport greasy, three-dollar flip-flops and wear their Thai hooker shorts." Even when the object of his interest is not available due to marriage or circumstance, Paul manages to weave himself into a pseudo romantic web, if for no other reason than just the intrigue.

Since our time together, Paul has become less depressed overall but still drifts in and out of mild depression. He continues to search for his next true love and is willing to let his heart hope and be crushed repeatedly until he finds her.

This same man who goes off on tirades against humanity at the slightest provocation (real or imagined) is also the man who shared with me on a car ride together his "private cat route." Paul has taken it upon himself to feed about a dozen stray cats in his surrounding neighborhood. He knows each one's peculiar quirks, and once he has gained their trust, he will conspire with a feral cat rescue team to capture the kitty and place it in a loving home. As I watched him fretting over a cat who was five minutes late for feeding time, and saw the anguish in his face transform to relief when the kitty appeared, my heart melted for this complex man. I found myself hoping that one day he will find a "special" woman who will find him eccentric and special enough to want to go cat rescuing together—and perhaps a little bit more.

When it comes to Individualists, the price of admission can be steep, but wow, what a ride!

5. *The INVESTIGATOR* (a.k.a. Thinker, Observer)

HIGH Norepinephrine—MEDIUM Serotonin
The Cerebral Type: *"Five fingers—count 'em."*
Basic Fear: Being useless, helpless, or incapable
Basic Desire: To be capable and competent
Key Motivation: To possess knowledge, to understand the environment, to have everything figured out as a way of defending the self from threats from the environment.
Favored Communication Style: Dissertations

Investigators are alert, curious, original learners. They want to understand everything around them. As they can easily become insecure in their environment, they need to be totally certain about something before they can do it. They sometimes prefer to think about doing something rather than doing it. Investigators are astute observers. They protect their privacy and maintain emotional distance from others. They may feel drained by commitment and by the needs of others. They are often considered odd or eccentric. Unhealthy Investigators tend to be isolated, paranoid, and antagonistic. Integrated Investigators are highly intellectual and excellent decision makers.

Examples: John Lennon, Lily Tomlin, Bobby Fischer, Stephen King, Clive Barker, Friedrich Vincent Van Gogh, Kurt Cobain, and the Unabomber.

• • • • •

The Investigator (also known as the Thinker or Observer due to his keen powers of observation) has also been affectionately referred to in our culture as the "nerd" because of—well—the look and all that goes with it. Many Investigators are attracted to science fiction, Star Trek, and weird science genres.

Let me tell you, some Investigator thoughts can be weird and creepy. I was married to a Thinker, so I would know. I remember saying to Dr. Eric Schulze, my husband and research partner of ten years, "I want to know everything you think for the next twenty-four hours." He replied, "No you don't." I insisted. I begged. I pleaded. I demanded in the name and spirit of research that he share with me completely uncensored "Eric Investigator thoughts" for at least one day.

Well, live and learn. After only an hour, I had had enough. I had been to "Creepy Bizarro Land" and back, and it was more than I could take. Eric smirked, looking pleased with himself. As for me, once I had that basic understanding of the inner life of the Investigator, it was frankly enough for me. I did not need to revisit that one!

This particular personality is not limited by social constraints of fashion and culture. Not every original thought found "outside the box" (the Investigator's specialty) is what we would call socially appropriate. But this is what allows them to be some of the most free and original thinkers in the world.

Their disregard or lack of interest in social norms may offer insight into why Investigators look as "nerdish" as they do. Take a look at Albert Einstein and then the Unabomber. Both fall on ends of the Investigator spectrum from high functioning to low, but you might see an interesting commonality—crazy hair! Again, complete disregard for social convention; and because they don't follow social convention, Investigators dress less for fashion than for practicality. So if a top button keeps them warmer, they may button it, even if it doesn't look "cool." Our Achievers (3) and Individualists (4) determine what is cool and trendy in this world, *not* the Investigators.

Under stress, Investigators can be intellectually arrogant and intolerant of what they view as stupidity and inefficiency, but on the whole, Investigators are very modest and humble people. If you ask an Investigator what she is a master at, the most likely answer will be "nothing." This is usually because she knows what she doesn't know. But if you ask her what she is *interested* in, you will have found the key to her mastery, because an Investigator is highly motivated to understand things at a deep level. And, that is why Investigators are very private people. Because to an Investigator knowledge is power, knowing about her, in her mind, will give you power over her.

When my son was in medical school, he noticed in the back of his medical school textbook references to my then new husband and research partner. He came to me one day and said, "Mom, is this *your* Dr. Eric Schulze?" I responded, "I doubt it; I'm sure if Eric had published this kind of outstanding work, I would have known it by now." But much to my surprise, Eric was quite accomplished. The very first time he published his research, it was published in *Science* magazine, something that is considered quite a feat. To this day, no one has surpassed his work in microtubules.

Ironically, when we met, I thought I was going to be able to teach *him* a thing or two about research. He never bothered to tell me that he trained at Harvard and had spent an invitation-only summer at Cold Harbor Springs hanging out with Nobel Prize winners. It took months before I learned that James Watson (of Watson and Crick, the guys who received the Nobel Prize for their work in discovering DNA) wrote Eric's medical school recommendation letter. Years later, I learned that Eric had personal relationships with Nobel Prize winners who fully expected that he too would win a Nobel Prize one day. I once overheard him speaking with one of those Nobel Prize winners and saying, "No, I haven't done anything Nobel worthy yet, but I believe that my wife has cracked the code of human personality, and one day *she* could be on the stage."

One of the additional blessings and curses of the Investigator personality is the ability to focus, which brings with it the ability to detach from feelings. This ability can be quite useful in high-stress situations requiring focus on intricate details, such as during brain surgery, but it could also present a disadvantage in an intimate relationship.

I think the biological purpose of the Investigator is to use intellect to advance our species, and in the past, that role was most likely held by a shaman who used his intellect to create potions, herbs, and medicines to keep the tribe healthy.

When Eric and I were researching the possibility that animals might also have personality, we were pleasantly surprised to find the Investigator personality occasionally presents in gorilla communities. These gorilla nerds hang out at the periphery of the community and tinker with novel ways to peel bananas or open up coconuts. And, get this: they seldom attract the gorilla "babes" early on. Sound familiar? But as time goes by, and the other male gorillas have died in battle or knocked each other off, and the nerd gorillas start getting a little silver on their backs, the females begin to take an interest in these surviving and somewhat eccentric gorillas. When Eric read this research, I heard him mutter, "Yep, Revenge of the Primal Nerds."

I believe Investigators have been stereotyped as unfeeling, but in fact, just the opposite is true. There is a great scene in the movie *Sherlock Holmes*, where

Robert Downey Jr. portrays Sherlock Holmes, purportedly an Investigator. In the scene, he is at a restaurant and he notices everything: the sights, the sounds, the waiter stealing a piece of silverware, and so forth. The viewer quickly gets an understanding as to how the Investigator also gets its other name, the Observer, and how keen powers of observation can quickly become over-stimulating and overwhelming.

The same process can happen with feelings. Eric and I noticed repeatedly and verified with countless other Investigators the phenomenon of "feeling in delayed time." In other words, when an overpowering emotion emerges, it is not uncommon for an Investigator to "shelve" that emotion in the present moment and process it minutes, hours, sometimes days later at a time and place when it feels "safer." This mechanism happens automatically and unconsciously and appears to protect the Investigator's brain from mental and emotional overload.

The Investigator with an Individualist wing (5 with a 4 wing) LOW dopamine — "The Iconoclast"

The traits of the Investigator and Individualist reinforce each other including that both are withdrawn types and tend to present as a more gentle and passive version of the Investigator. Rather than taking action The Iconoclast tends to internalize feelings making then one of the richest subtypes. They often combine outstanding creative and sometimes artistic ability with intellectual achievement. The Iconoclasts have a nice blend of intuition, knowledge, sensitivity and insight and are a bit more philosophical and sensitive to the human condition.

Examples: Albert Einstein, Nietzsche and Tim Burton

DR. HEARTLESS I PRESUMED

One of the most poignant moments I recall, which demonstrates this delayed-feeling phenomenon, occurred one night when Eric was working as a radiologist on a nightshift in Louisiana. He was called out to pronounce "fetal demise" in a full-term pregnancy before the obstetrician could safely begin the procedure to induce labor to abort the stillborn baby. The hospital was about a forty-five-minute drive from our home, so

continued on next page...

...continued from previous page

I rode with Eric to keep him company and also because I thought it would be an emotionally challenging task that night. Before he got out of the car, I reminded him that this was going to be a horrible night for this woman, and I encouraged him to give her time to talk or cry.

When he got back into the car, Eric seemed almost robotic. I asked him how it went. "Fine," he replied. "Did you talk to her?" I asked. "I said what I needed to say," he answered in a cool and clinical manner. I became upset by what I envisioned must have been a stiff and not very comforting bedside manner. "Dammit, Eric, that woman just lost her child. She carried that baby for nine months, and she just lost her baby, yet you walked in there like Dr. Insect—or Mr. Spock from Star Trek. That's what's wrong with doctors."

At that point, I thought about how Eric used to jokingly say that, when he married, me he decided he was going to "sleep with the enemy"—a nurse.

I didn't want to be his enemy; I was just disappointed in him and sad for that mother, whom I had never even met. I sat in icy silence for the next ten or fifteen minutes. And then, I saw Eric gripping the steering wheel as he pulled the car over.

He hung his head down and sighed. "Today, when I was driving to the grocery store . . . I hit a raccoon. I think it died." One big fat tear welled up from his eye and rolled down his cheek. At first, I couldn't make sense of it all. Then, I realized that he had already been very upset about killing a raccoon in the afternoon. That, coupled with the overwhelming task of dealing with the grief of a mother losing her firstborn baby, was too much for him to bear, and he had shut down his emotions. Instead of being upset with him, I was filled with compassion for this gentle man who was sometimes much more sensitive than I realized.

Oh, those Investigators . . . they are so weird and wacky and wired and wise.

6. *The LOYALIST* (a.k.a. Troubleshooter, Devil's Advocate)

HIGH Norepinephrine—LOW Serotonin

Committed, Security-Oriented Type: *"Six of one, half a dozen of the other."*

Basic Fear: Being unable to survive on their own

Basic Desire: To have security and support

Key Motivation: To have security, feel supported by others, have certitude and reassurance, fight against anxiety and insecurity

Favored Communication Style: Group thought and detailed descriptions

Loyalists are faithful, committed, and loyal to people or ideas with which they identify. Loyalists are responsible, conscientious, reliable, and dependable. They will work for a cause the way many others work for personal gain. At average levels, they become insecure and seek permission and approval from an authority figure (person or belief) before they act. They tend to be fearful, dutiful, and plagued by doubt and may not have enough self-confidence to make their own decisions or to act upon them. Unhealthy Loyalists tend to be extremely anxious and dependent. Integrated Loyalists can be good team players, loyal soldiers, and highly committed to family and friends.

Examples: Robert Kennedy, Malcolm X, Candice Bergen, Gilda Radner, Mel Gibson, Phil Donahue, Jay Leno, John Goodman, Diane Keaton, Woody Allen, Ellen DeGeneres, Andy Rooney, J. Edgar Hoover, Richard Nixon, Rush Limbaugh, "George Costanza," and "Archie Bunker."

• • • • •

I think the loyalist personality may be the second most challenging personality to have because it has an incredible amount of mental energy, but it is not necessarily pleasant energy. Remember how having high norepinephrine is like having a high brain engine idle, but low serotonin is like running low octane fuel? Rapid-fire questions like "What's wrong with this situation? What's not right about this? Who can I trust?" makes Loyalists incredibly good at troubleshooting. They can spot a problem long before most of us can. But this tendency also creates an incredible amount of discomfort and anxiety.

Rebecca, who describes herself as a "Loyalist and a half," says, "I even worry when everything is okay, because I start thinking, 'Oh, no, what if I'm missing something? What if I'm asleep at the wheel here and everything really *isn't* okay?'"

Back in the days of hunters and gatherers, a Loyalist would be the one who saw a broken branch that wasn't broken the day before, which would perhaps reveal a sleeping saber tooth tiger that could have wreaked havoc on the small hunting party.

Biologically speaking, I liken the Loyalist to a fighter ant, always on alert to the question "Who is with us, and who is not with us?" In an ant pile, the fighter ants react to and attack any invader that is "not us," whether it be a stick or a finger or another type of ant. Loyalists don't limit their "us/not us" type of thinking to people. I see a general tendency among Loyalists to categorize most concepts to black and white, all or nothing, good or bad, right or wrong.

Loyalists are extremely conscientious, responsible, and hyper-vigilant, and like any personality trait, these characteristics can be both a blessing and a curse. Always being on alert, especially for unpleasant things, can be wearisome. That goes for external circumstances too, in which a Loyalist worries about what might go wrong. Not only do Loyalists see what is not right or what is missing in the external world, but they also use that same critical lens internally, making self-esteem a challenge.

Speaking of criticism, this is a reminder that Loyalists, like the other two low-serotonin types (Individualists and Challengers), have a tendency to "hear" feedback more harshly than most other personality types. My pal Sal, a Super Six Loyalist, met me for lunch one day. When I saw him I said, "Hey Sal, you look great today!" His response: "What?! What does that mean? Does that mean I look terrible the *other* days?" In less than two seconds, Sal had taken a compliment and turned it into a criticism. Amazing. It sure can be tough being a Loyalist.

As I said, self-esteem can be an issue for a Loyalist. Upon completing a task, instead of feeling pride, a Loyalist can quickly tear herself down with self-talk that sounds something like this: "Oh, nice, I really did a good job with that. Well, I guess *anybody* could have done that. Actually, it's not *that* great of a job.

Oh, look—there's a mistake; what a mess. I'm sure somebody else could have done a much better job." When I suggested to a Loyalist client named Doug that he not criticize himself for one week, he came back the next week saying, "Well, I had absolutely nothing to say to myself for the entire week!"

But Loyalists are not just tough on themselves. They can also appear more negative to their friends and significant others, especially when someone is sharing an idea that he or she is excited about. Being a good troubleshooter, the Loyalist may point out all the things that could go wrong with the great idea, in order to protect the friend from being disappointed. The friend may interpret this as the Loyalist not having confidence in her, or not liking the idea, or not supporting her, when in fact the truth might be just the opposite.

Here's a tip when presenting an idea to a Loyalist, whether it be in a personal relationship or at a board meeting. Present the idea with this introduction: "I have an idea that has a few challenges, and I'm not sure that it will work." At this point, the Loyalist will already begin to think of ways that it *can* work. Once you have primed his brain in this way, you may proceed with guarded optimism. Overly optimistic presentations will make a Loyalist nervous!

Loyalists are sometimes referred to as having "ricochet brains." With extremely high levels of norepinephrine, their brains are constantly thinking and/or ricocheting from one idea or level to the next. Many report that reading, which requires a lot of focus in one place at one time, is quite a challenge. Sarah, a fast-talking, fast-thinking Loyalist, reports, "This is what reading sounds like to me: 'Oh, that's an interesting thought. I wonder how the author knows that? What are her credentials? Is she really an authority, or is that just her opinion? Was that a knock at the door, or was that the kids in the other room? If that's the kids, I wonder what they're up to? It's getting close to dinnertime. I wonder what we're going to do for dinner. Now, where was I on this page?' And then, I look at the same sentence and start all over again."

As tough as it is to be a Loyalist, you cannot find a more true-blue friend (hence the name Loyalist). Loyalists are wired to be faithful, uber-responsible, and conscientious. They are true team players and faithful sports fans. They will sacrifice themselves, often beyond what is healthy, for the sake of others (the team, the family, the church, or the cause, once they are committed). If you are friends with a Loyalist and happen to mention that you like chocolate ice cream, your Loyalist friend will run out as soon as possible to procure chocolate ice cream for your benefit. Unfortunately, he will also hope that you will be as loyal back and will find it confusing when you are not as loyal to him.

Over the years, I have noticed that Loyalists tend to relax in environments that are ordered and structured, and many Loyalists gravitate to bureaucratic environments. My best guess as to why this happens: high norepinephrine creates a hyperactive brain, experienced as chaotic, and law and order, rules and regulations may have a calming effect. All one has to do is make a decision as to which authority is the *right* authority to follow. This is why I think many low-functioning Loyalists are prone to becoming terrorists. All they have to do is choose a particular dogma they are willing to sacrifice their lives for and fight against anything that is "not us."

In addition to being faithful friends and loyal above and beyond most other types, another endearing trait of the Loyalist is his sense of humor. The fast-paced brain makes for quick wit, and the low serotonin often lends itself to sarcasm and/or self-deprecating humor, and that can be quite funny. Two classic Loyalist comedians are Ellen DeGeneres and Woody Allen. I thought it was priceless when Ellen described how she was so glad to finally come out of the closet and announce that she was gay. Seconds later, she started second-guessing herself, "Well, I *think* I'm glad I did that." And, what about Woody's famous line (borrowed from Groucho Marx)? "I don't want to belong to any club that will accept someone like me as a member." You have to admit that's funny, though at his expense.

Yes, the Loyalist is a true-blue friend, sitting on top of a tornado of norepinephrine, always on the alert for trouble and danger. Looking out for his people, his gang, his community, his country, or whatever other group he calls his family.

The Loyalist with an Investigator wing (6 with a 5 wing)
LOW dopamine — "The Defender"

The traits of the Loyalist and the Investigator are in conflict with each other, as the Loyalist's orientation is toward affiliation with others, whereas the orientation of the Investigator is toward detachment. Both types look for safety, but Loyalists look to alliances with others, and Investigators prefer to tinker with, or even dismantle, established systems of thought. Since both of these tendencies exist in the Defender, the resulting subtype often sees itself as fighting for the "little person" while at the same time being drawn to systems, alliances, and beliefs that often contain strong authoritarian elements. Defenders are generally attracted to professions such as medicine, law and engineering, since they desire to master system knowledge within a field where the rules and parameters are well defined. The Buddy is often seen helping with political causes and community service. Intense, highly committed and sometimes extremely partisan, they have great powers of concentration and loyal persistence to groups and causes.

Examples: George Bush, Bruce Springsteen and Billy Graham

The Loyalist with an Enthusiast wing (6 with a 7 wing)
HIGH dopamine — "The Buddy"

The Buddy subtype is more clearly extroverted, more interested in having good time, and (for better or worse) less intensely focused upon either the environment or themselves. There is a dynamic tension between the Loyalist personality and the Enthusiast wing. The Loyalist's focus is on commitment, responsibility and sacrifice of personal pursuits the sake of security, while Enthusiasts focus on experience, satisfaction, personal needs, and keeping options open. Despite (or pehaps because of the influence of this tension and the Enthusiast influence) The Buddy tends to be playful and sociable. They rely more on the opinions of others and struggle more with self-doubt and decision-making. They tend to be self-deprecating and often drawn to the expressive arts.

Examples: Tom Hanks, Princess Diana and the Cowardly Lion in the Wizard of Oz

---

NOT SURE IF I'M INDECISIVE OR NOT

My Loyalist friend named Becky is a marriage and family therapist, but she reports that she often feels "nuts" when she has to make a decision.

continued on next page...

...continued from previous page

The ricochet, "what ifs" kind of thinking typical of the Loyalist brain, makes decision making a challenge. In fact, we both agree that when we suspect someone as having the Loyalist personality, we often ask them, "Do you have a hard time making decisions?" When we see them struggling with the answer—"Well, I'm not sure; it depends; maybe, I don't know"—we are pretty certain that the answer is yes.

Oddly enough, Loyalists typically perform well in a crisis; it's the small decisions that are harder for them. One day over coffee, Becky and I discussed this phenomenon. She stated that in a family or professional crisis, she really shines. But according to her, "When I have to decide what to eat at a restaurant, I am just a wreck. My friends say they need to eat in advance of going out to dinner with me for fear of starving while they wait for me to decide what I want to eat!" We now believe the reason for that dilemma is because small decisions often don't yield significantly different outcomes. That leaves no *obvious* right or wrong choice, and a black-and-white thinker finds that tougher than a life-or-death decision. The trick is to recognize that inconsequential decisions are not worth brain space and energy, to learn to "flip a coin," and then override any second-guessing, knowing that the difference in outcomes is negligible, otherwise it would have been easy to make a choice.

That ricochet, multi-level thinking can be both useful and annoying. Becky was a hippie back in the sixties, and she did her share of mind-altering drugs (like all good card-carrying hippies). I had to chuckle when she said, "You want to know what it's like to have the Loyalist brain? Well, back in the day, when I did LSD, I looked around and everybody was tripping his or her fanny off, and I sat there and said, 'Nothing is different. *My* brain is tripping all the time!'"

Be good to Loyalists, and they will be good to you.

7. The ENTHUSIAST (a.k.a. the Generalist, Epicure)

HIGH Norepinephrine—HIGH Serotonin

The Busy, Fun-Loving Type: *"I'm seven, I'm in heaven!"*

Basic Fear: Being deprived or limited

Basic Desire: To be satisfied and content, to have their needs fulfilled

Key Motivation: To maintain their freedom and happiness and share their experiences with others

Favored Communication Style: Anecdotes

Enthusiasts are adventurous, with a contagious enthusiasm, and have a gourmet approach to life. They are typically accomplished in a wide range of fields. They seek novel experiences and sensations. Enthusiasts like to make others happy and to make the world a better place. Enthusiasts are future-oriented and enjoy making plans and willing to take risks because the assumption is that everything will work out well. Average level Enthusiasts can become scattered and avoid things that cause discomfort, either physically or psychologically. Unhealthy Enthusiasts may be compulsive, obnoxious, and offensive with little tolerance for anything serious or unpleasant. Integrated Enthusiasts are vivacious, accomplished people who can do many things well.

Examples: W.A. Mozart, Dolly Parton, Leonard Bernstein, Marianne Williamson, Timothy Leary, Jim Carey, Shania Twain, Howard Stern, and "Auntie Mame."

• • • • •

The Enthusiast is a seriously fun personality, highly adventurous—and rare. Probably less than 2.5 percent of the people in the world have the Enthusiast personality. (Dr. Eric Schulze has speculated, tongue-in-cheek, that there are even fewer Enthusiasts in the world than that, given that many Enthusiast children probably die jumping off rooftops while trying to be a real-life Mary Poppins or Spiderman.)

Enthusiasts are highly positive people. As an Enthusiast myself, I can vouch for that "high on life" attitude that comes with high serotonin. When I wake up in the morning (most mornings anyway), I truly wake up thinking, *Oh, yay! What else can go right today?* I have been told that I literally smile in my sleep. I love to dream big while asleep and awake, and I love to help make people's dreams come true.

And energy? One afternoon with that energizer bunny, and he'll be running back home crying to his mama, "I can't keep up! I can't keep up!"

Enthusiasts are future-oriented, but that can be a distraction. In my early twenties, I would often find myself working in a hospital while fantasizing about being on a Florida beach. When I finally made it to Florida, I would daydream about how everyone back at the hospital would be asking about my glorious tan when I returned. But where did the present moment go? I also remember eating a piece of chocolate and wondering which piece of chocolate in the box I would choose *next,* and what it might taste like—completely forgetting to enjoy the one that was in my mouth!

Why the positive outlook? Why the energy? Why the future orientation? Well, aside from the effects of high norepinephrine and serotonin, I believe the biological purpose of the Enthusiast might be like that of the scout ant. In an ant pile, the role of the scout ant is to go where no ant dares (or cares) to go and to find novel food or water. But get this: the scout ant does not eat the newly discovered food or water. No, it puts the food or water in its jaw and brings it back to the ant pile. It then gets very excited, shows the food and water to the other ants, and basically says, "Hey everybody, do you like this? Well, if you do, it's this way. Follow me to this new food and water!"

When I first read about the role of the scout ant, I nearly cried. It explained my life. No wonder I didn't follow the rules. No wonder I didn't go where everybody else always went. If I had, I wouldn't have been doing my biological "job." What a relief to realize that I wasn't trying to be different. I *was* different.

The Enthusiast loves novel experiences. It must be part of the scout ant wiring. A natural extension of that love of experiences extends into gift giving, including creating experiences for those we care about.

I now have quite a reputation in my family at Christmastime. One of the traditions in our family for Christmas is the Stealing Santa tradition of giving gifts, in which all the adults in our family each buy one present, which then goes into a pool of presents. On Christmas Day, everyone selects a number. Each adult in numerical order has a choice of selecting a present from the pool or "stealing" an already opened present from someone else. I have earned quite an infamous reputation based on the unusual, and some say would say freakish, presents I have purchased for my family members. My intention is always to come up with something that someone else might never imagine on his own. To give you an idea of my gift repertoire, my presents have ranged from a nose bowl for sinus irrigation to brainwave sessions for better brain control to a parachute jump to a high colonic. Needless to say, some years, my present is the last one to be chosen. Often, two relatives are left standing, clinging to each other like Miss America contestants—each consoling the other: "Well, if you get her present, I'll still support you."

Enthusiasts have the ability to transform even the most mundane of errands into an adventure. Another interesting feature of the Enthusiast personality is that we like to keep our options open. I think this is consistent with the scout ant theory. If a scout ant is limited or trapped, it cannot be of much benefit to the ant pile. So, limits and rules are something the Enthusiast, especially young Enthusiasts, tend to push against (stop signs, speed limits . . . puh-lease!).

Limits include when other people say they think I can't do something. When I was twenty-four years old, I parachuted for my first (and only) time. Midway between the plane and the ground, I thought to myself, *Now, exactly why am I doing this?* I was reminded that it was because a friend of mine didn't think I could. Note to self: it might not always be the best idea to do something just because someone thinks I can't or because someone says, "Don't!" Ah, lessons of a young Enthusiast.

But even as an aging Enthusiast, I have many lessons to learn. As a grandmother, one day, I found myself playing Go Fish with my then five-year-old grandson, Caleb. Somehow, I found myself about to lose the game. For a few moments, I thought about how I might steal a few cards and beat him; after all, he was so young, I could clearly sneak a few cards past him. First of all, I have to tell you that I was shocked at the thought. Enthusiasts are lovingly known as the "cheater babies" of this personality system because we do tend to push the envelope, and we don't like to lose. But still, as a positive grandparent, helping to build a child's healthy sense of self-esteem is critically important to me. So, why would I risk that by considering cheating at a silly card game? Interestingly, it is not that I want to win and beat other people; it is just that I don't like to lose. Losing feels like being trapped, and trapped, to an Enthusiast, feels like death. (After all, of what value is a scout ant if he can't scout?) "Give me liberty or give me death" is clearly a sentiment of an Enthusiast. Death is not a preferred choice, but lack of freedom is worse.

Of course, I let the little guy win. But I walked away with a much better understanding of why it is an Enthusiast needs to have options open. This awareness shed light on why my second marriage was my most favorite marriage structure of my three wonderful marriages. The second marriage was to Greg the Challenger. We created our marriage agreement to be renewed annually. In other words, June 26 every year was "easy out" day. We did not even have to have a good reason to terminate our marriage on that day. On any other day of the year, if either one of us was unhappy, we agreed to give a ninety-day notice and seek couple's counseling.

What I loved about that structure was that I never felt trapped. Every year was a choice, and every year was better than the next (except the last two, which, unbeknownst to us at the time, was suboptimal and related to perimenopausal symptoms—which would be a great subject for a whole other book).

The Enthusiast with the Loyalist wing (7 with a 6 wing)
LOW dopamine — "The Entertainer"

The Entertainer may be the most gregarious and high energy subtype of all.

Entertainers are playful and childlike and tend to be "uber" positive. Part of the challenge of having this personality is the tension between the Enthusiast's desire for adventure and the Loyalist's need for a sense of security. Since these two tendencies are diametrically opposed, the Entertainer is prone to a chronic undercurrent of anxiety. The Loyalist wing creates a little bit more of a people-oriented warmth, as compared with the Enthusiast with the Challenger wing; the latter is more focused on experiences and ideas. Entertainers tend to be "bouncy," some would say frenetic. (Think Tigger in Winnie the Pooh.)

Examples: Robin Williams and Bette Midler

The Enthusiast with the Challenger wing (7 with an 8 wing)
HIGH dopamine — "The Realist"
The high energy of the Enthusiast is often experienced as a high drive when combined with the focus and aggressiveness of the Challenger wing. This subtype has a large dose of confidence and willpower and at high levels of function is very capable of achieving goals and creating personal and material success. The Challenger wing adds elements of self-confidence, will power and assertiveness. Realists make very good leaders due to their quick minds and brilliant personal style. They present in a very adult-like manner and are perceived as earthy and persistent, some would say relentless, when in pursuit of something they want.

Examples: Joan Rivers, Larry King and Walt Disney

SPEED BUMPS, TIME WARPS, AND DOING MY JOB

One other interesting little feature about the Enthusiast is that we are described as disinhibited. (In psychology, disinhibition is a lack of restraint manifested in disregard for social conventions, impulsivity, and poor risk assessment.) We have an "open book" sort of personality, another one of those "what you see is what you get" types. If you were to look at the brain scan of an Enthusiast, we believe you would see a little less blood flow in the part of the brain that thinks through consequences (the prefrontal cortex, for you nerds out there). When Eric saw my brain SPECT scan (revealing blood circulation activity in the brain), he chuckled. "Aha! That explains it! You basically have a circulatory prefrontal lobotomy!"

In a layperson's terms, it means that my brain doesn't have a lot of "speed bumps"—another reason why Enthusiasts are also referred to as

continued on next page...

...continued from previous page

"bubblegum brains," meaning whatever is rolling around in our brains will just pop out of our mouths. (This is especially true for me if I've had a drink or if I am tired.) In my younger years people used to think I was trying to be outrageous. No, I was, according to my former daughter-in-law, "just saying what most people thought but didn't usually say." As a more mature Enthusiast, I have learned to pause (most of the time) and consider what I am about to say in delicate situations.

For the record, some experts in the field of the NPS system (including myself) do wonder if Enthusiasts *ever* present as totally "mature" adults. Many times, we seem like Labrador Retrievers, who appear like puppies even in our older years. In the movie *Harold and Maude*, the late Ruth Gordon was an Enthusiast in real life, and she portrayed an eighty-year-old Enthusiast character named Maude in the movie. When I saw that movie at age twenty-five, I was totally enthralled. It was not until almost a decade later that I realized it was because I had found a role model of the kind of woman I was going to be six decades later. As Maude was portrayed, even though Enthusiasts can become extremely wise and mature (because they amass so much experience due to their high energy and insatiable drive for collecting experiences), most paradoxically become more childlike and playful as they age.

And speaking of playful, if it isn't already apparent, while having the Enthusiast personality is a lot of fun, it can be exhausting for the people around me. My grandkids call time with me "Mia minutes," and my friends call it "Tina time." To them, a day or two with me feels like what they would typically experience in a few days.

In my younger years, my wanderlust used to be a source of concern, especially for my mother, who often asked me, "Why are you always on the move?" "What are you searching for?" "When are you going to get enough traveling?" It wasn't until I discovered this personality system and was able to explain my personality in terms of being a scout ant, that she

continued on next page...

...continued from previous page

and my family could understand that there was nothing "wrong" with me. I was just doing my "job."

Through the years, my understanding of this "job" has deepened. My quest for experiences is not only about traveling. I see it as a divine restlessness, a quest to learn. Over time, I have become more insatiable. How does one become the healthiest person possible? How does one become wealthy in the most elegant way? How does one create and maintain the most optimal relationships? It is clearly not enough for me to learn how to achieve these goals myself; it is extraordinarily important for me to come back to my human tribe and share that information. Otherwise, my circuit is not complete; my job is not done.

One of the best Christmas presents I have ever received was a gift from my son and his family, a beautiful piece of art by a famous local artist named Simon. It reads "Not All Who Wander Are Lost."

I think that sums it up.

And now, if you'll excuse me, it's time for another adventure . . .

Sevens . . . seriously fun, multitasking energizer bunnies on a mission from God to make the world a better place. Fasten your seatbelt!

How to Figure Out Your (and Others') Personality Type

Learning and remembering the NPS personality types can be overwhelming at first. The following chart is designed to help you remember the nine types by associating each type with at least one characteristic. It's designed to be a quick and fun tool; please don't take it too seriously!

An Easy-Peasy Cheat Sheet for Remembering the Nine Basic Types

1. The Reformer: "<u>One</u> way" (*the right way*)
2. The Helper: "Tea for <u>Two</u>" (*always serving others*)
3. The Achiever: "<u>Three</u>'s a crowd" (*-pleaser, wired to please and achieve*)
4. The Individualist: "<u>Four</u>-lorn and <u>four</u>-gotten" (*sigh, most prone to drama*)

5. The Investigator: "<u>Five</u> fingers—count 'em!)" (*counting, analyzing, the nerd*)

6. The Loyalist: "<u>Six</u> of one, half-dozen of the other" (*this or that, not sure, insecure*)

7. The Enthusiast: "<u>Seven</u>'s heaven" (*every day is a day in heaven if they can play*)

8. The Challenger: "I'm <u>Eight</u>, and I'm GREAT!" (*as a boss, it's my way or the highway*)

9. The Peacemaker: "Oh <u>Nine</u>; everything's fine." (*la, la-la, la, la*)

I wish I could tell you that it is always easy to figure out one's personality. It is not. Over the years, I have been surprised by how many people type themselves differently from how I or others perceive them. Many reasons underlie such differences in perception, including how different schools of thought describe the personality types and use different tests with varying ideas of this system. Sometimes, a person will misunderstand or focus on one aspect of a personality type and over- or under-identify with a single feature. For instance, someone might read that the Peacemaker personality tends to avoid confrontation. A person may think to herself, *Well, I don't like confrontation, so I must have a Peacemaker personality.* This particular quality is indeed one of the primary characteristics of the Peacemaker, but not the only one. Several personality types share this feature; in fact, most personalities do not like confrontation. What is important to understand here is that a cluster of traits appears in each specific personality that, when taken as a whole, creates the total makeup of that personality.

Part of the challenge in typing oneself or others relates to our own subjectivity and not being able to directly experience another person's thoughts or feelings. Recall, in Chapter 2, I described how people with a low pain threshold often describe themselves as having a high pain threshold, because it is impossible to objectively compare yourself with something outside your own experience, like someone else's pain threshold.

Aside from this challenge, terminology can also get tricky. Remember, also in Chapter 2, the story of the CEO who denied having a temper and stated that throwing a computer through the window was just "venting"? This is an example of how a person's judgment about another personality type will keep them from self-identifying with that type. For example, Individualists at low levels of functioning can be very dramatic and emotional—so much so that people often stereotype *all* Individualists as "drama queens." Sometimes, average and healthy Individualists do not identify with this personality because of negative associations with the low-functioning version of themselves.

Another personality typing challenge, at least until we can find reliable biomarkers, lies in the fact that the very nature of different personality types can cause confusion both within the person trying to type herself and also externally when she attempts to type others. For example, the Achiever personality can be very chameleon-like. I have seen many Achievers who, in written tests, score highest in the personality type of someone they admire.

For example, Frank (an average-functioning Achiever), was raised by an Investigator father who was a college professor. Frank spent his formative years in and around academic situations, during which time he learned to define success as being a thoughtful intellectual. As Frank developed into a young adult, he worked hard to develop his own intellectual persona. He even went through a period of wearing glasses (even though he didn't need them) because he thought it made him look smarter. It was no surprise, then, when Frank scored highest as an Investigator. Interestingly, a year later, after he began to function at a higher level of health (which involved a more authentic and introspective view of what he truly valued), he tested as an Achiever. Sometimes, because of their chameleon-like quality, Achievers can even be perceived to have the same personality as a person they are meeting for the first time.

But Achievers are not the only ones who can be confusing in this way. Peacemakers, who often "merge" with their partners, often test as the same personality types as their partners. I have also seen many occasions where a Peacemaker personality is typed as the same personality as the person doing the typing. Peacemakers, in the process of "merging" with another person, tend to reflect back, like a mirror, what another person expresses.

Sometimes, a person just likes the idea of being another type. I know a Reformer woman who has studied the personality system for over a decade and is adamant that she has the Challenger personality, but the only thing Challenger-like about her is her sense of fairness. She is soft-spoken and elegant, and although she experiences her own anger as Challenger-like, she never presents in an emotionally reactive way. Again, it is important not to focus on just one feature but rather on the cluster of traits.

Some other common challenges on mistyping include:

- Individualists (4) may identify with the "fun" aspects of the Enthusiast (7).
- Helpers (2) and Enthusiasts (7) are both energetic and often derive great satisfaction from helping others.
- Achievers (3) and Challengers (8) can both be very driven, Type A types.
- Individualists (4), Investigators (5), and Peacemakers (9) can often energetically be seen as somewhat withdrawn.
- Achievers (3) can present initially as the type of another personality that he or she most admires
- Loyalists (6) can sometimes be identified as Reformers (1) because they like to do things in a structured order (but for very different reasons).
- Depressed Individualists (4) can be experienced and test as Peacemakers (9) due to their lower energy level.
- Depressed Peacemakers (9) can also be experienced and test as Individualists (4).
- Individualists (4), Loyalists (6), and Challengers (8) can sometimes appear similar because of their shared tendency toward reactivity.
- Any type with a heavy wing can sometimes appear to be more like their wing than their core personality.

There are five basic ways of typing a person.

1. Pen and paper (or online) test. Numerous tests exist, but none of them to date, including our own, are as reliable as we would like for the very reasons listed above. It is my hope that, one day, we will have a way to test biomarkers (measuring brain scans, brainwaves, spoken words per minute, physiological reactivity, DNA testing,

neurotransmitters in blood or urine, and so on) as more accurate indicators. Until then, we will continue to look for and/or attempt to create the best test possible.

2. <u>Self-identification</u>. Self-identification involves reading about the different types and identifying with the primary cluster of one type. Some schools of thought studying the Enneagram believe that all typing should be self-identification, but as I mentioned earlier, I have seen people spend more than a decade thinking they have a specific personality type, only to learn they did not. Many have reported that their personal growth and relationship dynamics would have been easier had they had a more accurate understanding and acceptance of their true personality.

3. <u>Assessment by an expert in the Enneagram or NPS</u>. Again, this can be a tricky process. In my early years of typing others, I did not realize that many people were reflecting/mirroring my positive attitude in conversations with me. For years, whenever I liked someone, my first thought was that the person must have an Enthusiast or Peacemaker personality, the two personality types I identified with most easily in the beginning of my personality studies. Riso and Hudson and Dr. Schulze and I had several debates about well-known personality types as well. Even experts have their biases. It seems especially true the closer someone is to us. I was involved with an Achiever for six months and was convinced that he was a Helper because that's how he saw himself! Imagine that.

4. <u>Assessment by categorizing</u>. Categorizing involves learning the NPS types well enough to recognize the clusters and patterns of each type, then comparing the way a person presents himself with each of the nine types and selecting the one that seems to be the closest fit. Even experts get stumped and disagree about others' types, and given that personality begins on the inside, it is easy enough to be mistaken. The process resembles trying to guess someone's blood pressure.

One caveat, especially when learning, is to verify your guesses with the person you are attempting to type. Observe how the person resonates with your assessment and ask questions that the person will boldly say "no" to. For example, if you meet someone you think has a reactive personality (4, 6, or 8) you can verify by asking if she has a temper and/or anxiety; if the person calmly responds "no," it is unlikely that she has a reactive personality. If you meet someone you think might have the Enthusiast personality, ask if he has a problem following rules; if he replies, "No, not at all," you may want to revisit your assessment. If you think you have identified an Investigator, ask if she ever has a hard time turning her brain off at night; if she says, "No, I hit the pillow, and I'm out like a light," you may want to revisit your assessment again.

5. <u>Assessment by feelings.</u> Some people claim that this is the most accurate way to type someone; others say it is the worst way. (I bet it depends on personality. Imagine that!) The idea here is to pay attention to how you feel when you are with "certified" personality types that you know well. If, for instance, your Aunt Irma has the Helper personality, and every time she walks into the room, you feel somewhat uneasy—like a child being called into the principal's office—then, more likely than not, the next time you are in a room with someone who makes you feel somewhat uneasy (and specifically like a child being called into the principal's office), you may be in the presence of another person with the Helper personality.

Assessment by feelings can also be helpful as you review your own personal history. I know a very sweet Peacemaker who gets along well with all types. (What Peacemaker doesn't?) But internally, she has struggled with Challengers all her life. Whenever she had an "issue" with someone, I would question her about the characteristics of that person, and invariably, it would be a teacher, friend, or boss with a Challenger personality. What was particularly interesting about her situation was that she grew up with a rather *unhealthy* Challenger brother who bullied her and their siblings. Her Peacemaker attributes, coupled with a somewhat abusive relationship with her brother, caused her to have an extra sensitivity to any Challenger who happened to cross her path.

When she became aware of her sensitivity to this personality, she was reminded of an old uncle who had a *high-functioning* Challenger personality. Although he died when she was very young, she remembered feeling safe and protected when visiting his home and going on hunting trips with him. When she was able to see the high-functioning aspect of this personality and recognize the positive value and warm feelings associated with it, she started to value Challengers who appeared in her life.

THE THOMAS AND SCHULZE "METHOD" OF TYPING

Over the years, Dr. Schulze and I developed our own system for typing people. It usually begins with trying to figure out their basic norepinephrine level, so we ask, "Do you have a hard time turning your brain off at night, or do you generally fall asleep when your head hits the pillow? Or, is it somewhat unpredictable (that is, sometimes you have a hard time and sometimes you do not)?" If the person endorses the first option, we assume high norepinephrine set point; if he endorses the second option, we assume low norepinephrine set point; and if he endorses the third option, we assume moderate norepinephrine set point. We also pay attention to the speed of speech when listening to the person's response.

Next, we ask, "In your younger years, did you have a temper and/ or anxiety?" If the answer is a definitive yes, we conclude they most likely have a low serotonin set point; if the answer is a more thoughtful response, which reflects a moderate emotional state of being, we assess for a moderate serotonin set point; and if the answer falls into the range of a confident "Oh no, I rarely get upset about anything" type of response, it is fair to assume a high serotonin set point.

After combining the two set points, we use the chart below and match the responses to one of the nine basic types.

continued on next page...

...continued from previous page

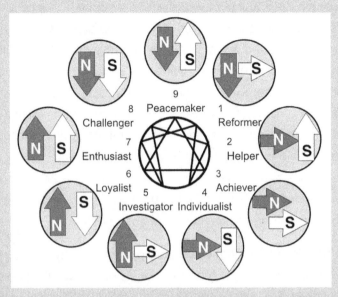

As noted earlier, all the possible combinations, starting at the top right, are:

1. Low Norepinephrine / Average Serotonin
2. Average Norepinephrine / High Serotonin
3. Average Norepinephrine / Average Serotonin
4. Average Norepinephrine / Low Serotonin
5. High Norepinephrine / Average Serotonin
6. High Norepinephrine / Low Serotonin
7. High Norepinephrine / High Serotonin
8. Low Norepinephrine / Low Serotonin
9. Low Norepinephrine / High Serotonin

Because of the subjective nature of human beings and the challenges involved in answering the above questions accurately, we would not make a definitive decision based on this input. It is essential, of course, to verify the assessment as often as possible. There comes a point, though, where,

continued on next page...

...continued from previous page

over time, we have found we reach an "aha" point. It happens when a person's actions and thoughts are totally consistent with the type we suspect they have, and at that point, we like to say they are "certifiable"!

If we don't reach the "aha" point in a reasonable amount of time, we might choose the top two or three personality types that are most likely and play around with them, comparing them to observations that Dr. Schulze and I have made over the years. Some of the observations below may seem a little quirky, but they have been surprisingly helpful, and at least they can get us somewhere in the ballpark of a person's specific type. The following is a condensed summary of key features we have used while attempting to ascertain someone's NPS type.

1. **The Reformer (One way).** The Reformer generally holds himself erect. Look for jaw tension. The Reformer usually presents as serious and steady; he tends to lecture and often employs a chopping motion with his hand when speaking. When asked if he is a perfectionist, he will often say, "No, I'm not perfect." He will resonate with having high standards and expectations, especially for himself.

2. **The Helper (Tea for Two).** She tends to be a "food pusher," often offering treats, foods, or comfort items, and often has a special drawer or place in her office or home that contains thoughtful gifts and cards. When asked if she has been told that she has more energy than almost anyone she knows, she is likely to say yes, and she has a difficult time asking for what she wants. When she gets what she asks for, it is often not appreciated because she had to ask for it.

3. **The Achiever (Three's a crowd [-pleaser]).** Good hair! He presents himself in a Hollywood style or GQ (Gentlemen's Quarterly) version of whatever he thinks is cool. Many Achievers

continued on next page...

...continued from previous page

have a "radio announcer" type speaking style, and almost all use trendy catchphrases such as "OMG" or "TMI." Look to their speech for newly trending catchphrases as well. This personality can be particularly charming—the more disarming, the more "dangerous." At average levels, he will be quick to name-drop and try to impress with accomplishments, experiences, and so forth.

4. **The Individualist (Four-lorn and four-gotten).** Often, she dresses in a way that is either beyond or outside of cultural standards (vintage clothing, a Bohemian style, designer fashions). She resonates with feeling "different" or misunderstood and is more sensitive than most people. She can relate to being sensitive to music, the environment, other people, and so on. Many Individualists are aware that they take things more personally than others. They tend to be very good wordsmiths, often journaling or engaging in creative writing. When speaking, they often touch themselves, including their chest and heart area.

5. **The Investigator (Five fingers; count 'em).** Usually, this personality type is easy to spot due to presenting as a typical nerd; that is, wearing clothing in a functional rather than stylish way. He may appear socially awkward and somewhat reticent when answering questions. He is not likely to volunteer much information, but he does resonate with having a dark sense of humor and being frustrated with others' stupidity and inefficiency. He also identifies with the idea of dropping "verbal hand grenades"—off-hand comments in a group—and he enjoys watching the reactions these create (often from a distance).

6. **The Loyalist (Six of one, half-dozen of the other).** This personality speaks very quickly and can get tangential in her speech. When asked if she has a hard time making decisions, she

continued on next page...

...continued from previous page

She will often initially disagree with this type identification (pointing out one or two small ways that she is *not* as described). She can display a rocking back-and-forth body motion or alternating hands and speech in a "on one hand this, but on the other hand that," type of pattern. Typically, the Loyalist has a hard time turning her brain off to go to sleep. Occasionally, after reporting that she sleeps well, upon further investigation, it is only after some type of bedtime ritual, such as watching TV or reading, or being physically exhausted.

7. **The Enthusiast (Seven's heaven).** This personality presents with high energy and sparkling eyes. When asked if he has been told he has more energy than almost anyone he knows, he says yes. He does not generally have a difficult time asking for what he wants. This type usually has a strong reaction to the question "What do you do if someone tells you that you can't do something or that something is impossible?" Most counter that question with a bold statement like, "Oh yeah, watch this!" He may also have a strong reaction to "How well do you deal with rules and structure?" And the answer is usually "Not well."

8. **The Challenger (I'm Eight, and I'm GREAT!).** This personality presents as solid and serious. Usually, she speaks in short sentences and does not over-think questions. Her voice seems to come from the gut. She's usually not interested in learning about the NPS when first discussing it with her.

9. **The Peacemaker (Oh, Nine; everything's fine).** This personality is soft-spoken, with a gentle smile. We often joke that he looks as though he has been smoking pot all his life. He may use the word "whatever" or some variation, and most answers to most questions have a "go with the flow" theme. Feeling peaceful, relaxed, or "at home" almost immediately is another feature we notice when in the presence of this type.

Once you have identified a specific personality type, you might ask questions to help confirm your best guess. We have what we call a list of "Rule/Out" observations—that is, certain traits that would absolutely rule out a type—to help determine if we have typed a person accurately. This is assuming, of course, that the person in question has not done an inordinate amount of personal "homework," such as introspection and/or therapy, to balance or counter his or her natural personality tendencies.

For example, if I believe someone has the Reformer personality, I will follow up by asking him if he has a hard time with mistakes (especially his own) and a difficult time relaxing. If he answers, "No, not really, I just take things as they come," then I go back to the drawing board and review my assessment. Perhaps he is a Peacemaker with a Reformer wing? Some other favorite Rule/Out observations follow:

- You are NOT a Challenger if you speak quickly or if you have trouble sleeping or problems with anxiety or second-guessing yourself.
- You are NOT a Peacemaker if you speak rapidly or if you have trouble sleeping or problems with anxiety or second-guessing yourself.
- You are NOT a Reformer if you speak rapidly or if you have trouble sleeping or problems with anxiety or second-guessing yourself.
- You are NOT a Helper if you feel comfortable asking for what you want or if, when you ask for something and get it, the value of it is not diminished *because* you had to ask for it.
- You are NOT an Achiever if you are quick to share your vulnerabilities or less-than-perfect attributes, or if you are not good at setting and achieving goals.
- You are NOT an Individualist if you don't identify with being more sensitive than most people and can't remember the last time you cried or if you have never had issues with depression and/or anxiety. You also don't "qualify" as an Individualist if you do not have some type of artistic ability.
- You are NOT an Investigator if you speak slowly, or if you have no trouble sleeping or crying easily, no problems with anxiety, or no problems sharing information about yourself quite freely.

- You are NOT a Loyalist if you speak slowly or if you have absolutely no trouble sleeping, or problems with anxiety, or issues with second-guessing yourself (especially with small, unimportant choices).

You are NOT an Enthusiast if you speak slowly or don't have any issues with structure and rules.

DOES YOUR PUPPY HAVE A PERSONALITY?

If you have ever wondered if animals have a personality, you could visit the website of Dr. Sam Gosling, founder of the Animal Personality Institute. Dr. Gosling holds the position of research professor in the Department of Psychology at the University of Texas in Austin.[13] Dr. Gosling is convinced that animals do in fact have personalities, and so am I.

The Puppy Personality Test
Following is a test I learned from training dogs. It is designed so that a person might choose a dog with the right traits for its owner. The similarity between this test and the NPS factors of personality in human beings is striking.

- Pinch the inside pad of the puppy's paw to see how the puppy reacts to pain. The more emotional response, the more emotionally reactive your puppy will be in life. (Sounds like a puppy test for serotonin.)
- Hold the puppy upside down and see how long it takes the puppy to calm down. The longer it takes to calm itself, the more mentally reactive your puppy will be in life. (This seems like a puppy test for norepinephrine.)
- Throw a ball or stick to the puppy and observe how energetic of a response this elicits and for how long the puppy plays with the)

continued on next page...

---

13   http://animalpersonalityinstitute.net

...*continued from previous page*

item. The more energetic and longer time spent in this activity, the more physically active your puppy will be in life. (And here we have an excellent puppy test for dopamine.

- When you walk into the room, crouch down close to the floor and call the puppy to you. The degree to which a puppy responds to you is an indication of its sociability and ability to relate to humans. (Voila, a puppy test for social orientation.)

Chapter 5

But Wait, There's More!

F or as long as human beings have been studying personality, there has been an ongoing debate about which factors and the actual number of factors required to capture the essence of personality. The most commonly accepted personality approaches range from two to sixteen factors.[14] Using the NPS, with its three-neurotransmitter pathways, creates a three-factor system (one factor per pathway related to thinking, feeling, and behavior).[15] But we believe a fourth dimension needs to be recognized for an optimally complete and accurate understanding of personality.[16] The fourth factor is known as social orientation.

Social orientation is the relational style a person uses to deal with the world and the people in it. The Social Orientation System is another set of variations outside of the nine basic types that can stand alone or be superimposed over the NPS types. Just as levels of health can be depicted using a photographer's gray

14 Eysenck proposed a two-factor model; Costa and McCrea have the NEO with five factors; Cattell's system has sixteen factors.
15 In Thomas and Shulze, NPS terminology for the factors are specifically called: mental activity—related to norepinephrine, outlook—related to serotonin, and assertiveness—related to dopamine.
16 Having done my post-doc studies at Duke University, I like to think of the four factors of personality as the "Final Four Factors."

scale analogy, the Social Orientation System can be depicted as modifying the hue of each type. The social orientation style can amplify or attenuate the basic personality types and also explain the sometimes subtle but significant differences within the same personality types. There are three social orientation styles in this system. We refer to them as Self-Preservation, Social, and Intimate.[17]

People with the Self-Preservation orientation are primarily concerned with issues related to self-preservation and meeting life's most basic survival needs. People with the Social orientation are primarily interested in getting along with others and forming secure social bonds. People with the Intimate orientation focus on making intimate connections with others.

As with other elements of personality structure, all people possess elements of all social orientation styles, although one social orientation style is usually more dominant than the other two. In addition, one or more of these social orientation styles can become imbalanced in some way and, to some degree, in childhood, thus becoming a significant arena for various related "issues" to arise.

Dr. Eric Schulze developed and refined our theory related to the origin of social orientation. It began when he attended undergraduate school at Berkeley and developed friendships with several people of diverse cultural backgrounds. During gatherings of his eastern Indian friends, he noticed that most of them were extremely social and group oriented, regardless of their specific personality types. As Dr. Schulze reported:

My Indian friends would often congregate for group lunches, dinners, and parties. The music there was rather loud, and there were multiple conversations (cross-talk within a cluster of people in conversation)

---

17 In several Enneagram circles the three social orientations are commonly called "subtypes" or "variants," and in the Riso and Hudson school the variants were referred to as: Self-Preservation, Social, and Sexual. (The label "Sexual" seemed confusing, so we chose the title "Intimate," which we find more conceptually descriptive of the relationship features.)

happening simultaneously. Having an Intimate Investigator personality, I personally found these gatherings somewhat taxing, if not completely exhausting. Sometimes, I would slip away for a while to remove myself from the sensory and social overload. It was during my times of "retreat" that I began to notice two other Indian friends who also slipped away and stayed on the periphery of those social gatherings. Being Intimate (and an Investigator), I eventually questioned them about their early upbringing. Unlike most of the Indians at the party, these two individuals were not raised in multigenerational families, which I had begun to suspect created a more Social orientation style. Instead, both of the two "Intimate" natives of India had parents who moved to the United States but did not relocate into an area where there was a strong Indian community. Therefore, both were raised in a standard Western-style "nuclear family," with the mother being the primary caregiver and the young men having only one or two other siblings.

I began to wonder if this kind of environment, being raised by a small number of caregivers in early life, might result in an Intimate orientation. If so, then what would lead a person to a Self-Preservation orientation?

It so happened that one other Indian friend of ours was typically less socially engaged as well. But unlike my Intimate friends, he almost always seemed more interested in having adequate food and comfortable sofa spots than the other people at the party. Upon further investigation, I learned that he had lost his mother to illness in his sixth month of infancy and was raised by an aunt and uncle who were very poor. He clearly had a Self-Preservation orientation, and I remember wondering at the time if it had to do with the disruption in his bond with a primary caregiver at an early age. After that time, I began to observe and question hundreds of people, and eventually, I was able to predict quite accurately a person's Social orientation based on their specific relationship with their primary caregiver(s) during the first three years of their life.

According to Dr. Schulze, it appears that while nature determines type, and nurture determines the level of functioning within the type, nurture also seems to determine social orientation. Dr. Schulze's theory is that the predominant social orientation style is shaped in the first three years and relates to the organization of the family unit and its overall health. Specifically, it appears that people with the Social orientation style of relating are raised in households with multiple caregivers, as is seen in multigenerational families living in close proximity and in split care (blended) families common these days where a child may be raised in multiple homes with many "moms and dads" due to divorce and economic influences.

On the other hand, people with an Intimate orientation may be products of either "traditional" (nuclear) families with two parents, and two to three children, or in single-parent households with strong ties with the primary caregiver. Moreover, people with the Self-Preservation orientation appear to reflect a disruption in the caretaking relationship due to separation, death, poverty, mental or physical illness, or sibling displacement during those critical first three years.

This theory would explain why there is a preponderance of certain social orientation styles in different cultures around the world, depending on the dominant family organization within that culture. It would also help to explain exceptions to the cultural norm related to exceptions among individual family circumstances.

THE CASE OF MAMIE

After years of observing and predicting the circumstances of social orientation styles, Dr. Schulze was stumped. He met Mamie, Dr. Thomas's mother, who was then a sixty-three-year-old gentlewoman living in southern Louisiana. According to him, Mamie clearly had the Self-Preservation orientation, but upon extensive questioning, there appeared to be no disruption of the caretaking bond. Her parents were relatively wealthy, and no major illness or catastrophe had occurred in her first

continued on next page...

...continued from previous page

three years, but Mamie, as an adult, had all the telltale features of Self-Preservation. She was frugal, always knew how much gas was in her car, lived a debt-free life, avoided most social opportunities whenever possible, and did not seem motivated to engage in intimate conversations.

For months, Dr. Thomas chided him, telling him he might need to go back to the drawing board of his theory since it was not holding up in Mamie's case. Dr. Schulze was perplexed but convinced he just did not have enough data. A year later, in a conversation with Mamie, Dr. Schulze inquired about her nickname "Mamie," the name her grandchildren used when they referred to her. At first, she said, "I don't know why I am called Mamie; I just always wanted to be somebody's Mamie, I guess." And then, almost as an afterthought, she said, "You know, when I was a little girl, I had a Mamie."

When he encouraged her to elaborate, she went on to describe how her parents hired a nanny to care for her and her brother from the time they were babies until she was about two years old. Around the time of her second birthday, her parents needed to relocate, and their nanny, whom they called Mamie, was unable to follow them to their new home. This gracious and emotionally reserved woman became slightly tearful and went on to say, "You know, I haven't thought of this in years, but I was told that, after we moved, I cried for months, especially at nighttime. Apparently, I was inconsolable because I missed my Mamie so much. I don't consciously remember her—I was too young then to even remember what she looked like—but just telling this story makes me feel so sad."

That afternoon, after describing the details of his conversation with Mamie, Dr. Schulze smugly proclaimed, "The case of Mamie is solved, and as far as my theory on social orientation goes—I rest my case."

How to Identify Your Social Orientation Style
INTIMATE ORIENTATION

The easiest way to determine if you have an Intimate orientation style is if you identify yourself as someone who feels shy on the inside. Even though you may appear gregarious and do quite well in social circumstances, the internal experience of shyness is a predominant indicator of Intimate orientation.

Intimate-oriented people can also be identified by the following characteristics:

- *Intimates tend to have only a handful of close friends.* Even though other people may consider an Intimate person a friend, an Intimate usually identifies her friends as those she would call to discuss a personal issue.
- *Intimates prefer to have meaningful conversations* with other people and find it tiring and tedious to have discussions about superficial subjects (such as the weather, television programs and characters, etc.).
- *Intimates commonly have nicknames for other people that are very specific in nature.* In other words, if an Intimate person nicknames a friend, that nickname will generally have a special, endearing meaning and typically will be used only for that friend.
- *Intimates often delay contact with others.* For example, most Intimates screen their phone calls. Intimates can become drained when overloaded by numerous conversations over the course of a day. Therefore, screening calls is an important way for them to manage feeling emotionally and socially overwhelmed.
- *Intimates feel stressed and dread initial contact when meeting new people.* This sense of dread can be elicited in social and business settings. The faster an Intimate can find common ground with a new

person, the more quickly he will feel relaxed, and that initial dread will quickly dissipate.

- **Intimates tend to avoid group gatherings.** Intimates generally feel stressed at the thought of a group vacation with many unknown people or going to a party. However, once an Intimate attends a group gathering and finds at least one other person with whom she feels a connection, and can have a meaningful conversation, the Intimate will feel comfortable and satisfied regardless of the group situation.

- **Intimates prefer to have partners who are also Intimate and thrive on intense connection.** Intimate people thrive on intensity (not to be confused with drama). Intensity in this context is defined as a deep, meaningful, multilevel, and usually complex connection. Many Intimate couples either work together or communicate with each other often throughout the day. It is not uncommon for Social or Self-Preservation ("Self-Pres") people to be somewhat surprised at the number of phone calls or texts that transpire between a couple who are both Intimates. Given a choice, an Intimate will usually prefer to do an activity with her Intimate partner rather than with another person or group. Sometimes Intimate couples will connect with another Intimate couple, and that will suffice for a "group" experience.

If an Intimate is aware of her social orientation style and shares that information with another Intimate, immediate recognition and connection is often the result. However, when an Intimate shares her sense of shyness with a Social or Self-Preservation person, she will usually be received with a look of confusion. The common response is, "But you don't seem shy at all." Some celebrity Intimates who have struggled with their discomfort in social settings include Johnny Carson, Barbara Walters, Barbra Streisand, Abraham Lincoln, and Albert Einstein. In fact, on the Internet, you can find websites dedicated to shyness and listing self-identified shy celebrities.

SOCIAL ORIENTATION

The easiest way to determine if you have a Social orientation style is if you identify yourself as a "people person"—the kind of person who feels comfortable with strangers and groups.

Social-oriented people can also be identified by the following characteristics:

- *Socials have many people they consider friends.* One Social person I know gave a birthday party for herself and told me that she invited "five hundred of my dearest, closest friends." To an Intimate, it would be impossible to have that many dear and close friends!
- *Socials are comfortable discussing almost any subject with almost anyone.* They are typically the masters of "small talk."
- *Socials commonly have generic nicknames for other people.* A Social person will often use a generic greeting, such as "How you doing, buddy?" or "Hey there, my friend." They also appear to be more comfortable calling someone by his name if it appears on a nametag. (An Intimate person often reports that it feels somewhat intrusive to do this and generally waits for someone to tell him his name before using it.)
- *Social people generally do not avoid or delay contact with others.* Therefore, they do not screen phone calls or put off returning phone calls.

- ***Socials look forward to meeting new people***. Most Social people describe feeling energized when they meet new people. A person with a Social orientation is the kind of person who sees strangers as "friends I just have not met yet."

- ***Socials initiate gatherings with other people***. By their social nature, it is common for Socials to initiate and attend social gatherings.

- ***Socials do not seem to prefer partners with a Social orientation***. While Social people often meet each other in social gatherings (not surprisingly), they do not have a strong preference for a Social versus an Intimate or Self-Preservation partner. Indeed, it seems easier for a Social to be involved with an Intimate than for an Intimate to be involved with a Social. This may be because most Socials are comfortable in all sorts of relationships, whereas the Intimate generally prefers to be with his significant other. Additional people require time and attention and can be perceived as stressors.

SELF-PRESERVATION ORIENTATION

The easiest way to determine if you have a Self-Preservation orientation style is if you identify yourself as someone who does not see relationships as central to your survival. You might perceive yourself as a simple and pragmatic person who is just as happy alone as when you are with others, so long as your basic survival needs are secure.

Self-Preservation-oriented people can also be identified by the following characteristics:

- ***Self-Preservers, like Intimates, tend to have only a handful of close friends.*** In a self-preservation world, however, friends are chosen more for their usefulness rather than the quality of intimacy. In fact, Self-Preservation people do not require much intimacy at all. They tend to be self-sufficient financially, mentally, and emotionally.
- ***Self-Preservers prefer to have conversations related to ideas that help them survive in the world.*** So, this person might be more interested in conversations related to gas mileage, how to save money on clothes, and the healthiest ways of eating as opposed to talking about another person's feelings. By the way, speaking of survival, we have noticed over the years that Self-Preservation personalities almost always know how much gas is in their car and are extremely uncomfortable with debt. Most will reduce their lifestyle to bare-bones living rather than take the financial risk of changing jobs or borrowing money and living in debt.
- ***Self-Preservers may or may not have nicknames for other people.*** This is a less predictable trait, although we have noticed that when nicknames are used they tend to be more descriptive of a person rather than sentimental. For example, I have a Self-Preservation friend who calls me "Nine Lives" to describe my multiple educational degrees and various life experiences. My Intimate friends are more likely to call me "T" or "Sweetness" or other such names that engender tenderness.

- ***Self-Preservers, like Socials, will not usually avoid or delay contact with others.*** This is especially true if contact with others means business opportunities. However, living in a self-sufficient world, contact with friends or family members is not as high a priority as it is for Socials or Intimates.

- ***Self-Preservers generally feel moderate stress when meeting new people.*** The stress of meeting new people may be related to undeveloped skill sets in making emotional contact with others. If there was a disruption in the caretaking bond in the early developmental stages, it is likely there was also a disruption in learning social skills needed for developing human connection, but there is also likely an underlying mistrust of others.

- ***Self-Preservers are willing to attend group gatherings when necessary.*** If a group gathering contributes to one's survival needs (e.g., a business party), a Self-Preservation personality will usually be willing to attend, at least for a reasonable period of time. You can be fairly certain, though, that when attending a group gathering, this person knows where the exits are and where the food table is, and he is generally looking for a "safe" place to land at the gathering.

- ***Self-Preservers prefer to have partners who are also valuable to them.*** Emotional connection is not as important as having a partner they can count on "through good times and bad." Self-Preservation personalities are "low maintenance" when it comes to their emotional needs since their highest priorities are related to physical and financial survival. Therefore, they may find it a bit of a struggle to fulfill their partner's emotional needs. For that reason, most find it easier to be with other Self-Preservation or Social personalities and have a more challenging time with the "higher maintenance" Intimate, who desires and thrives on intense emotional connection.

THREE SIBLINGS AND THREE DIFFERENT
WAYS OF RELATING TO THE WORLD

Even though I am socially quite capable and even appear gregarious to others, on the inside I feel extraordinarily shy. I dread meeting new people, whether they are potential friends or clients. And, the idea of attending a party or, worse yet, going on a group vacation makes me feel like throwing up. I screen all my phone calls, and when overwhelmed, I find it challenging to even return calls to friends and family. I am one of the most extreme examples of Intimate orientation that I know. Despite the fact that I have repeatedly shared my inner angst with several friends and family members, to this day many still do not believe that I feel shy on the inside. However, my first few years and identification with being an Intimate personality are extremely consistent with Dr. Schulze's theory.

I was the firstborn child, and I spent my first two years of life in a small trailer with my parents at a Marine barracks in North Carolina while my father served his country (both of my parents are from Louisiana). So for the first two years of my life, I had the undivided mother and father. When I was about two years old, we returned to Louisiana, and my brother, Michael, was born into a very social network. My uncle and cousins lived next door, my grandparents lived very close by, and my mother's twin siblings moved in with us when their parents (my grandparents) passed away. So, again, based on Dr. Schulze's theory, it was no surprise that Michael turned out to be a very Social person. It took Michael most of his adult life to accept that I did not like to have people (even family members) drop by unannounced at my home. It was also hard for him to understand that my lack of visits to his home had nothing to do with my lack of feelings for him. In fact, it was just my way of showing respect for his privacy (that he did not require!).

continued on next page...

...continued from previous page

My sister, Ann, was born five years after my brother, and my mother nearly died from complications of childbirth. Ann lived with our aunt and uncle for an extended period of time during those first few months after her birth, and we believe that this disruption of her caretaking bond accounts for her high Self-Preservation orientation. Same parents, three siblings, three different social orientations. Fascinating, eh?

In communicating with others, it is helpful to know both their personality and social orientation style. For example, an Intimate Individualist (introverted and emotionally aware) might feel honored to have someone ask him to share intimate details about his personal life. But if that same Individualist were to ask a Self-Preservation Investigator (somewhat reclusive and private) similar questions, the Investigator might find such questioning intrusive and uncomfortable. Knowing another person's personality and preferred social orientation style makes it much more likely that we can apply the Platinum Rule, which is "Do unto others as *they* would like us to do unto them." [18]

The social orientation style can amplify or attenuate your basic personality. For example, the basic nature of the Investigator is to be somewhat shy and withdrawn. So, an Investigator with the Self-Preservation orientation style is going to be less interested in people and more interested in things, and that will amplify his predisposition to be detached from his emotions and connecting with other people. Therefore, an Investigator with Self-Preservation style is going to present as an *extreme* version of an Investigator and might be quite fine living in a cardboard box under a bridge. On the other hand, an Investigator with a Social orientation will appear a little more approachable and comfortable around others, and an Investigator with an Intimate orientation tends to find sharing one's inner feelings and thoughts a little easier than his other two counterparts.

---

18 This is as opposed to the Golden Rule: "Do unto others as you would have them do unto you."

Another example is the Helper tendency to be "other oriented" and self-sacrificing; this is amplified with the Social orientation style. Social Helpers are sometimes referred to as Caretakers on steroids!

If social orientation is not taken into account, certain traits of a person's personality will seem contradictory. For example, take the Enthusiast—a normally disinhibited and open personality who will talk about almost anything.[19] If this particular type has an Intimate orientation, she will be much less of a "party girl" and sometimes may even appear aloof due to her shyness. If you ever "capture" an Intimate Enthusiast, watch her in moments of silence, and you may catch a glimpse of shyness. Pay attention—it is usually fleeting!

As you become more familiar with the system, eventually you may notice that there are stereotypes of the basic types, and when people conjure up the "average" function of any given personality type, they often unknowingly attach a social orientation to it. Below are what I think are the most common stereotypical pairings of personality type with social orientation. When these pairings of personality type and social orientation occur (whether it is in our minds or the actual real-life pairings) the personality type becomes amplified.

The most common stereotypes of social orientations with the basic personality:

- The Reformer—self-preservation
- The Helper—social
- The Achiever—social
- The Individualist—intimate
- The Investigator—self-preservation
- The Loyalist—self-preservation
- The Enthusiast—social
- The Challenger—self-preservation
- The Peacemaker—intimate

---

19 Believe me on this one. As an Enthusiast I have often received feedback, especially in my early years, about "trying to be outrageous." I think a better explanation is that a disinhibited person could be described as someone who doesn't have many speed bumps between their brain and mouth! In other words, whatever is rolling around in the brain often comes out uncensored in young, tired, or inebriated Enthusiasts. Hint: don't take a young, tired, drunk Enthusiast out to dinner if you want to impress others around you!

If we agree that social orientation results from the first three years of one's environment and creates an imprint and preference for one of the social styles, then we can assume there is an opportunity for growth here as well. Just like personality, where we have the capacity to experience all personality types within ourselves, we have the capacity to experience all three social orientation styles as well.

Most people have a clearly predominant social orientation style, but the percentages can vary greatly. For instance, one person whose predominant style is Intimate might be extremely Intimate, with perhaps 80% of interactions experienced as an Intimate and 15% as Social and only 5% as Self-Preservation; whereas another person whose predominant style is Intimate might experience 50% of her interactions as Intimate, 30% Social, and 20% as Self-Preservation. Unlike personality, in which the set point itself does not change (that is, we believe if you were born with a Loyalist personality type, you *always* have the Loyalist personality—short of brain injury, of course), we believe that, in certain situations, the predominant social orientation style *can* change.

Since the origin of social orientation style seems to be created by the past environment, a change in the social orientation style may also be created by a notable change in the later environment. For instance, I have a friend named Dorothy who, for most of her life, considered herself to be a very strong Social Helper. At the age of sixty, she was severely injured in a car accident and developed chronic, intense back pain. From then on, she became much less Social and much more aware of Self-Preservation issues. In her case, before attending a social event, she needed to know how much standing would be involved, if there were comfortable chairs, if there would be a lot of stairs to climb, etc. So, understandably, self-preservation issues became the focus of her life, and Social orientation became her second favored style of relating.

Although I am an extreme Intimate, recently I have come to terms with the realization that getting my message[20] out to you and the world is more

---

20   My "message" is how to train your brain for a change and how to understand your
      personality to become the ultimate you.

important than my personal comfort level. In the last year or two, I have done more public speaking than usual, and I have noticed that I am at least more willing to be social than I have been in the past. I am consciously spending more time with other people and now feel more comfortable doing so. I have actually created a "family of choice" (as opposed to a family of creation) who are friends of mine that I interact with as a group. Unlike many social groups that meet to party, my "family" goes on trips together. These trips are often related to personal growth. Or, we might work on personally meaningful and significant projects to help each other. We usually end up in deeply intimate and often philosophical discussions as we "play" together. And even though it might not be a Social style's idea of a group vacation, it is a stretch for me to travel and wake up with several people as opposed to one Intimate partner.

When it comes to mate selection, Riso and Hudson believe that matching social orientation styles was the single most necessary element for relationship success. I disagree with that, however, and believe that while matching the social orientations might create easier and less stressful connections, if a couple were to have mismatched social orientations, then understanding and accepting those differences can still allow for a rich relationship. In fact, unmatched styles might allow for opportunities of greater personal growth for both parties, in very much the same way that understanding and accepting differences in personality can lead to personal growth.

Although I do not believe that social orientation is as important a factor in mate selection as level of functioning (more on this in the next chapter), I do believe it is still a factor that impacts relationships and needs to be taken into consideration.

Roger, a strong Intimate, complained constantly because his partner, Helen, a strong Self-Preservation personality, seemed more interested in taking care of the house and creating her teaching plans for the next day than she cared for him. Helen felt burdened by Roger's insistence that they have more of what she described as "24/7, in-your-face couple time." Once they discovered what their social orientation styles were and how they were developed (Helen lost her mother at the age of eighteen months, and Roger was raised as an only child by two doting parents), they were able to have compassion for each other and began to respect that neither one was purposely being "difficult." They merely had different social orientation styles that shaped their ideas of how a relationship should be. They sought counseling, and during their first session, both agreed that Roger was more negatively impacted by Helen's lack of sharing than Helen would be by sharing her inner emotions. They started a process of couple journaling in the morning, and not only did they grow as individuals, but they became a much stronger couple and much happier and well-developed people.

Another example is the relationship of Harry and Paula. Harry is an Intimate, and Paula is a Social. When Harry met Paula, it was love at first sight for both of them. But within a couple of months, they were both frustrated with their relationship, particularly as it related to how to spent their free time together. Harry, an "off the chart" Intimate, hated the Sunday parties that Paula enjoyed. He felt slighted whenever Paula suggested they attend the Sunday events. He interpreted her requests as an indication that she did not think he was enough for her. (Specifically, he worried that she might think he was not smart enough or interesting enough and that she needed the Sunday gatherings to "complete her.") Paula was oblivious to how uncomfortable gearing up for Sunday was for Harry. Instead of looking forward to the weekend, Harry had begun to dread Fridays because it reminded him that Saturday was close at hand and that Sunday would follow immediately behind it!

In much the same way that Roger and Helen worked out their differences, Harry and Paula determined that Harry was much more negatively impacted by going to the Sunday parties than Paula was by not going. They decided that because Harry was most negatively impacted, he could choose not to go to the parties. As it is with most couples, with greater understanding and less pressure, Harry became more comfortable choosing to attend the parties with Paula, and Paula became more sensitive to Harry's discomfort. In the end, they probably attended more parties than Harry would have cared for and fewer than Paula would generally have attended, but they were happy with their compromise. They also worked out a signal so that when Harry felt overwhelmed and had reached his tolerance for hanging out in the Social world, they would excuse themselves and return to their cozy couple Intimate world.

Once you identify your social orientation style (see below for the TASSO test—the Thomas and Schulze Social Orientation test) and would like to experience a more complete version of yourself, you can "visit" the other styles by spending time with someone who has a style that does not match your own. Then, simply experiment with those same types of behaviors and notice how you become more aware of a different way of relating to yourself and others.

The TASSO Test
(Thomas and Schulze Social Orientation Test)

Circle the letter (A, B, or C) for the sentence that most closely describes you for the majority of your adult life.

1.

A _____ I tend to avoid parties and groups whenever possible, but once I go I usually do fine, especially if I connect with someone and have a meaningful exchange.

B _____ I often initiate group activities.

C _____ I go to great lengths to avoid social situations that I don't care for. I avoid group activities unless they are important to my work or social relationships.

2.

In a group situation:

B _____ I try to "touch base" with as many people as possible.

A _____ I prefer to have one or two intimate conversations.

C _____ I feel more comfortable if food and drinks are available, and I have a good excuse to leave early or when I have fulfilled my obligation.

3.

B _____ I often have nicknames for people.

A _____ tend to find out what a person likes to be called and then call them by that name.

C _____ I am very conscious of respecting people's privacy.

4.

A _____ I wait until someone tells me their name, even if they are wearing a nametag.

B _____ I use people's names often, even if I have just met them.

C _____ I usually don't volunteer my name unless asked.

5.

C _____ I spend a fair amount of time in search of sales and good deals.

B _____ I like to shop with friends.

A _____ I don't care for the experience of shopping and use catalogs or the Internet whenever possible. If I have to shop myself, I do it as efficiently as possible.

6.

C _____ I have a tendency to stockpile food in my refrigerator (my pantry could easily sustain me for two weeks if necessary).

B _____ I enjoy eating out with people, even if I don't know them well.

A _____ I'd rather eat alone than with someone I don't know that well. I enjoy eating alone or with a good book if the ambience is nice.

7.

C _____ My friends consider me a packrat. It's hard for me to let go of things for fear that I may need them or want them in the future.

A _____ I tend to hold on to a few meaningful mementos. Almost all of my decorations have some symbolic meaning.

B _____ I enjoy decorating with lots of photographs of my friends and family.

8.

B _____ I enjoy the idea of hanging out at coffeehouses.

A _____ I prefer having coffee with a friend or two rather than with a group of people.

C _____ Coffee at coffeehouses is not a good value; I'd just as soon have coffee at home.

9.

B _____ I generally enjoy group vacations.

A _____ I prefer vacations to be "getaways" with one or two intimate friends.

C _____ I think of vacations as a luxury and can even feel a little guilty when taking them.

10.

C _____ I feel very uncomfortable when my gas tank is below a quarter full, and I can tell you how much gas I have in the tank almost any time.

B _____ I enjoy long rides alone regardless of my gas tank status. In general, I don't know how much gas is in my car, even at the start of a long trip.

A _____ I much prefer to have at least one person in the car wherever I go to keep me company.

11.

C _____ I almost always answer the phone if it is work related.

A _____ I screen my calls habitually; I'm often afraid I'll get roped into lengthy conversations.

B _____ I almost always answer the phone; you never know who might be calling.

12.

B _____ I often initiate "cross talk" in restaurants (talking to people at other tables).

A _____ I prefer quiet cozy places to eat.

C _____ I prefer to eat at familiar places that offer a good value.

13.

B _____ I like to have music or TV on most of the day to keep me company.

A _____ I like music at medium to low volume levels so that I can converse easily with another.

C _____ I am careful to keep my music at medium to low levels in order not to hurt my hearing.

14.

C _____ When I am involved in an intimate relationship, if I have my way, I prefer to be at home or with my significant other.

B _____ When involved in an intimate relationship, if I have my way, my significant other and I often go out together with others.

A _____ When I am involved in an intimate relationship, if I have my way, it doesn't really matter what we do; I just prefer to be with my significant other.

15.

A _____ Even though I feel very "shy" internally, people are often surprised when I tell them this.

C _____ Almost everyone I know perceives me as shy.

B _____ I do not consider myself shy and feel comfortable in the presence of people I do not know well.

16.

B _____ All of my friends know at least at little bit about all of my other friends.

A _____ I tend to compartmentalize my friends; many have nothing in common with the others.

C _____ I tend to be very private even with my friends—a lot of my friends are not aware of at least a few significant aspects of my life.

17.

B _____ I have more than a dozen people that I consider current friends.

A _____ I have a handful of people that I consider to be intimate friends.

C _____ I can go for months, maybe even years, without contacting friends.

18.

B _____ My significant other and I develop "couple" and group friends together.

C _____ It takes a long time for me to feel safe when starting new relationships.

A _____ My significant other and I develop our friends separately, although there is a lot of overlap.

19.

B _____ Spontaneous vacation sounds like fun, especially if I'll be meeting lots of new people.

C _____ Spontaneous vacation sounds like potential danger; I prefer planned vacations.

A _____ Spontaneous vacation sounds like fun, especially if I'll be learning something new about myself.

20.

A _____ I was raised primarily by one or two significant caretakers and have fewer than three siblings.

B _____ I was raised in a multigenerational family or had more than two significant caretakers.

C I experienced what most people would consider unusual threats to my caretakers or self in the first five years of my life (serious illness or death of a caretaker, hospitalization, loss of income, etc.).

21.

A ____ I fall in love deeply and easily and intensely.

C ____ I am cautious about who I become involved with romantically and who I choose to invest in romantically.

B ____ I have had many romantic relationships, including ones that I know from the start may not be long term.

A majority of A's indicates you most likely have an Intimate orientation.

A majority of B's indicates you most likely have a Social orientation.

A majority of C's indicates you most likely have a Self-Preservation orientation.

Intimate, Social, or Self-Preservation?

If you spend time with an Intimate, you will notice that he puts his focus on you and shares his feelings more freely and deeply than your Social and Self-Preservation friends. So if intimacy is something you want to develop, pay attention to the types of questions that person asks and the situations he creates. Most likely, an Intimate will suggest a quiet place to meet for coffee or lunch and will ask what most people consider "personal questions"—like "How do you feel about losing your job?" as opposed to "What are you going to do to find another job?"

If you spend time with a Social, you will notice that her attitude seems to be one of "every stranger is a friend I just haven't met yet." She may take you to her favorite spot to eat, where she knows many people who have a tendency to stop by to say "hi."

If you spend time with a Self-Preservation person, you may notice that the conversation focuses on "survival-type" (matter-of-fact, non-abstract) topics such as the weather, the price of real estate, her bad back or dental exam results, what places to eat are good deals, the cost of living, etc. You may also notice that if your Self-Preservation friend chooses a restaurant as a place to meet, it will most likely be one that is perceived to be of good value (large portions and reasonably priced!).

Now that you have a better understanding of the "Final Four Factors" of human personality, let's put it all together in the next chapter to explore how you might take this information and apply it to your life to become the Ultimate You.

Chapter 6

How to Utilize the NPS
to Create an Awesome Life

N
ow that you understand the theory of the biological basis of NPS, the next question becomes: how can you take this information and create the Ultimate You and the most awesome life possible?

How can you create a better life? Better relationships? How can you use this information to attract and create the healthiest relationships possible? How can you become a better contributor to the world? How can you use this information to improve your parenting, grandparenting, teaching, or leadership skills in a way that will leave a rich legacy for future generations?

On the other hand, if you feel like you are already your most Ultimate You and living an awesome life, or if you just want to have a more peaceful life, it may be enough for you to accept the theory of the biological basis of personality. There is no need to memorize the types and learn the biological set points beneath them; you can simply know that based on that theory, there is a biological purpose for each personality and a need to respect biodiversity. From that premise, you can also make the assumption that every single person on the planet is "doing the best they can with what they've got to work with," and you will experience the true meaning of compassion summed up in the sentence, "There, but for the grace of God, go I."

A Better Life

If you were not fortunate enough to be born into a high-functioning, healthy family or you want to go to the next level of functioning (or become the Ultimate You, using this system), there are two ways to experience that kind of integration. The first way is by practicing modes of thinking and behaving that create opportunities to experience or "visit" a more integrated personality, which then temporarily affects your brain chemistry. The second is to directly manipulate your brain chemistry (through medications, supplements, food, specific exercises, music, etc.). This also temporarily allows you to "visit" your integration point.

Let's look at the first way. Prescriptive exercises that help you develop the lesser-developed aspects of your personality will create balance and higher functioning. To accomplish this, you need to look at where your personality currently "lives" and then compare this to the aspects of where your personality temporarily "visits" under optimal conditions (your integration point).

Then the challenge is to create opportunities for yourself, to "stretch into" experiencing more of your integration qualities. For example, Investigators visit Challengers under optimal conditions, so if you have the Investigator personality, it would be growth-producing to put yourself in situations that involve power-promoting traits, such as wilderness adventures, to get in touch with taking action and feeling your strength and using physical resources rather than sitting at home or in the office experiencing life mentally. If you have trouble thinking of what kinds of opportunities you can create, Riso and Hudson give more detailed prescriptions for integration in their book *The Wisdom of the Enneagram*.[21]

---

21 Sometimes you may find that even though you want to experience other aspects of yourself, there seems to be an unconscious block to your ability to immerse yourself in another way of being. If you feel stuck and unable to embrace other aspects of yourself, it may be because you have unconscious imprints that are self-sabotaging and telling you that you can't be whatever it is you hope to be. Or, if you find you are still unable to forgive someone (including yourself), or that you do not feel like you are otherwise able to accomplish your goals, then I suggest you read my first book, *The Ultimate Edge: How to Be, Do and Have Anything You Want*. Combining the strategies of *The Ultimate Edge* with the NPS is the über elegant way to the Ultimate You!

Below are a few ideas for starters. I encourage you to be creative and enjoy the process as much as you can.

Adapted from *Wisdom of the Enneagram*, Riso and Hudson

Type	The Direction of Integration
1	For Reformers to become more spontaneous and joyful, like healthy Enthusiasts (7): Consider taking up a hobby you don't need to be accomplished in, something that is fun and relaxing to do that has no apparent goal. Once a month, consider doing something silly just for the silliness of it—wear a clown nose to work.
2	For Helpers to become more self-nurturing and emotionally aware, like healthy Individualists (4): Schedule a couple of hours a week for "just you" time which might include activities such as getting a massage or going to a therapist for personal exploration just for the health of it.
3	For Achievers to become more cooperative and committed to others, like healthy Loyalists (6): Practice daily random acts of kindness, making sure that you are invisible. Have a conversation with someone at least once a week in which you do not try to one-up the other person to impress them but actually make them feel like they have something special that you might not have in a genuine and authentic way; find their gift.
4	For Individualists to become more objective and principled, like healthy Reformers (1): Practice showing up at whatever craft you enjoy, whether it is music or art or journaling, and rather than waiting to feel inspired, just begin despite how you feel. Just show up. Make an agreement to do your craft for a given period of time regardless of your results.
5	For Investigators to become more self-confident and decisive, like healthy Challengers (8): Try being bold. Take up martial arts, or go to a dance class or Toastmasters; push against your tendency to be private and notice what happens when you are seen. Hint: you are still breathing.

6	For Loyalists to become more relaxed and optimistic, like healthy Peacemakers (9): Get involved in a sport or activity that involves vigorous exercise and then follow it with yoga or meditation. Keep a journal of self-talk and imagine how you would speak to a child that you care about. How closely does your self-talk match that conversation? Track your progress.
7	For Enthusiasts to become more focused and profound, like healthy Investigators (5): Practice mindfulness—do one thing at one time once or twice a day. For example, when drinking your morning beverage, pay attention to the flavor, aroma, and temperature rather than multitasking or paying attention to your multitude of thoughts.
8	For Challengers to become more openhearted and caring, like healthy Helpers (2): Spend time with a child or children or pets. Allow yourself to be vulnerable with a trusted friend or mentor— share your vulnerable feelings rather than talk about your ideas. Encourage other cars to go ahead of you in traffic.
9	For Peacemakers to become more self-developing and energetic, like healthy Achievers (3): Write down some goals every month and take action steps to accomplish them. Declare your goals to a trusted friend or buddy, and be accountable for those goals.

An important note here is that ultimately you can work on "visiting" *all* personality types within yourself to develop "neuronal plasticity"; a.k.a. "flexible brain." When you can consciously visit each personality within yourself, you can consciously choose to visit a specific personality that works best in a specific environment or situation. For instance, if you are working on a project that requires intense focus, consciously creating the Investigator mindset will help you to function more optimally in that setting. Remember, unless you have the Investigator personality, you do not "become" an Investigator. You are whatever your personality set point is; you are simply a temporary visitor to the Investigator mindset.

Since you have three main neurotransmitter pathways in the brain that affect you and can be affected by your choices, I don't think it too farfetched that you might have access to multiple personality styles and that you can and do "visit" more than just your integration and disintegration personality points.

PERSONALITY FLOOD

Simply spending time with someone who has a different personality can cause your chemistry to temporarily reflect the other person's chemistry — and you temporarily "visit" that personality within yourself. For example, people often report that they feel more peaceful and happy after spending an extended period of time with a Peacemaker; or that they feel thoughtful, philosophical, and sensitive after being in the presence of an Individualist; or more bold when spending time with an Achiever; and more cheerful and warm after being nourished by a Helper and so forth.

One day, we may be able to demonstrate what we call a "personality flood" — that is, if you were to take your brain scan at rest and then spend two to three hours with someone who has a different personality from yours, on taking a second brain scan, we would anticipate that your brain would temporarily light up in places of activity that reflect the personality of the person with whom you just interacted. Perhaps this would be a demonstration of mirror neurons at work.

But you don't have to take my word for it. Just think about the last time you spent a significant amount of time with someone who had a very different personality from you and how you became, at least temporarily, a little bit more like them. I first got this insight after a visit of a few hours with a highly stressed Loyalist friend of mine. He second-guessed every answer I gave him during what felt like an "interrogation" about a relationship choice I had made. That evening, even though I was no longer with him, I found myself obsessing about different aspects of our conversation and second-guessing some of the comments I had made during our earlier discussion. By the end of the night, I had a stomachache, could not get to sleep, and had a general feeling of dread and anxiety.

I called a friend of mine to talk with her about my situation. Toward the end of the conversation, she became frustrated because I kept taking counterpoints to whatever suggestion she made to help me relax. She finally became quite flustered and asked, "What's happened to you?" I

continued on next page...

...continued from previous page

shook my head and realized that I had been "sixed." It took me a little while after that to settle my brain down. If I had known about GABA at the time, I probably would have taken one or two of those to get to sleep. But since I didn't, I asked myself a series of questions until I was able to calm myself.

The next morning, my Loyalist friend called to report that he felt much better having shared his concerns with me. I responded, "I guess you did—now that you dropped off some of your excess norepinephrine with me and took a little of my serotonin!" We had a good laugh about it, but I learned an important lesson about the dynamics of personality floods that day and also the importance of surrounding myself with healthy, functioning people regardless of their personality type.

When we surround ourselves with different personality types, we may notice that some are more challenging to be around. For many years I had issues with average Reformers. There's a big difference between not liking someone versus not liking what they do and having an emotionally charged reaction to that person. And when it came to the Reformer, I noticed that I often felt edgy and annoyed when I had interactions with someone at an average to low level of functioning. I was particularly annoyed with their sense of righteousness and superiority. In fact, I felt indignant and secretly superior to them in their righteousness. How embarrassed I was when I realized that I was feeling more righteous than they were!

This experience reminded me of the day I realized how prejudiced I was about prejudiced people. On that day, I became aware that I felt superior to people who were prejudiced, but when I saw the irony and hypocrisy in that attitude, I was humbled. In a moment of clarity, I realized that people who are prejudiced just don't have enough information, and I am no exception to that rule. As soon as I was able to understand and have compassion for my own lack of information, I felt connected to rather than better than others who lacked information. I then began to pay attention to what aspects of other people irritated or annoyed me, and I came to better understand the term "projection." Basically, if there is some unknown aspect of myself that I don't like but have not fully recognized, I will project it onto others who seem to be mirroring that aspect of myself. As soon as I "own it," that is, accept that the very reason it is bothering me is because it is a reflection of some aspect of myself I don't acknowledge, I am amazed at how quickly my upset dissipates and I feel compassion for that other person and myself.

The same process happens with personality. The day I "owned" my self-righteousness about self-righteousness happened at Jazz Fest in New Orleans—the story I told in the narrative of the Reformer in Chapter 4 (where I was judging a Reformer for judging me only to discover she was frowning at the mud and grass on my white dress). Before that day, I used to say, "I *love* Investigators, Enthusiasts, Challengers, and Peacemakers. I'm not wild about Helpers and Loyalists. And, I struggle with Reformers, Achievers, and Individualists." My goal after that was to be able to genuinely say about *every* personality type, "I *love* that type," because then I would know I had embraced, honored, and celebrated *all* aspects of myself! Today, by the way, I can truly say I *adore* each type at its highest level of functioning, am amused at each type at its average level of functioning, and have compassion for all at their lowest levels of functioning. It's a very sweet place to be indeed.

While you are paying attention to the people you associate with, keep in mind a quote from the late Jim Rohn, an American entrepreneur, author, and motivational speaker who influenced others in the personal development industry. Jim was probably most well known for saying, "You are the average of the five people you spend the most time with." When I heard those words, my first reaction was one of concern. Because I have the Intimate Social orientation, I don't really spend that much time with five people intimately in any given week! I later learned that spending time with people can also include being influenced by the media, as in which books we read, which movies we watch, which television shows we watch, and so forth, so make sure that you are surrounding yourself with high-functioning people, regardless of their personality type, and high-functioning programming, such as high-quality books, YouTube video clips, talk show radio, and even music. As sophisticated as our brains are, they can be unconsciously influenced by the average of the "people/media/programs" we expose ourselves to on a regular basis.

So now that we have covered ways of thinking, feeling, and behaving that can help you to become your Ultimate You, as I mentioned before, there is a second pathway to experiencing your ultimate self. You can use this pathway separately or in conjunction with the first. (Combining them is the most elegant and dynamic way!) The second pathway involves spending a little more time understanding the chemical configurations of your personality. Once you have an understanding of how these neurotransmitters affect you, you can manipulate your own brain chemistry and thereby alter your emotional, mental, spiritual, and physical states toward optimal functioning. The key idea here is balance and common sense.[22]

The following is an example of how a client of mine named Sarah used this information to optimize her personality potential. Sarah described herself as a "Super Social Six" (Loyalist). When we first met, she was plagued with anxiety, and her family was concerned about her alcohol consumption, which seemed to be steadily increasing. She also had occasional angry outbursts with her husband, Ned (a Peacemaker), when he offered suggestions for how she might better manage her life and emotions. He complained that she was being overly sensitive, and he felt discouraged about their relationship. In addition to that, she was upset because she was overweight and gaining a few pounds steadily every few months.

I explained to Sarah that her biological set point was most likely high norepinephrine and low serotonin. I then discussed how stress increases norepinephrine levels and decreases serotonin levels. In fact, as norepinephrine increases, it creates its own sensory overload, which in turn decreases serotonin even more; then, as serotonin decreases, it makes people with this chemical makeup more vulnerable to pain, stress, and fatigue, which causes them to lose even more serotonin. Eventually, this becomes a vicious cycle, with norepinephrine skyrocketing and serotonin plunging. The gap between them is what we call "reactive land"—the bigger the gap, the greater the reactivity

---

22 NOTE: I do not prescribe medications or supplements. But, under the care of your physician or mental health provider, I am sure you can create a personalized plan of care to optimize your specific personality chemistry for supporting the Ultimate You.

that shows up, either as a temper or anxiety. I then showed Sarah the periodic table of personality and pointed out that her integration point is precisely where her husband Ned "lives." The nine's chemical configuration is exactly opposite of the six's chemical configuration, being characterized by low norepinephrine and high serotonin set points. So, Sarah created the following plan for herself based on the above information and her knowledge about the neurotransmitters:

- To reduce norepinephrine:
  - Take GABA supplements twice a day
  - Go to the gym three times a week with friends to do kickboxing and salsa class, to relieve frustrations of the day, and also to spend some girl time together to debrief about stressors of life in general
  - Turn the TV off at 7 p.m. (to decrease sensory input at night) and spend more time with her husband—she was pretty confident that this ritual would ensure that they would be able to make love more often. (And, you know what that does to norepinephrine—wink!)
  - Limit coffee to one cup in the morning and a diet soda to once in the afternoon
  - Listen to happy jazz station while driving into work rather than talk radio
- To increase serotonin:
  - Take SAMe supplements twice a day.
  - Limit phone conversations with her energy-draining mother (a low-functioning Reformer who had a bad habit of lecturing Sarah on all the things she should and should not be doing with her family)
  - Spend more time with her best friend, Megan, a quirky Investigator who was not interested in gossip or negativity and often helped Sarah figure out elegant solutions to life challenges
  - Follow the Burn Fat Forever program[23] to reduce or eliminate carbohydrate and alcohol craving

---

23   BurnFatForever.org is a program co-designed by a colleague and friend of mine that promotes a high-fat, moderate protein, low-carb eating program. Following this program not only promotes weight loss, but it also reduces cravings for carbohydrates and alcohol,

Within one week, Sarah was noticeably calmer and happier, sleeping better, and having a better relationship with her husband (in every way!). By six weeks, she was taking extra walks to reduce stress rather than eating carbohydrates; losing weight steadily; feeling much more in control of her life; enjoying her time with her family; and looking and feeling much healthier, happier, and younger!

Personality and Nutrition

You can run, but you cannot hide from the fact that your body and brain are inextricably connected. How you exercise and feed yourself can contribute to becoming your healthiest emotional self on your way to becoming the Ultimate You. Therefore, I think it is extremely important to educate yourself in the basics of nutrition and brain/body health.

Unfortunately, almost everyone *thinks* they know what healthy eating is, but research is starting to reveal some surprising findings that are turning the world of "healthy nutrition" upside down—and just in time, too. Many of the commonly accepted "truths" and "nutrition facts" are not only inaccurate but actually dangerous and leading us to all sorts of ills, including diabetes, obesity, heart disease, certain types of cancer, Alzheimer's, mood swings, and depression.

I have learned from Nora Gedgaudas, author of *Primal Body, Primal Mind*, that there's no such thing as an *essential* carb; not only are carbohydrates not necessary, they can actually be very harmful. According to Gedgaudas, "Telling someone that they need to eat a balanced amount of carbohydrates is like telling someone that they need to have a balanced amount of cigarettes." I strongly encourage you to consider that carbohydrates, especially refined carbohydrates, are not good for your body or your personality.

Not only do refined sugars and processed foods stimulate release of insulin, which has an inflammatory effect on your body and brain, but ingesting such foods increases the odds of experiencing the detrimental effects of hypoglycemia.

---

and research is indicating that it decreases the risk of diabetes, heart disease, stroke, obesity, Alzheimer's, and certain cancers.

Hypoglycemia is low blood sugar and can happen in response to not eating enough food or to an overactive response of the pancreas, which secretes insulin to prepare the body for incoming carbohydrates.

Hypoglycemia seems to exaggerate or exacerbate the low-functioning traits of all personality types, but I believe that people who are already low in serotonin set point activity are more prone to experience the downside of hypoglycemia side effects than the medium and high set point types. Regardless, it is very helpful for *all* personality types to recognize the signs and symptoms of hypoglycemia, which can include weakness, shakiness, edginess, confusion, lightheadedness, blurry vision, rapid heartbeat, unexplained fatigue, headache, and hunger. These symptoms can creep up insidiously or catch you off guard by happening very suddenly.

One of the tricky things about hypoglycemia is that when you're in the middle of it, you may not recognize the symptoms. And because of this, if you are experiencing a hypoglycemic-induced edginess, you may actually believe that a situation you are in is causing you to be upset when it's actually that you are in an upset state, and some poor person just happens to cross your path at the wrong time! Think about fussiness that comes upon young children; a vigilant mother will know to feed the child a nutritious snack to get the child back on track, but if that doesn't happen, the child is likely to blame the bad mood on a sibling. Like an accident looking for a place to happen, hypoglycemic edginess is an upset looking for a person, place, or situation to blame the upset on.

When a person is in the middle of a hypoglycemic state, it is generally *not* the time to encourage them to eat since they will probably find your suggestion annoying or insulting. "What? I'm not the one with a problem. *You* are!" It is better to have a procedure set up in advance. I suggest the following policy: make an agreement in *advance* of a hypoglycemic event that if you seem to be crankier than the situation warrants, and the person suspects hypoglycemic-induced edginess, then even if you don't particularly feel like it, you will trust that person's judgment and have at least a few morsels of protein and/or fat.

CODE ORANGE

Years ago, when my son, Matthew, and I were on a weeklong road trip in California, we discovered the powerful impact of hypoglycemia and its effect on our personalities and our relationship. On the first three days of our trip, we noticed that we were getting annoyed with each other, which was not typical for us. We found ourselves making statements like, "Hey, whatever you're saying right now is really bothering me" or "You are really starting to get on my nerves right now." Because it wasn't common for us to have this kind of tension between us, we started to pay attention to see if we could figure out what this edginess was about.

On the fourth day, we realized that our feelings of aggravation with each other seemed to occur about an hour before lunchtime or dinner each day. So, we created a couple of new policies. First, we modified our language. Instead of saying "You are bothering me right now," we agreed to say something like, "I'm feeling edgy, so this may not be the best time to have this discussion."

Then, we came up with a code word for hypoglycemia. We chose the word "orange" and used it in the following manner:

"I'm feeling a little yellow" means "I'm getting hungry."

"I am getting orange" means "I am feeling hypoglycemic [weak, edgy, etc.]."

And, God help us all if either one of us says, "I'm red!" which translates to "Get me to some food *now,* or else!"

Once we had smoothed out the wrinkles to our little system, we cleverly would ask, when observing that the other was a little grumpy, "I notice you seem a little tired or grouchy. *Orange* you getting a little hungry?"

While the low serotonin types may respond to the decrease in carbohydrates and an increase in protein and fat more dramatically than the other types, all personality types—I repeat *all*—will benefit from this regime.

continued on next page...

...continued from previous page

Since that infamous road trip, both Matthew and I have helped many parents, children, and couples have a less stressful relationship by teaching the cause, effect, and prevention of hypoglycemia.

My second research interest after personality addresses how to help females over forty fight fat. I can't tell you how many postmenopausal women (including myself) lament over how our male partners lose weight easily, but we struggle with losing the same five pounds again and again. In my quest to crack the code of that fat puzzle, I learned that our brain is the fattest organ in our body and consists of at least 60 percent fat. It makes sense that feeding it will help our brain to function more effectively.

I also think that, as a fat-phobic society, we are not only afraid of becoming obese but also afraid of ingesting the "wrong" kind of fat, assuming that fat will make us fat and hurt our health. The most current research is now indicating that eating fat will actually help you to lose weight (more on that in my e-book *Burn Fat Forever and Grow Young*) and has a healthy anti-inflammatory effect on the body, in addition to helping your organs perform more efficiently. As my clients add more fat to their diets, not only do they lose weight, but they also experience decreased emotional reactivity, fewer mood swings, and a greater sense of well-being.

Mate Selection

In addition to being able to "speak" another person's language more easily, the process of choosing a mate can be much more elegant with this information.

In choosing a partner, the level of functioning is probably the most important aspect that will affect the future of the relationship. Relationships always operate at the level of the lesser of the two people's level of functioning. Just as a college professor has to use a simple and less complicated vocabulary when speaking to a kindergartner, a higher functioning partner is forced to relate to his partner at a lower level of functioning—simply because higher functioning health and relationships require greater degrees of maturity and more sophisticated communication.

It is also extraordinarily helpful to know which types of personalities we resonate with and what the challenges might be for us with the same and different types. Some people spend their entire lives being attracted to and getting involved with one type of personality. When that is the case, the storyline and issues tend to follow similar patterns. The themes stay the same; only the names change.

An example of this is Michael, an Achiever who was always attracted to petite, seductive, and low-functioning Individualist women. Wired to be a hero, he attracted low-functioning Individualist women who were looking for a hero to rescue them from their miserable lives. So, the pattern was love at first sight, a passionate whirlwind romance, a quick engagement or marriage, and then a rapid cool-off period, with the woman bashing him because he wasn't what she thought he was going to be (her savior), and him feeling disgusted because she was "just like all women"—moody, temperamental, and hard to please. Unfortunately, because that was the only kind of woman he found himself attracted to, he believed that all women were this way, and he eventually concluded that "all relationships are doomed" from the very beginning.

Some of us may find that we desire different personality types at different stages in our lives. For instance, Mary, an Achiever, ended a relationship with a low-functioning Loyalist. Her initial attraction to him was his extreme loyalty, but over time, she became disillusioned with his negative, critical comments that she interpreted as "lack of trust in and support for" her. She then became involved with an easygoing Peacemaker. When she met him, she was attracted to his mellow "go with the flow" attitude, which was quite a pleasant contrast to her former partner's hyper-vigilance. During the honeymoon phase of that relationship, she was thrilled, but as the newness of the relationship wore off, she became discouraged and disillusioned because her easygoing partner was not motivated to join forces with her in accomplishing many of her high-energy goals and tasks. She hopped right out of that relationship and into one with a high-powered "make it happen" Challenger man. As you might guess by now, she was quite smitten with someone who seemed to be as driven as she was, but over time—sigh—she felt embarrassed and uncomfortable in social situations with him, as he would react angrily when he felt threatened. She also began to feel like she was missing a partner sensitive to her emotional needs (especially because she herself was not), and the last I heard, she had gotten involved with an emotionally sensitive Individualist—but was starting to get annoyed because he was "always processing" their relationship!

The take-home message here is this: it is extremely useful to know the "price of admission" for each personality. In other words, whatever "blessing" we are attracted to will also have its corresponding "curse" or challenge, depending on that specific personality type. Not only is it unfair, but it is also quite damaging to both parties if you enter into a relationship thinking or hoping your partner will be "perfect" in every way while, over time, expecting him or her to change that very personality to accommodate you.

In choosing a partner, the level of functioning is probably the most important aspect to look for. As I stated earlier, the relationship will always play out at the level of the lesser of the two's level of functioning.

FORMULA FOR FINDING THE PERFECT PARTNER FOR YOU[24]

Create a list of ten to thirty of the most important non-negotiable traits, values, circumstances, etc. that you desire in a partner. Make an agreement with yourself that your future partner needs to BE, DO, or HAVE those things on your non-negotiable list when you meet that person and not just have the *potential* to be, do, or have those non-negotiable items.

Here's a sample of *potential* non-negotiables (this is only an example; your list will likely be quite different):

1. Radically honest
2. Communicates well
3. Travels well and really enjoys it
4. Has good chemistry
5. Loves to dance
6. No history of addiction or ten years sober

continued on next page...

---

24 Taken for my e-book, *How to Find the Perfect Partner*

...continued from previous page

7. Romantic—treats me like a queen and is comfortable being adored
8. Good sense of humor; laughs freely
9. Open to new possibilities like costuming, spontaneous trips, personal growth workshops
10. Healthy body weight—eats well
11. Financially successful and responsible
12. Emotionally available

Then, review your list, and make sure that YOU are everything you are asking for in a partner. This can be tricky. Many times, when helping people to find a suitable partner, I have noticed that what a person wants and what a person actually *is* can be very different. For example, several of my male clients have listed that they want an extremely attractive, "hot" woman. That is all fine and good, except that most of these men have not looked at themselves in the mirror since high school. Some of them are grossly overweight, do not dress well, and do not appear confident or sexy. Perhaps the desire for an attractive woman is to validate that they are attractive or successful. In these instances, I suggest that they lower their attractiveness standard for their partner or go to the gym and wear clothes that belong in this decade! Likewise, some of my female clients insist on having partners who have a good sense of humor, but they wouldn't know a joke if it slapped them on the fanny! I remind these women that men with a good sense of humor are looking for the same in their mate.

Once you are clear about what you want, and certain that you personally are everything on your list, inform everyone you know that you are looking for a partner, and share your list with them (not necessarily in writing, but in conversation).

Once you begin dating, be sure to assess your potential mate's qualities (as per your checklist), *and*, most importantly, take into consideration this person's personality, level of functioning, and social orientation. I plan to create an app soon that will quickly give you the strengths and liabilities of each type.

Improved Relationships

Speaking of social orientation and intimacy, another powerful way to utilize this information is in your personal relationships. From working relationships to parenting relationships to romantic relationships, understanding how the different personality types interact with each other takes a lot of the unpleasant mystery out of the relationship. It also helps to predict the strengths and "issues" that different combinations of personalities create.

Without getting into too much detail, based on some preliminary research we did studying SPECT scan images of brains, Dr. Schulze and I found that different types of personalities activated different parts of their brains at periods of rest and concentration. The implications of this are profound. But when it comes to human relationships, the bottom line is this: different personality types *live* in different areas of the brain, meaning they utilize different areas of the brain, and therefore, different personality types see and experience the world very differently. That means the Golden Rule ("Do unto others as you would have them do unto you") is not necessarily the most helpful rule in dealing with others, as we have already noted. Knowing another person's personality and social orientation makes it much more likely that we can apply the Platinum Rule: "Do unto others as *they* would like us to do unto them."

It is my hope that with a better understanding of the biological basis of personality, we will be less inclined to take someone's reaction (or what might *appear* to be an under- or over-reaction, given the circumstances) personally if we know that the person has a different set point from our own personality. If you happen to be on the other side of a very upset reactive type, you might even have a sense of compassion for them in their moment of reactivity, thinking perhaps, *Yep, I can see you are a little serotonin depleted at this moment; it must be hard to be you at this time.*

Parenting

I have noticed that when people (especially from Westernized cultures) can understand a biological or scientific reason for something, they more easily embrace people and situations that seem different, "weird," or even threatening. For example, for nearly a decade, mothers who had schizophrenic children were thought to be mothers with a "schizophrenogenic" personality type. (Say that ten times fast.) A schizophrenogenic personality type was described as a mother who was cold, withdrawn, and did not nurture her child. Imagine the way she was treated by the medical and psychiatric community for "creating" a schizophrenic child. Imagine the guilt she might have experienced by being labeled (either openly or through others' attitudes) a poor mother.

Research now shows us that infants actually influence a parent's response. Babies born with early onset schizophrenia do not respond to social cues of the mother, meaning that when the mother smiles and coos to her infant, the infant does not maintain eye contact or smile and coo back. Eventually, without that feedback and communication, the mother loses a maternal sense of connection and may appear to be distant and not caring. With a scientific understanding of the process of parenting and delayed development, parents of schizophrenic children are now treated with the respect and compassion they deserve.

With a better understanding of their children's biologically based assets and liabilities, I believe that all parents and their offspring will benefit. I once counseled a young mother and father who were distressed by their seven-year-old child's poor school performance. By the time I saw the parents, they had grounded their son for his entire school year. He was not allowed to watch TV or spend time with his friends and was on the verge of losing desserts with dinner due to his "bad attitude and poor performance" in school.

Despite his consequences, Ronnie continued to get Ds and Cs in all his subjects, and according to his parents, he was becoming "more and more lazy and difficult." They were distraught and wondered if I could help them to "straighten him out."

I do not specialize in working with children, but because this couple came to me as a favor for one of my friends, I agreed to at least meet with Ronnie. During my first session with Ronnie, I noticed that as he described how he felt when taking a test, he became visibly shaken; he looked pale and sweated profusely. Just describing the testing process induced a panic attack. It was very clear to me that he was not "trying to be difficult." I suspected that he had a learning disorder and recommended to the parents that he be tested for that.

When the test results came in, the parents were shocked—their son Ronnie, whom they loved dearly but were so disappointed in, was three points above being labeled mentally retarded. Ultimately, the cause of his mental limitations was traced back to a time in his early infancy when he experienced a high fever; from then on, he began to show some indications of developmental delay. The parents misinterpreted his lack of development as being lazy and difficult, and they pressured him to achieve milestones that were too challenging for him.

Initially, when they learned that their child did not have an "attitude problem" but rather a genuinely challenged brain, they felt incredibly guilty for having pressured him beyond his capability. However, once they acknowledged and accepted that, they were loving and devoted parents. From then on, every time Ronnie took a test and came back with a C or D, he was praised—a hero in his family, rather than a failure.

Interestingly, Ronnie's grades improved slightly, and when he occasionally scored a B, it was quite a treat. But believe me, whether he brought home a B, C, or a D, you couldn't have met two prouder parents! Had I not had the opportunity to intervene, Ronnie would have become an adult who saw himself as a failure. This would have crushed his self-esteem and may have led him to develop into all sorts of undesired outcomes—from juvenile delinquency to poor relationships to depression and possibly even suicide.

How do I know that his poor self-esteem might have led to such outcomes? Well, you see, almost thirty years ago, I sat in a psychiatric hospital for a year (as a staff member, not a patient) and listened to one patient after another tell me how horrible they felt about themselves. There was the man whose mother wanted him to be a third-generation attorney, but he was more of a musician and, therefore, felt like a failure. There was the woman whose father wanted his firstborn to be a boy; she never recovered from feeling like she was a "mistake." Believe it or not, high self-esteem is a cornerstone to mental health. But I cannot tell you how many parents, in the name of good intentions and even love, have damaged their children by inadvertently trying to impose their own personalities' distinct values and perceptions on their children. Parents who unwittingly try to force their personality characteristics on their children can create devastating consequences.

In my book *The Ultimate Edge*, I mention a story about my pet pig, Peggy Suey, and how we were both crazy about each other but driving each other crazy because we didn't understand each other's language. The more I tried to show my affection toward her in a humane way, and the more she tried to be affectionate with me in her porcine way, the more we upset each other. Luckily, only one of us had to understand the other to make our relationship "work." The same is true in parenting.

Some parenting combinations might naturally be easier or more challenging, depending on the personalities themselves. For instance, because of the adult-to-child power imbalance, it might be more difficult for a Reformer child to have an overbearing Helper parent. Whereas, if the adult-to-child power roles were reversed, a Helper child might be softened by the influence of an Individualist parent, who could possibly coax her little Helper to be more in touch with her feelings. Another example could be an average Reformer parent who gets annoyed with an Achiever child who tries to do things for a certain effect, as opposed to doing it for the "right reason." Contrast this with a Peacemaker parent who encourages his little Reformer to lighten up a bit and to relax and not stress about having perfect grades in school or in extracurricular activities.

Regardless of the different personalities between parent and child, the most important aspect is to remember that there is no "right" or "wrong" way of perceiving the world. It's all about context. Some ways are more useful and beneficial in some contexts, and some are more useful and beneficial in other contexts. The most successful children, and adults, are those who are open to exploring all aspects of themselves and choosing the most appropriate traits for the specific situation.

THE TRIALS AND TRIBULATIONS OF BEING THE MOTHER OF TINA

Having the Enthusiast personality with the Leader wing is like having a tiny tornado for a personality. Now that I have a better understanding of *my* personality, when I reflect back on my life, I see what a challenge it

continued on next page…

...continued from previous page

must have been for my Peacemaker mom to have had me as a daughter. When I was a little girl, she would occasionally say to me, "You think too much." I remember thinking, *What does that mean? Doesn't everybody think all the time? How does she know that I'm thinking? Why does she think that I'm thinking too much?* And then, I would think about thinking. Imagine that! How could I know as a child that not everybody thought as much as I did? I started thinking from the moment I woke up until the time I went to sleep, and I just assumed everybody else did too.

Later, as adults, both my mother and I would come to appreciate that aspect of me. We would later learn that my mom had a low norepinephrine set point—which explained her ability to sit down in the middle of the day, close her eyes, and within seconds fall into a deep twenty-minute nap.

For as long as I could remember, she and I had been at odds because of our very different personalities. We both had positive outlook personalities, but unlike her, my personality has high physical and mental energy and an insatiable drive to go on adventures, explore, and experience change. When I say that we were at odds, it wasn't like we argued or fussed at each other a lot. We were both just befuddled as to what might be "wrong" with the other one. Each of us wondered how the other could see and experience the world so differently, and each of us would often try to "help" the other. I don't know about her, but I secretly thought I was "right" and that, one day, she would "come around" to seeing the world my way.

Well, I was certainly wrong about that! I recall the day we were working in my garden in Abita Springs. She was working at one end of the garden weeding, methodically moving from left to right one square foot at a time. I was working a bit more randomly. I would start in one area of the garden, weed a little bit, see something else that needed to be done in another area, attend to that, then move over to another spot and water a plant that looked a little thirsty, and then perhaps return to weeding. My mom

continued on next page...

...continued from previous page

thought my way seemed inefficient. I thought her way seemed boring. I suggested that I try her way and she try mine. We both tried the other one's way, and by the end of the afternoon we reached the same conclusion. We had each figured out the best way to weed the garden. It was obvious that *her* way was the better way for *her*. And, *my* way was the better way for *me*!

My mom also was troubled by my wanderlust. I was twenty-four years old when I took my first trip out of the country, to Mexico. When I returned, my mother was quite relieved that I was back safely and said, "Well, now that you have that [travel] out of your system, I suppose you're ready to settle down?" That question did not compute. I was dumbfounded. "Are you kidding? That trip just whet my appetite. I'm already trying to figure out how to save money to go to Canada now!" Then, I looked at my mother and felt horrible. She looked visibly distressed. I could not understand why she seemed so troubled by my statement. Later, I would learn that she associated my traveling with searching, and searching with unrest, and unrest with a lack of peacefulness or unhappiness. From time to time she would ask me, "What are you searching for?" or "When do you think you're going to settle down?" Not until she understood my personality— many years and discussions later—did she begin to consider that perhaps nothing was wrong with me.

Once, when I announced that I was going on a month-long trip to India, I could see that she was very concerned about my safety, but I also sensed there was something else disturbing her. Upon further investigation, I learned that she was wondering where *she* might have gone wrong as a parent to have a daughter who was always "doing crazy things" and "taking unnecessary risks" and "going to dangerous parts of the world for no good reason." I assured her that my trip was going to be a very safely planned and protected trip and that she had contributed to a "healthy little bird who felt confident enough to fly out of the nest and land safely on the ground."

continued on next page...

...continued from previous page

"Hmmm," she said as she smiled, "I never thought of it that way." Embracing the concept of my personality as a scout ant and seeing her role as a healthy mother bird who helped her little bird fly out of the nest seemed to comfort her as I continued with my never-ending adventures.

One of the keys of good parenting is the understanding that there is no one-size-fits-all way to raise a child. Granted, there are basic foundational principles that apply to all human children; however, those principles need to be tailored and delivered in a way that gives the child the best chance to flourish. In addition, if parents understand their children from the inside out—that is, if they know their child's neurotransmitter set points—they will be able to make more informed decisions about the care and nourishment of that child. It would be most helpful if certain annoying or confusing behaviors in children could be explained through the lens of their personality, so that those behaviors might actually be appreciated as part of the "price of admission" for having that particular personality.

Patricia, a twenty-eight-year-old Individualist mother, described her first child, Missy, as "perfect." According to her, Missy slept well from early infancy on, was rarely fussy, and had grown into a child who, at five years old, was easygoing and could entertain herself for hours on end. Patricia's second child, Brandon, was her "difficult" child. From birth on, he seemed "irritable" to her; was difficult to soothe; and at two years old, was turning into a "whining, crying, angry little demon." It didn't take long to discover that Missy was probably a Peacemaker child and that Brandon was probably a stressed Loyalist.

On further investigation, I learned that the household was rather chaotic at times. Patricia and her husband lived in a small apartment on a busy street with lots of activity and noise occurring even into the early morning hours. They also housed two poorly trained dogs, a cat, and a hamster. Patricia was enrolled in school, and her husband had a second job; both felt stressed by their financial situation and somewhat erratic schedules. They often ate out or picked up fast food for themselves and the children.

Once Patricia learned that both she and her son had "reactive" personalities, she was able to understand that all the sensory stimulation occurring in their home was most likely creating stress that decreased serotonin in both of them, and this, in turn, negatively impacted them both, causing them not only to be irritable and reactive to their environment but also to each other. The more upset Brandon became, the more frustrated Patricia would get, and the next thing you knew, they were like two cats in a pillow case—each reacting to the other and both escalating their already upset states. With this new knowledge, Patricia also began to make a connection between Brandon's intake of caffeine and his whining and temper tantrums. She became aware that she had been comparing the two children and that she secretly resented Brandon for upsetting the peacefulness of their home since his birth. She worried that ultimately his self-esteem would be damaged because she realized that she had become much more critical of almost everything he did.

Once she became involved in protecting him from sensory overload, feeding him more carefully, and providing a more structured schedule, Brandon responded quite favorably to his new environment. The greatest healing occurred, however, because Patricia began to appreciate the gifts of his personality. Even her language reflected her newfound appreciation. For instance, instead of saying that he was "fussy," she now said he had a personality similar to her own and described it as a "spicy" personality; she actually bragged about what a "Ferrari kind of a kid" she had as she described how quickly his brain (and body) responded to many situations. Patricia began to appreciate her son's remarkable ability for pattern recognition and other attributes associated with his personality. She stopped feeling guilty for her emotional responses and understood that she too was sensitive not only to the environment but to his emotional outbursts. As she embraced the blessings and challenges of Brandon's personality, they both began to relax and enjoy a more loving and fulfilling relationship.

To Sum It Up

If you do nothing more than accept that your personality is biologically based, you will probably find over time (if not immediately) a sense of relief and increased compassion for yourself. The more you understand the basic personality system, the more you will understand what motivates you and how you are wired to perceive yourself and the world around you. Once you can accept that your personality is biologically based, you are just a step away from accepting that *everyone's* personality is also a result of biology.

At this point, most people begin to feel compassion for others as they realize that everyone is simply doing the best they can, given their circumstances and resources. Those circumstances for all of us start with being born as a biologically-based personality; then being raised in whatever high-, medium-, or low-functioning family we were born into; then being affected either positively or negatively by our environment; and finally, having (or not having) and utilizing (or not being able to utilize) resources that further shape our personality, level of functioning, and ultimately the course of our life.

I cannot overemphasize how profound this change in perception can be. If you really "get" that everyone, and I mean every single person on the planet, is "doing the best they can with what they've got," and you experience the true meaning of compassion summed up in the sentence "There but for the grace of God go I," then you will no longer believe that people are jerks or idiots. Instead, you will have learned that when people behave in ways that seem rude, self-centered, mean, or self-destructive, and you judge them, it is because you don't have enough information.

OBSERVATION VS. JUDGMENT

Please note that *observing* and *judging* are two very different processes. Observation is simply noting that a person's behavior appears to be whatever it is, and it is free of emotion. Judgment, on the other hand, is emotionally charged and has a sense of self-righteousness. Judgment also separates you from the person or situation you judge. Compassion results from observing *without* judgment and either understanding the person's situation or at least giving the person and situation the benefit of the doubt (trusting that he is indeed doing the best he can, given his circumstances and resources).

One of the best places to experiment with this life-improving concept is in your car. Now, I spend a fair amount of time on the road, and I have observed people behind the wheel engaging in some dangerous and crazy moves, but I have not been upset in traffic for over thirty years!

My "peace in traffic" began as a result of a terrible upset in my life. The short story is that, thirty years ago, I was extremely upset while driving on the interstate and unknowingly changed lanes without looking carefully, causing a driver to have to swerve off onto the shoulder. I was quite shaken when I heard him blowing his horn, and then, I looked into my rearview mirror to see him driving off the road. What happened after that, though, was even more upsetting. The driver was able to maintain control of his car and then sped up to my car and screamed obscenities at me. I doubt he saw the tears streaming down my face, but if he had, perhaps instead of angry gestures he would have gestured for me to pull over. If he had given me the benefit of the doubt, he might've said, "Hey there, you really scared me just now. You seem really upset. I don't know what's going on in your life right now, but you and I (and the rest of the drivers on the road) might be a little safer if you took a few minutes to collect yourself rather than driving while you are this emotionally distraught." He might even have given me a hug. Although that might sound farfetched (giving someone a hug after accidentally running into me), that was, in fact, something I personally did on a few occasions after that day.

By extending compassion rather than blame at the scene of an accident, we were all able to recover more quickly from the shock of what had just occurred. More importantly, I was reminded that day that I was not trying to cause an accident by any means, so I learned to extend the benefit of the doubt to other drivers on the road. Now, you too can pay forward the benefits of the new knowledge you have gained. Here is my invitation to you:

When you get a chance to sit in a quiet place, consider a real or imagined person who you believe has made bad choices. Consider what personality type they might have, what type of unhealthy family they may have been born into, and what resources they might not have been able to access. Imagine that this person made the best choice at the moment, even if it meant taking a drug to cope with an unbearable situation or acting in a mean or cruel way because they were not healthy enough to handle the situation differently. Consider how that person's personality type may have influenced the way he perceived himself and his situation. And then, do the following thought exercise: say to yourself, "If I were this person and had this person's personality, and was born into this person's family, and had the same life circumstances as this person, I would not be looking at this situation in the same way that I currently am. Rather, I would see and experience the world through that person's eyes, personality, and experiences, and therefore, I would likely be doing exactly what this person is doing now."

You may or may not decide to change or to manipulate your own neurotransmitters directly. You may or may not devote yourself to better understanding personality theory. But I do hope that, by the time you finish this book, you will at least be willing to accept the simple fact that people are doing the best they can. Just being open to this possibility will help you to become the Ultimate You!

Chapter 7

Clinical Implications

T his chapter is intended for researchers, educators, and clinicians—and also recommended for nerds and non-technical people who are having trouble getting to sleep. I will start with a request from the East and a challenge from the West. First, from the East (an excerpt from Timothy Leary's book *Flashbacks* (italics added):

> [Lama Govinda[25] speaking to Timothy Leary]: I have discussed with you how wisdom must be acquired at the same rate as knowledge. Now, I should like to charge you with a mission that is close to my heart and that you are well qualified to perform. The premise underlying this mission is a self-evident one: that any system of personality classification that has endured for centuries in many different cultures has passed the test of place and time. It must tell us something valid about the various types and sub-species of humans. Thus, there must be meaningful correspondence among all the personality classification systems that have survived from antiquity, such as the Tarot, the I Ching, the Olympian

---

25 Lama Govinda (1898–1985) was a German-born scholar of Tibetan Buddhism and the spiritual head of the Buddhist Order of Vajrayana in India. His twenty-two books include *The Foundations of Tibetan Mysticism* and *The Way of the White Clouds*.

gods and goddesses, and Hindu castes. *A successful demonstration of correspondences among the great systems of human mentation would help to harmonize East and West, science and yoga, past and future.* Would you work on this problem?

[Timothy Leary]: I was interested in the task but despaired of finding the time for such arcane research. One would have to live like the Lama, withdrawn from the world, like a medieval scholar in a monastery. The assignment of this mission brought my studies with the Lama to a close.

And from the West: in 2000, the United States' Committee on Doctrine produced a draft report on the origins of the Enneagram to aid bishops in their evaluation of its use in their dioceses. The report identified aspects of the intersection between the Enneagram and Catholicism which, in their opinion, warranted particular scrutiny and were seen as potential areas of concern, stating that "While the Enneagram system shares little with traditional Christian doctrine or spirituality, it also shares little with the methods and criteria of modern science . . . The burden of proof is on proponents of the Enneagram to furnish scientific evidence for their claims."

The request has been made, the gauntlet thrown! If you are a professional in the field of psychology or education, please consider the following thoughts and suggestions. My neurotransmitter theory of personality proposes that the NPS provides an accurate reflection of the genetically determined, beautifully symmetric biology of the human mind. The neurotransmitter theory, and the NPS from which it evolved, could stimulate and advance research into human personality. Areas in which the NPS could be most useful include, but are not limited to, personality types at risk for specific personality disorders or major mental illness, personality-tailored clinical and pharmacological treatment, and development of biomarkers for more rapid diagnosis and evaluation of personality type.

More immediately, applying the NPS as a tool in clinical psychology could also have significant implications. Using the NPS as a tool provides both the client and therapist with an objective map of stress states and optimal states of integration. This knowledge can empower the client, who would no longer have to rely only upon the therapist's intuition for assessment of areas of concentration for balance and growth. In addition, one of the most useful aspects of the NPS is the inclusion of healthy and optimal states of personality. The current fields of psychology and medicine tend to focus primarily on illness and dysfunction. Increased awareness of optimal states of human potential may encourage research and development of technology for enhanced states of being.

System Overview for Clinicians

Unlike most personality systems, the NPS is *both* categorical and dimensional. It is categorical in the sense that all individuals can be placed into one of nine distinct personality types. It is also dimensional in that the specification of what NPS type a person has relates directly to their relative position along three psychological dimensions. For purposes of definition, in psychology, categorical personality theories suggest that individuals can be placed into specific and mutually exclusive categories, whereas dimensional models suggest that individuals have personality traits that exist as points along a continuum of specific personality trait dimensions. A trait is a cross-situational individual difference that remains stable across the lifespan but can change through adaptive processes. The theory underlying the NPS suggests that an individual's personality can be determined by their position along three personality trait dimensions, which then determine their NPS type. Therefore, the NPS, which at first glance appears to be merely a categorical typology system, can actually be deconstructed into groupings of dimensional traits.

Based on McCrae and Yang's suggestion that "the current categorical system should be replaced by a more comprehensive system of personality traits and personality-related problems," the following is a proposal for a novel set of dimensions based on the NPS subdivisions. I like to call the "new" set of dimensions the Final Four Factors.[26] These Final Four dimensions are Outlook, Mental Activity, Assertiveness, and Sociability.

---

26 My nod to Duke University.

Outlook (OL)

The dimension of Outlook (OL) relates to the degree of orientation of attitude related to optimism versus pessimism and a consistent, pleasant demeanor versus a moody. temperamental demeanor. The OL axis appears to be related most closely to the Harmonic Triads and ranges from Positive OL (the Positive Outlook types), exhibiting a high sense of well-being and a predisposition to an optimistic outlook, to Neutral OL (the Competent Outlook types), exhibiting a neutral sense of well-being and a predisposition to a realistic outlook, to Reactive OL (the Reactive Outlook types), exhibiting a low sense of well-being and a predisposition to a pessimistic outlook.

Mental Activity (MA)

The dimension of Mental Activity (MA) relates to mental processing speed and a sense of continuous mental engagement. The MA axis appears to be most closely related to the Processing Triad and ranges from High MA—exhibiting high-speed mental processing with almost constant mental engagement (the Thinking Triad), to Medium MA—exhibiting medium-speed mental processing with intermittent mental engagement (the Feeling Triad), to Low MA—exhibiting low-speed mental processing with situation-induced engagement (the Instinctual Triad).

Assertiveness (AS)

The dimension of Assertiveness (AS) relates to the degree of assertive action, physical energy, and drive used under stress. Locus of control ranges from internal to external and parallels the continuum of high to low assertiveness, respectively (Williams, 1985). This means that if an individual has an internal locus of control, she does not blame others for her experiences but rather perceives her life circumstances as being influenced by her own choices and personal responsibility. An individual with low AS would also lean to the external pole of locus of control, perceiving her circumstances as a result of outside influences over which she has little or no control.

The AS axis appears to be related most closely to Riso and Hudson's Hornevian Grouping of the Enneagram and ranges from High AS (the Assertive types), exhibiting a high level of physical energy and drive with a predisposition to a predominantly internal locus of control, to Average AS (the Compliant types), exhibiting a moderate level of physical energy and drive with a predisposition to a mix of internal and external locus of control, to Low AS (the Withdrawn types), exhibiting a low level of physical energy and drive with a predisposition to a predominantly external locus of control.

Ultimately, I believe these differences are related to dopamine levels and account for the "wings," which, if true, also accounts for pockets of concentration of high and low dopamine around the NPS circle of personalities. After my dissertation, Dr. Schulze and I came to believe that average dopamine levels create what we refer to as a "core" type; that is, having very little "wings" or characteristics from the personality type adjacent to it on either side. We also came to the conclusion that a high dopamine level creates a wing that shares characteristics with the more energetic of the adjacent two personalities. That would leave the low dopamine level, creating a wing that shares characteristics with the less energetic of the adjacent two personalities. The wings could ultimately help explain co-morbidity of personality disorders, as will be discussed later in this chapter.

Sociability (SO)

The Sociability dimension (SO) relates to the preferred method of relating to others and to the world. This dimension can stand alone or be superimposed on the personality types, and the continuum would range from High SO (the Social style), to Average SO (the Intimate style), to Low SO (the Self-Preservation style).

The Nine-Point Personality System and SPECT Scans

One of my all-time favorite research heroes is the psychiatrist Dr. Daniel Amen. About twenty years ago, Dr. Amen asked the question, "Why are we, as psychiatrists, the only physicians who don't look at the organ we treat?" He was considered a quack by his colleagues and almost lost his license due to his practice of treating his patients based on SPECT scans, which created images of the brain that reflected relative blood flow, believed to correlate with brain activity. These days, he is considered a pioneer in brain research and was eventually invited to be a keynote speaker for his colleagues at the American Medical Association conference. Dr. Amen's groundbreaking work included identifying six different types of attention deficit disorder (ADD) and noting that each type responded very differently to various treatment modalities. I believe that Dr. Amen also inadvertently identified biomarkers to personality.

After the completion of my dissertation, I contacted Dr. Amen and asked him if Dr. Schulze and I could visit with him and take resting and concentration SPECT scans of our brains. I predicted, based on Dr. Amen's work and our understanding of the NPS types, which parts of our brain would be hypo- and hyper-perfused. You might imagine our excitement when my predictions proved accurate.

The basis for my predictions traced back to Dr. Amen's descriptions of patients with attention deficit disorders. For example, Dr. Amen described the over-focused ADD child as one who was usually very smart, socially awkward, and had a tendency to be interested in things rather than people. He described how the anterior cingulate gyrus, the brain's "gear shifter," was hyper-perfused and made it difficult to change focus. His description sounded like a very stressed Investigator, so I predicted that a healthy Investigator (like Dr. Schulze) would have a higher perfusion in this area but not to the degree of the ADD child. Sure enough, that's exactly what we saw when our scans were done.

Furthermore, the difference between rest and concentration SPECT scans on both of us, we believe, captured the biological changes that the brain makes to reflect integration patterns. In other words, my cingulate gyrus showed more pronounced circulation when I concentrated, which made it more "five-like" in that scan.

Interestingly, the NPS system predicts that my personality temporarily visits the "five" when I focus, which is exactly what happened in the SPECT scan. Dr. Schulze, on the other hand, in order to accomplish the task (an inhibit/disinhibit computer task), reported that he had to *relax* his brain to be successful. His concentration SPECT scan shows a decrease in cingulate gyrus activity, which makes his brain appear more "eight-like" as in "less over-thinking and more doing." Important to note, both of us scored above 95 percent in ability to focus. If we had not factored in our different brain baselines related to our personalities, statistically speaking, the SPECT scans would have had zero significance. However, given what our prediction was, this set of scans is not only significant but also has incredible implications for further study that could contribute greatly to the fields of communication and learning.

Below and on the left is an image of the over-focused ADD brain with relatively high activity in the cingulate gyrus (the brain's "gear shifter"). We think this shows a stressed Investigator (5) child's brain.

Over focused ADD vs. Healthy "5" brain

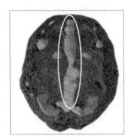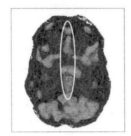

By contrast, the image on the right shows the brain of a healthy adult (Dr. Eric Schulze) at rest and concentrating. Notice that, at rest, the cingulate gyrus is still quite active, but not nearly as pronounced as the over-focused ADD brain. Then, notice how the cingulate gyrus becomes much less perfused in the concentration scan.

Now, look below at an image of the HD/ADD brain (on the left), which Dr. Amen describes as belonging to a child who has excessive physical energy and is prone to impulsive behavior, like blurting out answers in class. The prefrontal cortex here appears deeply pitted, meaning there is not much relative circulation in that area. It just so happens that this part of the brain is where executive judgment takes place, and with decreased circulation to that area, impulsivity becomes pronounced. Looking next at the Enthusiast (my brain), one sees slight pitting in the same areas, producing a personality that has high physical energy and is prone to what I call "spontaneous" behavior.

Impulsive vs. Spontaneous?

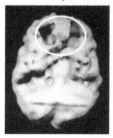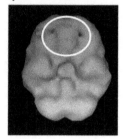

This next image, below, is a computer-generated representation of my brain at rest and then concentrating. The arrow in the second picture points to the increase in circulation related to the cingulate gyrus. Could this be a SPECT scan illustration of integration of the Enthusiast (7) personality to the Investigator (5)?

An inner view of a
card carrying "7" brain

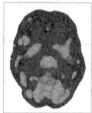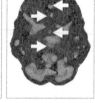

At rest   Concentration

Interestingly, Dr. Schulze's Thinker (5) brain showed an anterior cingulate gyrus that calmed down under concentration conditions. Could this be evidence of integration of the Thinker (5) to the less thinking and more action oriented Challenger (8)? Hmmm . . . very interesting . . .

An inner view of a certifiable "5" brain

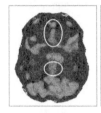 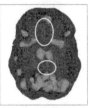

At rest   Concentration

The Nine-Point Personality System and the DSM IV

The DSM-IV employed a categorical model for the classification of personality disorders. In developing diagnostic criteria for personality disorders for the recently released DSM-V, it is noteworthy that the DSM-V work group initially proposed a somewhat dramatic new approach: maintain six personality disorder diagnoses from the prior ten in the DSM-IV and also move from a categorical to a trait-based, dimensional classification system. Per the categorical system, a patient either has a diagnosis or not, whereas a dimensional system better captures the nuances of human personality by measuring a variety of traits on a continuum. Unfortunately, the proposal was ultimately voted down; however, the authors did place an alternative hybrid dimensional-categorical model in a separate chapter in Section 3 of the DSM-V to stimulate further research on this modified classification system.

In my view, a dimensional model offers clear advantages in understanding personality. While DSM-IV descriptions of personality disorders (PDs) represented a major advance in classification in its day,[27] as John Livesley,

---

27 General diagnostic criteria for a personality disorder:
   A. An enduring pattern of inner experience and behavior that deviates markedly from the expectations of the individual's culture. This pattern is manifested in two (or more) of the following areas: (1) cognition (i.e., ways of perceiving and interpreting self, other people, and events), (2) affectivity (i.e.. the range, intensity, lability, and appropriateness of emotional response), (3) interpersonal functioning, and (4) impulse control.
   B. The enduring pattern is inflexible and pervasive across a broad range of situations.
   C. The enduring pattern leads to clinically significant distress or impairment in social, occupational, or other important areas of functioning.

author of *DSM-IV Personality Disorders*, observes, "It is still far from adequate in describing the phenomena that constitute the clinical core of personality disturbance." Livesley contends, as do the vast majority of researchers in the field, that the degree of overlap between and among the disorders is too great. He further insists that use of the term "co-morbidity" hides diagnostic confusion.

The promising trend in the movement toward a "dimensional" approach is highlighted in the most recent contribution of Costa and McCrae's five-factor model (consisting of neuroticism, extraversion, openness, agreeableness, and conscientiousness). All of the current models seek to identify the essential components of personality, and all assume a continuum between normal personality and abnormal personality disorders.

The NPS is in a unique position to contribute to our understanding of the personality continuum, ranging from self-actualized states to average levels of functioning to psychopathy. This feature in the NPS may bring personality disorders into sharper focus if in fact the distinctions of the nine types are truer to *in vivo* human personality than the current typology systems, as I believe they are. There are some significant correlations between the DSM-IV criteria for personality disorders and the descriptions of low average to low levels of functioning within the NPS.

The reader may notice that there is potential overlap and redundancy among the NPS types. According to Livesley, "Diagnostic overlap among Axis II disorders is the rule rather than the exception."

The overlap of diagnoses that occurs in the DSM-IV classification system can be more easily understood through each NPS type and its corresponding wing. For example, a paranoid PD appears to be extremely similar to the low-functioning Loyalist (6) personality. A paranoid person with a co-morbidity of schizotypal PD would translate, in NPS terms, to a Loyalist with a "five" (Investigator) wing.

D. The pattern is stable and of long duration and its onset can be traced back at least to adolescence or early adulthood.

E. The enduring pattern is not better accounted for as a manifestation or consequence of another mental disorder.

F. The enduring pattern is not due to the direct physiological effects of a substance (e.g. a drug of abuse or a medication) or a general medical condition (e.g., head trauma).

Using the NPS type, wing, and level of functioning might help clinicians and researchers to simplify diagnoses and pinpoint the primary and co-morbid (or secondary) PD. For example, the DSM-IV states, "Individuals with Antisocial Personality Disorder also often have features that meet the criteria for other Personality Disorders, particularly Borderline, Histrionic and Narcissistic Personality Disorders."

The antisocial personality disorder criteria could be descriptive of either the Achiever (3) or the Challenger (8) in a low-functioning state. The dual diagnosis of narcissistic PD and antisocial PD might distinguish the NPS Achiever from the Challenger, since the Achiever personality, at average to low levels, tends to be self-absorbed and self-referential. The Challenger personality does not share the narcissistic feature. Furthermore, the same dual diagnosis of narcissistic PD with antisocial PD and a co-morbid diagnosis of borderline PD could more simply be described in NPS terms as an Achiever with an Individualist wing. Likewise, a narcissistic PD with antisocial PD and a co-morbid diagnosis of histrionic PD could more simply be described in NPS terms as an Achiever with a Helper wing. If you would like more information in this vein, Riso and Hudson's Enneagram teacher training manual includes a chapter with a brief discussion of the role of the NPS in the diagnosis and treatment of DSM-IV Axis I disorders.

In addition to the direct potential correlations between the NPS and Axis II disorders, the NPS has implications for Axis I disorders as well. A vast body of research is quickly growing with accounts of numerous Axis I diagnoses and high correlations with disturbances of neurotransmitter activity. In addition, recent research has revealed a high frequency of co-morbidity between Axis II and Axis I disorders. It is not within the scope of this book to provide an exhaustive review of correlation between the Axis I and Axis II classifications and the NPS. However, it should be noted that the research is expanding rapidly, and many correlations have been drawn that include, but are not limited to, personality disorders and alcohol dependency (Basiaux 2001), eating disorders (Heaven, 2001) (Phillips & McElroy, 2000), chronic pain (Weisberg, 2000), and depression (Joyce, 1999). In fact, Clonniger has already suggested that personality assessment may allow reliable measurement of risk of mood disorders and other psychopathologies, including psychosis (Clonniger, 1999). Not only might there be co-morbidity between Axis I and Axis II disorders, but there may also be a few Axis I disorders that are, in fact, misdiagnosed Axis II personality disorders. For example, at least one Axis I disorder, cyclothymia, may be a misdiagnosed personality disorder for a low-functioning Enthusiast personality.

Researchers are also beginning to identify subgroups of certain Axis I disorders, such as bulimia, alcoholism, and depression. These new findings of co-morbidity and sub-groupings may actually be explained as different levels of functioning of separate NPS types with similar phenotypic expressions based on entirely different motivations and neurochemistry.

Clinical Applications

A better understanding of the NPS process may eventually help clinicians to prescribe personality-tailored medication, diets, exercise, and spiritual practices. For decades, researchers and psychiatrists alike have attempted to solve the seemingly unsolvable conundrum of the unpredictability of psychoactive medications and their effects on patients. To date, psychopharmacotherapy of personality disorders is still in its infancy and remains one of the less explored areas of research (Pelissolo, 1999).

The field of pharmacokinetics is an even newer area of study. While the focus of pharmacodynamics is the study of the effect of a drug on the body, pharmacokinetics is the study of what effect the body has on the drug. Grilly states, "Differences among organisms in their pharmacokinetics, due to genetic differences, the presence of other drugs, disease and physiological and psychological status, can result in 5-20 fold differences in their reaction to a given amount of a drug within that species" (Grilly, 2000). Recently, Tanum and Malt indicated "personality traits were better predictors of treatment outcome than serotonergic sensitivity assessed with the fenfluramine test" (Tanum & Malt, 2000).

Perhaps a more accurate map of personality would result in more accurate predictions of treatment outcome and may lead to rational drug treatments based on solid neurobiological profiles for each of the NPS types. If accurate, the neurotransmitter tables could explain why certain psychoactive medications such as Prozac, a selective serotonin reuptake inhibitor (SSRI), work on some people, cause unwanted side effects on others, and have no effect at all on others (Stokes, 1997).

Our modern society has created many circumstances that increase stress and fatigue. Such stressors may exacerbate serotonin depletion (Kramer, 1993). If the hypothetical neurotransmitter theory is correct, then some personality types would be at higher risk for depression based on the lower activity of their endogenous serotonin pathways. Analysis of specific personality traits and preemptive institution of coping strategies could potentially avert chronic depression in certain segments of the population (Tauscher, Bagby et al., 2001). Another potential outcome of researching the NPS might be developing an improved screening process to identify at-risk individuals in their work and home environments.

Decreased serotonin levels have not only been implicated in depression but have also been consistently correlated with aggressiveness and alcoholism (Lovinger, 1997). Serotonin depletion may also have an effect on sensation seeking and criminal behavior (Fuller, 1996) (Heinz, Mann et al., 2001). This model suggests a need to study personality types that might be prone to serotonin depletion and therefore more susceptible than others to alcoholism under stressful circumstances. For instance, a personality type that shows an affiliation with the Positive Outlook group would be least likely to commit violent crimes, while personality types that show affiliation with the Reactive groups would have a higher potential for violence. Low socioeconomic status could be a stressor that causes decreased serotonin levels. Therefore, low serotonin activity coupled with a neurological predisposition for violence and environmental stressors could lead to violence in a stressed or even semi-stressed environment.

In the future, correctly typing personality and corresponding relative levels of dopamine may prove to be crucial in areas related to the so-called "natural rewards" of eating, love, and reproduction, as well as to the "unnatural rewards" of alcohol, other drugs of substance abuse, and compulsive activities, such as gambling, eating, sex, and risk-taking behaviors.

As mentioned previously, dopamine activity has been implicated in reward and motivation pathways in the brain. Because of this, it is under considerable scrutiny in the area of addiction. Comings has proposed that "defects in various combinations of the genes for these neurotransmitters [dopaminergic genes and genes that modulate dopamine pathways] result in a Reward Deficiency Syndrome (RDS) and that such individuals are at risk to abuse the unnatural rewards" (Comings, 2000). The efforts to attain "unnatural rewards" that impair healthy functioning of the individual account for a number of the DSM-IV Axis I diagnoses. Once again, NPS typing may help to identify individuals at risk for many of the Axis I disorders.

Suggestions for Research

The following are areas in which the validity of the Nine-Point Personality System might benefit from further investigation.

- *Twin Studies.* Since it appears that a person's personality is governed by that individual's genetic heritage, one of the most powerful tests of the theory would be to test identical twins for their nine-point personality types. A test group of ten to twenty twin pairs could be located and tested for NPS type relatively easily. It might be hypothesized that identical twins should demonstrate high heritability.

- *DSM-IV Axis II Personality Disorder Studies.* Since specific NPS types may be at risk for developing specific PDs, one research approach would be to test populations of individuals with specific PDs for correlations with their NPS types. This model may also help to explain co-morbidity of PDs. Furthermore, use of the NPS may help to isolate the primary personality disorder with the primary NPS type and the secondary disorder with the NPS "wing." A sharper understanding of primary and secondary disorders could significantly help clinicians to target the treatment modality best suited for the primary personality. It is predicted that overrepresentation of NPS types will appear in the PD categories similar to the PD/NPS chart below.

- *Pharmaceuticals.* Since this theory suggests a correlation between the NPS type and a predisposition to Axis I diagnoses, it might be useful to test a group of men and women between the ages of eighteen and sixty years old, who have been under treatment for depression, to determine the relative prevalence of their NPS type. We might predict that the Positive Outlook Types (those personalities high in serotonin) would be underrepresented in patient populations and/or would demonstrate a more robust response to certain treatments. Further, the Reactive Triad personalities might be overrepresented and demonstrate more resistance to certain treatments.

- *Substance Abuse and Recreational Drug Use.* The theory predicts that an individual's NPS type is based on the relative strength or weakness of the three major distributed neurotransmitter systems. Since most recreational drugs appear to modulate one or more of these systems, it is possible that certain nine-point types might take certain drugs to temporarily strengthen a relatively weak pathway, while others might "self-medicate" to decrease overactive pathways. A project likely to yield fruitful results would be to evaluate the recreational drug preferences of each of the nine types. It would be my prediction that drug usage and preference would not be evenly distributed across the NPS types.

- *Social Relevance.* Demonstrating a biological basis for personality in a system that is easily understandable would not only help to determine more precise and effective medication, nutrition, and treatment modalities, but it would also foster greater interpersonal and cultural understanding. Demonstrating a biological basis for personality could help to remove judgment and prejudice caused by lack of information. Furthermore, having a universal and scientifically validated system would encourage development of tools for communication that could address the different motivations and needs of different personalities. When we as a society can embrace our differences, understand the positive intentions of personality, have compassion for the stressed levels of each personality, and develop communication skills to reach all personalities at various levels of health, we will be well on our way to a healthier and more peaceful world.

In addition to the many dimensions of personality psychology, there are interests in the spiritual aspects and implications of this field. One such interest is in the area of personality and how to apply the acquired scientific knowledge in this field to enhance human potential. Students of the NPS report that when they reach a deeper understanding of the system, they cannot help but become more compassionate and less judgmental. Through this process of study, they have noticed that observation and understanding replace judgment and upset. The ability to observe without judgment and to distance oneself, at least somewhat, from total identification with the personality has long been a recommendation of spiritual teachers (as well as those in the helping professions) and many, if not all, spiritual traditions. This creates a chance for the "seeker" to transcend the personality and its many neurotic needs in order to become aware of a more subtle level of existence and to achieve a self-actualized state.

One reason the NPS has been so useful and consistent may be because it is intuitively based on a biological connection. If that biological basis can be demonstrated, perhaps then the Western world, which relies heavily on science for validation of theories, will be willing to study personality and human nature in a more systematic and objective manner. This process could ultimately lead to the same compassionate and nonjudgmental view of self and others that Eastern traditions have embraced for centuries. If personality is something we, as a culture, come to see as something a person *has*, as opposed to what a person *is*, then we move closer to an integrated system of embracing science and spirituality in a mature and holistic way.

All one need do is look at our changing views of the causes of schizophrenia, which, in the past, were considered everything from demonic possession to the result of a "schizophrenigenic" type of mother, judged as distant and non-nurturing. The "schizophrenigenic" (detached and aloof) effect that mothers exhibit with their schizophrenic children is now believed to be a result of repeatedly frustrated attempts to make social contact with a child, not a cause or contributing factor in the etiology of schizophrenia. With more scientific understanding, schizophrenia is being understood as a multi-causal disease related to a chemical imbalance. Because of this new information, no longer is there an emotionally charged judgment and affront to the newly diagnosed patient and family members. Rather, treatment now involves supporting the patient's self-esteem, maintaining a continued partnership with significant others and the health team, while exploring medication and treatment options that work best with the patient's physiology.

Ethical Considerations

Finally, a very important area to be addressed is the ethical and moral responsibility of the researcher who proposes that personality and/or aspects of personality might be biologically based to disseminate this information in a socially responsible manner.

Inherent in the ethical considerations is the need to be precise and careful with the terminology involved in theory creation and explanation. Imprecise or negatively charged terminology could seriously impact those people who are "typed" into one of the nine-point personalities. For instance, the Individualist (4) personality has, in some cases, been labeled as the "drama queen" rather than the "Individualist" or the "Artist." The term "drama queen" bears negative connotations, and widespread use of such terminology could have serious negative consequences, not only on the individuals with that personality type, but also on society as a whole. We might lose perspective on the value of Individualist personalities.

In addition, care must be taken to avoid presenting any particular personality or trait as "better" than any other. Any hint of such a suggestion carries potential concern for inadvertent and highly charged issues and, at the extreme, to the area of eugenics. What I have come to appreciate over time is the absolute need for biodiversity in all areas of life, including personality. In the end, whether any single personality characteristic is more or less useful depends entirely on context. For example, while anxiety is not considered a pleasant or desirable characteristic, anxiety tends to create a hyper-vigilant awareness of one's surroundings that could mean the difference between life and death, if detecting danger sooner rather than later was needed for survival in a specific situation. That same feature of anxiety could create life-threatening hesitancy in a situation that requires immediate action.

Due to the extraordinary social relevance and potential for extreme social impact, anyone who teaches this system is charged with the solemn responsibility to uphold the highest standards possible. This involves making a commitment to self-assessing personal biases and relentlessly seeking a deeper understanding of oneself and all sentient beings.

Conclusion

The opportunity for research in the area of personality psychology is as limitless as the variations of personality. As human beings, our entire experience of the world is colored by our personality. As such, the exploration of the genesis of our personality is one of the great frontiers of human knowledge. It is my hope that the ideas contained in this book will stimulate an interest among scientists to explore the potential of both the NPS and my neurotransmitter theory of human personality based on the NPS. The implications of a theory that can lead to a fundamental shift in the understanding of "why we behave as we do" is worthy of consensual and empirical verification.

In conclusion, I quote my now-favorite textbook author, Dr. Funder: ". . . So, in the end you may not have to choose. This single, major, integrated theory of personality that includes all of these viewpoints does not exist yet, and if it is ever invented, it will stand as one of the major intellectual accomplishments of all time."

I would never be so audacious as to say that I have created or even discovered the jeweled One Big Theory. But I have been privileged (and at times burdened) to have a perspective that few seem to have at this present time, which has allowed me to make what I believe is an important contribution to this field. In as humble a way as I know how, I am taking a bold leap in suggesting that the OBT already exists. I believe the elephant, the Rosetta Stone, the OBT of the six current personality psychology approaches—the Enneagram and the NPS periodic table of human personality—are all facets of the one and same diamond. Hopefully, in exploring and researching this together, we may find a better way of learning, loving, and living.

About Dr. Tina Thomas

Dr. Tina Thomas, a.k.a. "Dr. T," is an internationally renowned author and motivational speaker specializing in the field of self-development. Her endearing, charismatic style has garnered Dr. Thomas a reputation as one of the most dynamic speakers on the circuit today. Her proven innovative programs enable people to quickly achieve their goals, be they business success, personal growth, or competitive edge. Dr. Thomas has been featured as a personality expert on ABC, CBS, Fox, and NBC.

Dr. Thomas was propelled into the international spotlight when she was credited with "cracking the code of human personality," a feat that has been referred to by some as the "Holy Grail of Psychology." The significance of this psychological breakthrough is immense; in fact, many feel it could revolutionize the entire thought process of how humans reach their potential.

Practicing what she calls the "magic" of science and psychology, Dr. Thomas authored *A Gentle Path: A Guide to Peace, Passion and Power*, which was re-released as *The Ultimate Edge: How to Be, Do and Get Anything You Want*, along with *Who Do You Think You Are? Understanding Personality from the Inside Out* and four e-books: *How to Find the Perfect Partner*, *Radical Relationships*, *Burn Fat Forever . . . and Grow Younger Every Day!*, *The G-word*, and *The Little Book (The Missing Pieces of AA's Big Book)*.

As a speaker, Dr. Thomas relates her scientifically-based formula that translates into success in everyday life, which includes increased sales, higher employee retention, and an overall healthier lifestyle. She helps people develop a clear plan of action to accelerate their success, whether they are looking to become the top salesperson in their company, increase their bottom line, improve employee relations, or make their first million dollars.

She holds a PhD in biopsychology and is a licensed clinical social worker, a registered nurse, and a TEDx speaker. Formerly, the clinical director of the prestigious Tulane University Cancer Counseling Center and a research professor at Duke University, Dr. Thomas is currently the director of the Gestalt Institute and Relationship Center of New Orleans and New York. Known among friends and colleagues as a "professional fairy godmother," she has a well-earned reputation for empowering others to reach their goals in an elegant and dynamic way. She has a private practice, is a corporate consultant, and offers personalized workshops that have changed the lives of entrepreneurs, educators, CEOs, medical professionals, and people from all walks of life. Dr. Thomas maps the path to success and transforms lives forever!

Bibliography

Amen, D. G. and B. D. Carmichael (1997). High-Resolution Brain SPECT
Imaging in ADHD. Annals of Clinical Psychiatry 9(2): 81-6.

Amen, D. G., F. Paldi, et al. (1993). Brain SPECT imaging. J Am Acad Child
Adolesc Psychiatry 32(5): 1080-1.

Amen, D. G., M. Stubblefield, et al. (1996). Brain SPECT findings and
aggressiveness. Ann Clin Psychiatry 8(3): 129-37.

Amen, D. G., S. Yantis, et al. (1997). Visualizing the firestorms in the brain: an
inside look at the clinical and physiological connections between drugs and
violence using brain SPECT imaging. J Psychoactive Drugs 29(4): 307-19.

Anton, R. F., D. H. Moak, et al. (1996). The obsessive compulsive drinking
scale: A new method of assessing outcome in alcoholism treatment studies.
Arch Gen Psychiatry 53(3): 225-31.

Baron R, Wagele E (1994). The Enneagram Made Easy, Harper San Francisco, CA

Basiaux, P., O. le Bon, et al. (2001). Temperament and Character Inventory
(TCI) personality profile and sub-typing in alcoholic patients: a controlled
study. Alcohol 36(6): 584-7.

Beauvais, P (1973). Claudio Naranjo and SAT: A Modern Manifestation of
Sufism? PhD Dissertation. The Hartford Seminary Foundation

Benjamin, J., R. P. Ebstein, et al. (1998). Genes for personality traits: implications for psychopathology. Int J Neuropsychopharmacol 1(2): 153-168.

Carlson, J. G. (1985). Recent assessments of the Myers-Briggs Type Indicator. J Pers Assess 49(4): 356-65.

Carrasco, J. L. (1997). [Psychobiological approach to personality disorders]. Actas Luso Esp Neurol Psiquiatr Cienc Afines 25(4): 207-16.

Chou, Tom (1999). Tom's Enneagram Page, Graduate Program in Neuroscience, Harvard www.people.fas.harvard.edu/~tchou/ennea_intro. html#2 University Boston, MA

Cloninger, C. R. (2000). A practical way to diagnosis personality disorder: A proposal. Journal of Personality Disorders, 14(2), 99-108.

Cloninger, C. R., D. M. Svrakic, et al. (1999). Measurement of psychopathology as variants of personality. Personality and psychopathology. C. R. Cloninger, et al. Washington, DC, American Psychiatric Press: 33-65.

Cloninger, C. R., C. Bayon, et al. (1998). Measurement of temperament and character in mood disorders: A model of fundamental states as personality types. Journal of Affective Disorders 51(1): 21-32.

Cloninger, C. R. and D. M. Svrakic (1997). Integrative psychobiological approach to psychiatric assessment and treatment. Psychiatry 60(2): 120-41.

Comer, Ronald J. (2002). *Fundamentals of Abnormal Psychology*, Worth Publishing: New York, NY

Comings, D. E. and K. Blum (2000). Reward deficiency syndrome: genetic aspects of behavioral disorders. Prog Brain Res 126: 325-41.

Costa, P.T, McCrea, R.R. (1992). The five-factor model of personality and its relevance to personality disorders. Journal of Personality Disorders, 6, 343-359.

American Psychiatric Association (2013). Diagnostic and statistical manual of mental disorders (5th ed.). Washington, DC

Di Chiara, G (1997). The Neurobiology of Addiction - an Overview, Alcohol Health and Research World, Volume 21, No.2 108-113

Ellason, J. W., C. A. Ross, et al. (1996). Axis I and II comorbidity and childhood trauma history in chemical dependency. Bull Menninger Clin 60(1): 39-51.

Enoch, M. A. and D. Goldman (2002). Problem drinking and alcoholism: diagnosis and treatment. Am Fam Physician 65(3): 441-8.

Froehlich, J. C. (1977). Opioid Peptides Alcohol Health & Research World Vol. 21, No 2.

Finn, P. R., E. J. Sharkansky, et al. (1997). Heterogeneity in the families of sons of alcoholics: the impact of familial vulnerability type on offspring characteristics. J Abnorm Psychol 106(1): 26-36.

Fuller, R. W. (1996). The influence of fluoxetine on aggressive behavior. Neuropsychopharmacology 14(2): 77-81.

Funder, David C. (2000). *The Personality Puzzle*, Second edition. W.W. Norton and Company: New York, NY

Gedgaudas, Nora T. (2011). *Primal Body, Primal Mind: Beyond the Paleo Diet for Total Health and a Longer Life*, Second edition. Healing Arts Press: Rochester, NY

George, D. T., J. C. Umhau, et al. (2001). Serotonin, testosterone and alcohol in the etiology of domestic violence. Psychiatry Res 104(1): 27-37.

Goldstein, B. I., J. R. Abela, et al. (2000). Attributional style and life events: a diathesis-stress theory of alcohol consumption. Psychol Rep 87(3 Pt 1): 949-55.

Grilly, David M. (2002). *Drugs and Human Behavior*, Fourth edition. Allyn and Bacon: Boston, MA

Hallman, J., L. von Knorring, et al. (1996). "Personality disorders according to DSM-III-R and thrombocyte monoamine oxidase activity in type 1 and type 2 alcoholics." J Stud Alcohol 57(2): 155-61.

Hamer, D. H., B. D. Greenberg, et al. (1999). "Role of the serotonin transporter gene in temperament and character." J Personal Disord 13(4): 312-27.

Havens, S. (1995). "Comparisons of Myers-Briggs and Enneagram Types of Registered Nurses." Master's thesis for University of Florida

Heaven, P. C., K. Mulligan, et al. (2001). "Neuroticism and conscientiousness as predictors of emotional, external, and restrained eating behaviors." Int J Eat Disord 30(2): 161-6.

Heinz, A., K. Mann, et al. (2001). Serotonergic dysfunction, negative mood states, and response to alcohol. Alcohol Clin Exp Res 25(4): 487-95.

Higley, J. D. and A. J. Bennett (1999). Central nervous system serotonin and personality as variables contributing to excessive alcohol consumption in non-human primates. Alcohol [??] Alcohol 34(3): 402-18.

Hill, E. M., S. F. Stoltenberg, et al. (1999). Potential associations among genetic markers in the serotonergic system and the antisocial alcoholism subtype. Exp Clin Psychopharmacol 7(2): 103-21.

Heinz, A., K. Mann, et al. (2001). Serotonergic dysfunction, negative mood states, and response to alcohol. Alcohol Clin Exp Res 25(4): 487-95.

Horney, K. (1945) (reissued 1992). *Our Inner Conflicts*. W.W. Norton & Co., Inc.: New York, NY

Joyce, P. R., R. T. Mulder, et al. (1999). Temperament and the pharmacotherapy of depression. Personality and psychopathology. C. R. Cloninger, et al. Washington, DC, American Psychiatric Press: 457-473.

Kandel, Schwartz and Jessel (2000). *Principles of Neuroscience*, Fourth edition. McGraw-Hill: New York, NY: 896

Keller, M. (2001). Role of serotonin and noradrenaline in social dysfunction: a review of data on reboxetine and the Social Adaptation Self-evaluation Scale (SASS). Gen Hosp Psychiatry 23(1): 15-9.

Kramer, P (1997). *Listening to Prozac*. Penguin Books: New York, NY

LeDoux, J. (2002). *Synaptic Self: How Our Brains Become Who We Are*. Viking: New York, NY

Livesley, W. J. (2002). Department of Psychiatry, University of British Columbia http://www.ikttp.de/html/livesley.html

Livesley, W. J. (1995). *The DSM-IV Personality Disorders*. The Guilford Press: New York, NY

Lovinger, D (1997). The Neurobiology of Addiction - an Overview. Alcohol Health and Research World Volume 21, No.2 114-119

Mazur, A. and A. Booth (1998). Testosterone and dominance in men. Behav Brain Sci 21(3): 353-63; discussion 363-97.

McCrae, R. R., & Costa, P. T., Jr. (1997). Personality trait structure as a human universal. American Psychologist, 52, 509-516.

McCrae and John (1992). McCrae R.R., and John O.P. An Introduction to the Five-Factor Model and Its Applications. Special Issue: The Five Factor Model: Issues and Applications, Journal of Personality 60:175-215, 1992.

McCrae, R. R., J. Yang, et al. (2001). "Personality profiles and the prediction of categorical personality disorders." J Pers 69(2): 155-74.

Merikangas, K. R., L. C. Dierker, et al. (1998). Psychopathology among offspring of parents with substance abuse and/or anxiety disorders: a high-risk study. J Child Psychol Psychiatry 39(5): 711-20.

Meszaros, K., E. Lenzinger, et al. (1999). The Tridimensional Personality Questionnaire as a predictor of relapse in detoxified alcohol dependents. The European Fluvoxamine in Alcoholism Study Group. Alcohol Clin Exp Res 23(3): 483-6.

Mihic, S. & Harris, A. (1997). The Neurobiology of Addiction - an Overview. Alcohol Health and Research World Volume 21, No.2 127-131

Miller, J. D., D. R. Lynam, et al. (2001). Personality disorders as extreme variants of common personality dimensions: can the Five-Factor Model adequately represent psychopathy? J Pers 69(2): 253-76.

Millon, T. (1991). Normality: What may we learn from evolutionary theory. In D. Offer & M. Sabshin (Eds). *The Diversity of Normal Behavior*. Basic Books: New York, NY

Mikheev, V. F. (1979). Role of genetic factors in the formation of trace reactions in man. Zh Vyssh Nerv Deiat Im I P Pavlova 29(3): 510-7.

Nakazawa, T. (1999). Dependence and obsession V.C Nihon Arukoru Yakubutsu Igakkai Zasshi 34(1): 27-35.

Needleman Jacob (1996). G. I. Gurdjieff and His School, Professor of Philosophy, San Francisco State University, San Francisco, CA www.bmrc. berkeley.edu/people/misc/School.html

Newgent, R. (2001). An Investigation of the Reliability and Validity of the Riso-Hudson Enneagram Type Indicator, PhD dissertation, University of Akron.

Oxenstierna, G., G. Edman, et al. (1986). Concentrations of monoamine metabolites in the cerebrospinal fluid of twins and unrelated individuals—a genetic study. J Psychiatr Res 20(1): 19-29.

Panzer, A. (1998). Depression or cancer: the choice between serotonin or melatonin? Med Hypotheses 50(5): 385-7.

Paunonen, S. V. and M. C. Ashton (2001). Big five factors and facets and the prediction of behavior. J Pers Soc Psychol 81(3): 524-39.

Peirson, A. R., J. W. Heuchert, et al. (1999). Relationship between serotonin and the temperament and character inventory. Psychiatry Res 89(1): 29-37.

Pelissolo, A. and J. P. Lepine (1999). Pharmacotherapy in personality disorders: methodological issues and results. Encephale 25(5): 496-507.

Rasanen, P. (1997). Testosterone and Mental Disorders. Duodecim 113(5): 395-9.

Reynolds, S. K. and L. A. Clark (2001). Predicting dimensions of personality disorder from domains and facets of the Five-Factor Model. J Pers 69(2): 199-222.

Roberts, A. and Koob, G. (1997). The Neurobiology of Addiction - an Overview. Alcohol Health and Research World Volume 21, No.2 101-106.

Randall, S. (1979). The Development of an Inventory to Assess Enneagram Personality Type, PhD dissertation. California Institute of Asian Studies.

Reynolds, Susan (2007). *The Everything Enneagram Book: Identify Your Type, Gain Insight into Your Personality, and Find Success in Life, Love, and Business*. Adams Media

Riso, D. R., & Hudson, R. (1996). *Personality Types: Using the Enneagram for Self-Discovery*. Houghton Mifflin Co.

Riso, D. R., & Hudson, R. (1999). *The Wisdom of the Enneagram: The Complete Guide to Psychological and Spiritual Growth for the Nine Personality Types*. Bantam Books

Riso, D. R., & Hudson, R. (1999). Enneagram Teacher Certification Training. Kirkridge Retreat Center. Bangor, PA

Roy, A. (1999). Neuroticism and depression in alcoholics. J Affect Disord 52(1-3): 243-5.

Salvadora, A., F. Suay, et al. (1999). Correlating testosterone and fighting in male participants in judo contests. Physiol Behav 68(1-2): 205-9.

Samochowiec, J., F. Rybakowski, et al. (2001). Polymorphisms in the Dopamine, Serotonin, and Norepinepherine Transporter Genes and their Relationship to Temperamental Dimensions Measured by the Temperament and Character Inventory in Healthy Volunteers. Neuropsychobiology 43(4): 248-53.

Sannibale, C. (1998). An evaluation of Cloninger's typology of alcohol abuse. Addiction Volume 93 Issue 8 1241-9

Schreiber, B., Shannon, J. (2000). *Enneagram Workbook - Leading from any Position.* Self-published. Placitas, NM

Schulze, E.S., Thomas, T.M. Biological Basis of Type. The Enneagram Monthly Number 66 Volume 6 November 2000

Schmidt, L. G., P. Dufeu, et al. (1997). Serotonergic dysfunction in addiction: effects of alcohol, cigarette smoking and heroin on platelet 5-HT content. Psychiatry Res 72(3): 177-85.

Siever, L. J., H. W. Koenigsberg, et al. (2002). Cognitive and brain function in schizotypal personality disorder. Schizophr Res 54(1-2): 157-67.

Slutske, W. S., A. C. Heath, et al. (2002). Personality and the Genetic Risk for Alcohol Dependence. J Abnorm Psychol 111(1): 124-33.

Soloff, P. H., K. G. Lynch, et al. (2000). Serotonin, impulsivity, and alcohol use disorders in the older adolescent: a psychobiological study. Alcohol Clin Exp Res 24(11): 1609-19.

Soloff, P. (1997). Special feature: psychobiologic perspectives on treatment of personality disorders. J Personal Disord 11(4): 336-44.

Stahl, Stephen M. (2000). Essential Psychopharmacology: Neuroscientific Basis and Practical Applications, Cambridge University Press: New York, NY

Stokes, P. E. & A. Holtz (1997). Fluoxetine tenth anniversary update: the progress continues. Clin Ther 19(5): 1135-250.

Stoltenberg, S. F., G. R. Twitchell, et al. (2002). Serotonin transporter promoter polymorphism, peripheral indexes of serotonin function, and personality measures in families with alcoholism. Am J Med Genet 114(2): 230-4.

Stough, C., C. Donaldson, et al. (2001). Psychophysiological correlates of the NEO PI-R openness, agreeableness and conscientiousness: preliminary results. Int J Psychophysiol 41(1): 87-91.

Tanum, L. and U. F. Malt (2000). Personality traits predict treatment outcome with an antidepressant in patients with functional gastrointestinal disorder. Scand J Gastroenterol 35(9): 935-41.

Tauscher, J., R. M. Bagby, et al. (2001). Inverse relationship between serotonin 5-HT(1A) receptor binding and anxiety: a [(11)C]WAY-100635 PET investigation in healthy volunteers. Am J Psychiatry 158(8): 1326-8.

Thome, J., H. G. Weijers, et al. (1999). Dopamine D3 receptor gene polymorphism and alcohol dependence: relation to personality rating. Psychiatr Genet 9(1): 17-21.

Torgersen, A. M. and H. Janson (2002). Why do identical twins differ in personality: shared environment reconsidered. Twin Res 5(1): 44-52.

Verheul, R., W. van den Brink, et al. (1999). A three-pathway psychobiological model of craving for alcohol. Alcohol 34(2): 197-222.

Vogel, F. (1986). [Principles and significance of genetically-induced variability of the normal human EEG]. EEG EMG Z Elektroenzephalogr Elektromyogr Verwandte Geb 17(4): 173-88.

Vogel, F. and E. Schalt (1979). The electroencephalogram (EEG) as a research tool in human behavior genetics: psychological examinations in healthy males with various inherited EEG variants. III. Interpretation of the results. Hum Genet 47(1): 81-111.

Vogel, F., E. Schalt, et al. (1982). Relationship between behavioral maturation measured by the "Baum" test and EEG frequency. A pilot study on monozygotic and dizygotic twins. Hum Genet 62(1): 60-5.

Wagner, Jerome & Walker R.E. (1983). Reliability and Validity Study of a Sufi personality typology: the Enneagram, Journal of Clinical Psychology 39(5) September

Wagner, Jerome & Walker R.E. (1981). A Descriptive, Reliability, and Validity Study of the Enneagram Personality Typology, PhD dissertation, Loyola University of Chicago

Walch JM1 et al (2005). The effect of sunlight on postoperative analgesic medication use: a prospective study of patients undergoing spinal surgery._ Psychosom Med. 2005 Jan-Feb;67(1):156-63.

Weijers, H. G., G. A. Wiesbeck, et al. (2001). Neuroendocrine responses to fenfluramine and its relationship to personality in alcoholism. J Neural Transm 108(8-9): 1093-105

Weisberg, J. N. (2000). Personality and personality disorders in chronic pain. Curr Rev Pain 4(1): 60-70.

Widiger, T. A. (1991). Personality disorder dimensional and models proposed for DSM-IV. Journal of Personality Disorders, 5, 386-398

Widiger, T. A., T. J. Trull, et al. (1987). A multidimensional scaling of the DSM-III personality disorders. Arch Gen Psychiatry 44(6): 557-63.

Williams, J. M. & J. K. Stout (1985). The effect of high and low assertiveness on locus of control and health problems. J Psychol 119(2): 169-73.

Young, J. & R. Persell (2000). On the evolution of misunderstandings about evolutionary psychology. Ann N Y Acad Sci 907: 218-23.

Young, S. N. and M. Leyton (2002). The role of serotonin in human mood and social interaction. Insight from altered tryptophan levels. Pharmacol Biochem Behav 71(4): 857-65.

Zuckerman, M. (1985). Psychobiology of Personality, Cambridge University Press: New York, NY

Zuckerman, M. (1985). Sensation seeking, mania, and monoamines. Neuropsychobiology 13(3): 121-8.

Zinkle, T.E., (1975). A pilot study toward the validation of the Sufi personality typology. PhD thesis, United States International University.

Appendix A

A Little History (of the Enneagram)

The Enneagram is translated from the Greek root word *ennea* meaning "nine" and "grammos," which means "points" (Wagner, 1981). The symbol (see Diagram #1) that represents this personality typing system is ancient, but no definitive reference to the origin of the symbol is known.

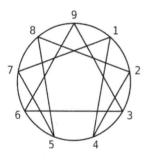

Several Enneagram scholars suggest that the symbol may have originated in Babylon around 2500 BC (Riso & Hudson, 1999). These same authors also state, "The theories underlying the diagram can be found in the ideas of Pythagoras, Plato, and some of the Neo-Platonic philosophers" (Riso & Hudson, 1999). Other Enneagram scholars believe the Enneagram has Sufi roots (Wagner, 1981) and originated in Afghanistan two thousand years ago. According to these scholars, the knowledge was passed down as "an oral tradition" (Zinkle, 1975). Regardless of the symbol's origin, what is known is that the symbol was first brought to the attention of the Western world by George Ivanovich Gurdjieff (ca. 1877-1949), a spiritual teacher of his day and creator of a spiritual practice known as the Fourth Way (Riso & Hudson, 1999).

Dr. Oscar Ichazo

From this time onward, there is little dispute that the modern Enneagram System began with a synthesis of the Enneagram symbol and certain aspects of the Hebrew Kabbalah and the "Desert Fathers" by Oscar Ichazo, founder of the Arica Institute in Chile (Zinkle, 1975; Riso & Hudson, 1999). It is believed that Ichazo independently developed this personality typology (*The Enneagram of Personality*, Randall S., 1979) along with its wings and lines of integration and disintegration. Ichazo has not described how he came up with this construct, nor has he written of any theoretical basis for the exact number of personality types, existence of wings, and the rationale for the specific arrangement of types and wings around the Enneagram diagram. Ichazo also identified what he labeled the three instincts, now referred to as the three variants, also called "subtypes" by various Enneagram teachers. Again, this system of variants was an independent development by Ichazo, and he has not described his thought process related to the development or theoretical underpinning of this concept. Later, Ichazo taught the Enneagram of personality to Dr. Claudio Naranjo, a psychiatrist associated with the Esalen Institute in Big Sur, California.

Dr. Claudio Naranjo

Dr. Naranjo expanded his understanding of the Enneagram to include aspects of modern psychiatry. His interest was in labeling the types and wings and correlating the descriptions of Enneagram personalities with psychiatric categories (Riso & Hudson, 1999). In the early 1970s, one of Naranjo's students, the Rev. Robert Ochs, S.J., taught the Enneagram to other Jesuits at Loyola University of Chicago. It was well received in the Jesuit community in the United States. In fact, the Jesuits were largely responsible for its nationwide exposure. In 1974, Don Riso, a Jesuit seminarian, discovered the system, which at that time was not much more than an impressionistic description of the nine individual personality types—something that, according to Riso, could be written on a single piece of paper in its unabridged version. More extensive descriptions, of two to five pages per type, actually existed during the time of Riso's introduction to the system. However, he apparently did not have access to these versions at that time. Since then, Riso dedicated his life to developing the Enneagram. He and his partner, Russ Hudson, further refined the system by adding the dimensions of the nine levels of development within each personality. Riso and Hudson further refined the variant system as well, along with the subdivisions of the Enneagram, into the Hornevian and Harmonic Triads.

Don Riso & Russ Hudson

Ken Wilber is a current leader in transpersonal psychology, philosopher, and the author of more than a dozen books, including *The Spectrum of Consciousness*. According to Don Riso, Wilber has indicated that the addition of the nine levels of function have transformed the NPS from an interesting but "flat" two-dimensional typology system—composed of types and lines of integration and disintegration—into a powerful, precise, and dynamically alive three-dimensional representation of the human personality (Riso, 1999).

Riso and his partner, Russ Hudson, have written several books and produced several audiotapes that describe in great detail all aspects of the Enneagram, including personality-specific prescriptions for emotional and spiritual development unique to each type.

Dr. Eric Schulze & Dr. Tina Thomas

In 1997, two students of Riso and Hudson, Tina Thomas and Eric Schulze, attended Part 2 of the Enneagram Teacher Training Workshop at Kirkridge Retreat Center in Pennsylvania. During this training, they shared their belief in a biological basis for Enneagram and agreed to be research partners. Shortly thereafter, Schulze moved from California to be with Thomas in Louisiana, and they began their self-funded research. Through their partnership, they developed an elegant theory for the biological underpinnings of the Enneagram and also for the influence of early environment on the social orientation (also referred to as the variants or subtypes of other schools). Thomas and Schulze prefer to refer to the Enneagram and combined biological theory as the Nine-Point Personality System (NPS) because they believe it is a more straightforward name and easier to assimilate. They also prefer using the term NPS because it helps distinguish it from the Enneagram as a biologically-based system that differs in several, sometimes subtle, but significant ways.

Appendix B

Resources

Books

The Wisdom of the Enneagram
Personality Types
Similar Minds
The Enneagram in Love and Work
A Gentle Path: A Guide to Peace, Passion and Power

Scientific Articles

Life Sciences
Food reward and cocaine increase extracellular dopamine in the nucleus accumbens as measured by microdialysis; Luis Hernandez and Bartley G. Hoebel; March 1988

Psychopharmacology
Synergistic dopamine increase in the rat prefrontal cortex with the combination of quetiapine and fluvoxamine; Damiaan Denys, et al.; November 2004

Neuroscience Letters
Scheduled eating increases dopamine release in the nucleus accumbens of food-deprived rats as assessed with on-line brain dialysis; Fenny S. Radhakishun, et al.; March 1988

PNAS
Tyrosine administration increases striatal dopamine release in rats with partial nigrostriatal lesions; E. Melamed, et al.; July 1980

Brain Research
Sexual behavior enhances central dopamine transmission in the male rat; J. Pfaus, et al.; October 1990

Websites

Nate's Website:
tinathomas.com
www.enneagraminstitute.com

Enneagram Blog:
http://ewagele.wordpress.com

The Happy Introvert on YouTube:
http://bit.ly/HapInt

The Creative Enneagram on YouTube:
http://www.youtube.com/watch?v=P9c38dNs5KI&lr=1

Wagele Cartoons and Books:
http://www.wagele.com

For how to deal with Intimate and Self-Pres social orientations:
https://www.psychologytoday.com/blog/the-career-within-you/201203/how-get-along-introverts-part-iasbb.com

Further Reading

University of Texas College of Pharmacy:

Dopamine: A Sample Neurotransmitter

MayoClinic.com:

Schizophrenia Treatment and Drugs

Western Washington University Residences:

Caffeine: What Every College Student Should Know

Read More:

http://www.livestrong.com/article/113977-increases-dopamine/#ixzz2GragMJbI

Read More:

How to Reduce Dopamine | eHow.com http://www.ehow.com/how_5095275_reduce-dopamine.html#ixzz2GrdkCMd9

Read More:

http://www.livestrong.com/article/324523-how-do-i-decrease-dopamine-levels/#ixzz2GrefZD6A

Printed in the USA
CPSIA information can be obtained
at www.ICGtesting.com
JSHW022219140824
68134JS00018B/1144